The Vested
OUTSOURCING MANUAL

Also by Kate Vitasek

Vested Outsourcing: Five Rules That Will Transform *Outsourcing*
(with Mike Ledyard and Karl Manrodt)

The Vested
OUTSOURCING MANUAL

A Guide for Creating Successful Business and Outsourcing Agreements

Kate Vitasek
with
Jacqui Crawford, Jeanette Nyden, and
Katherine Kawamoto

THE VESTED OUTSOURCING MANUAL

First published in 2011 by
PALGRAVE MACMILLAN®
in the United States—a division of St. Martin's Press LLC,
175 Fifth Avenue, New York, NY 10010.

Where this book is distributed in the UK, Europe and the rest of the world,
this is by Palgrave Macmillan, a division of Macmillan Publishers Limited,
registered in England, company number 785998, of Houndmills,
Basingstoke, Hampshire RG21 6XS.

Palgrave Macmillan is the global academic imprint of the above companies
and has companies and representatives throughout the world.

Palgrave® and Macmillan® are registered trademarks in the United States,
the United Kingdom, Europe and other countries.

ISBN: 978–0–230–11268–1

Library of Congress Cataloging-in-Publication Data

Vitasek, Kate.
    The vested outsourcing manual / by Kate Vitasek with Jacqui
    Crawford, Jeanette Nyden, and Katherine Kawamoto.
      p. cm.
    ISBN 978–0–230–11268–1 (hardback)
    1. Contracting out. I. Title.
HD2365.V59 2011
658.4'058—dc22   2011005465

A catalogue record of the book is available from the British Library.

Design by Newgen Imaging Systems (P) Ltd., Chennai, India.

First edition: June 2011

10 9 8 7 6 5 4 3 2

Printed in the United States of America.

DEDICATION

We would like to dedicate this book to our partners, who have selflessly given us time, support and encouragement throughout our careers. We are firsthand believers that win-win principles are a foundation for success in our personal lives. Our marriages and relationships are a testament that together is indeed better.

Greg, Tim, Jonathan, and John: we are in your debt and appreciate all that you have done for us.

Greg Picinich
Vested to Kate Vitasek

Tim Lohraff
Vested to Jeanette Nyden

Jonathan Archer
Vested to Jacqui Crawford

John Kawamoto
Vested to Katherine Kawamoto

CONTENTS

FIGURES

INTRODUCTION: IMPLEMENTING THE BETTER WAY

n the first book in this series,[1] we asked, and then answered, the question: "Is there a better way to outsource?" The result was the pioneering *Vested Outsourcing: Five Rules that Will Transform Outsourcing*, which outlined the need for a new, modern way to outsource based on trust, collaboration, and working together to achieve mutually beneficial goals.

The good news is that companies such as Microsoft, Intel, UPS, and P&G are embracing the concept. But this acceptance has led quickly to the next, challenging series of questions: "Exactly how do you craft a Vested Outsourcing agreement based on the Five Rules? Where do we begin? Is there a template or roadmap you can give me for guidance and success?"

This manual is your resource to answer those questions.

We found that practitioners have a real need for guidance on how to move beyond conventional approaches for developing agreements with strategic suppliers, such as complex outsourcing arrangements with service providers.

For those of you still on the fence, consider the success that Microsoft is having with facilities management with Grubb & Ellis[2] and back-office procure to pay with Accenture.[3] Grubb & Ellis won Microsoft's Supplier of the Year award for increasing service levels by 47 percent and decreasing costs by 21.7 percent. Grubb & Ellis has also received Microsoft's Environmental Supplier of the Year and Diversity Award for exceeding Microsoft supplier diversity goals and a Value Award for its leadership in generating cumulative cost reductions to Microsoft in excess of $34 million.[4] Microsoft has also deployed Vested Outsourcing for back-office procure-to-pay operations with Accenture.[5] The joint Microsoft/Accenture team has taken the Triple Crown in the world of outsourcing, winning the industry's top awards from the Outsourcing Center,[6] the Shared Services Outsourcing Network[7], and the International Association of Outsourcing Professionals.[8] "We are definitely realizing benefits from our collaborative and mutually aligned relationships with our strategic suppliers that the vested outsourcing model creates. The key is maximizing the areas where we both are aligned and minimizing the areas of divergence. Vested Outsourcing helps us do that," says Tim McBride, Microsoft's chief procurement officer.[9]

OVERVIEW OF THIS BOOK'S STRUCTURE

Developing a Vested agreement that creates successful and true vested supplier relationships is not as simple as it seems. Why? Companies lack a proper roadmap that details in a straightforward and clear manner how to create a practical system that works in a technological and global world. We wanted to develop such a roadmap that allows a company to move beyond merely paying lip service to the idea of a partnership by creating true win-win agreements where all the parties have a vested interest in mutually defined Desired Outcomes.

A foundation of this manual is the seminal work of the 2009 Nobel laureate Oliver E. Williamson in Transaction Cost Economics and economic governance.[10] He advocates that companies develop a plan and a contract that are flexible frameworks, where companies work collaboratively and proactively to address their ever-changing business needs rather than create rigid processes that put suppliers in a box, with every change being "out of scope" and causing tensions.

We believe that this manual represents the essence of Williamson's thought and teachings, especially that a Vested agreement be a flexible framework.

The University of Tennessee's work in the area of Vested Outsourcing shows that the best companies develop relationships whereby they and their suppliers or service providers have a vested interest in each other's success: creating a flexible operating structure that aims at embracing business changes, flexibility, and innovation while avoiding writing agreements that force risk onto one party or the other.

Consider this book a roadmap to crafting, implementing, and arriving at a successful collaborative Vested agreement and governance structure to manage the Vested relationship. The book drives the principles of Vested Outsourcing beyond theory into implementation and practice.

Each part is a sort of Global Positioning System that provides practical guidance and advice, along with real examples that demonstrate how to develop a sound, flexible, plan aimed to drive mutual advantage for the company and the outsourcing provider.

Like a traveler with a destination in mind, this book travels to an end result: development of an actual Vested agreement that can be used in a new relationship. We use the University of Tennessee's Five Rules of Vested Outsourcing and map ten key elements that all companies should address in any agreement between a company and its suppliers.

This manual is structured into three distinct parts, each serving a different purpose to help you with your journey to build a collaborative, mutually beneficial agreement.

Part I, "Laying the Foundation," provides an overview of Vested Outsourcing and the Five Rules while stressing the importance of a flexible framework, building trust, working collaboratively, and moving beyond transaction-based mindsets. It gets the journey to mutually Desired Outcomes and the win-win relationship started.

Part II, "Creating the Rules of Engagement," is the heart of the manual. The path you will take to design your Vested Outsourcing agreement, it has in-depth discussions of each of the elements to include in your agreement.

In Part III, "Getting to We," you reach your goal: a collaborative and flexible joint Vested framework.

A NOTE ON TERMINOLOGY

The word *vested* is used to describe many facets of a successful outsourcing relationship, and there are significant nuances to Vested Outsourcing's definition of the word. Throughout this manual, we use the word *Vested* independent of "Vested Outsourcing" to connote the principal thinking and philosophy of the Vested Outsourcing methodology. Therefore, we have chosen to capitalize the term *Vested* when it applies to the overall principles established under Vested Outsourcing.

It is also important to understand what outsourcing is and what can be outsourced.

Outsourcing refers to having a service provider perform a process or function on behalf of a company. In today's market, almost anything can be outsourced. It is not uncommon for companies to buy services and not realize that in fact they are outsourcing. Many mature professions such as logistics and facilities management are predominantly outsourced. For example, 83 percent of all companies outsource their logistics and transportation work to third-party service providers.[11] Other types of outsourced services range from technical support, call centers, maintenance, product returns, food service/cafeteria management, and even facilities management for an entire campus of buildings. Usually, if a process is not core to the organization, it is a candidate for outsourcing.

We use the terms *procure, source, purchase, buy,* and *acquisition* interchangeably. In all cases, the terms are meant in the context of a company that is buying outsourced services.

In addition, we refer to the parties involved in an outsource agreement in specific ways. The company that is outsourcing is the *outsourcing company* or, most often, the *company*. The provider of these services is referred to as the *service provider*.

We use the terms *relationship, partnership,* and *arrangement* interchangeably to refer to the coming together of a company that is outsourcing with one or more of its service providers under a common agreement or contract.

Those involved in a Vested Outsourcing agreement are the *parties.* Generally such agreements are between two parties and are independent, stand-alone agreements. However, we have seen outsourcing relationships that include more than one service provider. For example, a construction project can include any number of separate parallel agreements between the owner and multiple expert service providers such as an architect, engineer, or builder, along with subcontracts between those providers and the organizations that provide services and supplies to them.

Along the way you might find it useful to check the glossary, which provides comprehensive and helpful definitions of many terms used in the outsourcing and logistics arena.

Before beginning the journey, we would like to make two important distinctions: This manual is not just another legalese-ridden guide to effective contracting. In fact, we rarely use legal terms. There are bookshelves full of those types of books. Where possible we even try to avoid the use of the term *contract.* We do this for a reason, because a good business agreement with a service provider goes well beyond the contract. This manual is not intended to address or resolve every business situation you encounter; it is about agreeing collaboratively and effectively, about successfully realizing your Vested Outsourcing agreement.

Enjoy your journey!

PART I

LAYING THE FOUNDATION

CHAPTER 1

ARE YOU READY?

When an outsourcing relationship goes wrong, it can cost millions of dollars, result in lost market share, and have a disastrous impact on consumer confidence in a company or brand. The University of Tennessee faculty outlined perverse incentives that result in poor outsourcing agreements in their research and first book, *Vested Outsourcing: Five Rules that Will Transform Outsourcing.*[1]

Although it is safe to say that companies want to improve their outsourcing practices, most are not sure where to begin and how to make systematic changes. The University of Tennessee researched this challenge and incorporated the lessons it learned to outline a systematic model to improve outsourcing as a business practice. This model is called Vested Outsourcing because the core principle is to create an outsourcing relationship where companies and service providers become "vested," or mutually committed to each other's success, creating the true win-win solution that goes beyond the mere feel-good lip service often espoused in the first blush of a new agreement.

The findings of the University of Tennessee's research are embodied in *five key rules.* When applied to a business outsourcing practice, the Five Rules (reviewed in chapter 2) will transform outsourcing relationships, increase innovation, and improve efficiency. The approach and the thinking are laid out in the first book; this second book is your manual, your detailed guide to implementing a successful, Vested Outsourcing business model and agreement.

We start from the premise that you are using this manual because you are committed to developing a Vested Outsourcing agreement. We assume that you have already finished the necessary deliverables to complete Steps 1 through 3 of the Vested Outsourcing implementation process[2] and are ready to roll up your sleeves and begin crafting a successful business agreement that will motivate the parties to deliver transformational results.

TRANSFORMATIONAL RESULTS ARE WHERE WE START THE STORY

The University of Tennessee has researched outsourcing relationships that use the outcome-based approach for more than five years. Although some outcome-based deals failed miserably, the university researchers found that the majority of the outcome-based relationships they studied performed well, meeting or exceeding performance targets.

Researchers became intrigued with a select group of outcome-based outsourcing agreements that were wildly successful,[3] bringing transformational results to the company that is outsourcing and to the service provider. The United States Air Force was so intrigued with this small group of successful "outliers"[4] that it funded a secondary research project for the university to determine what factors drove the transformational success.

The university's research revealed that the most successful outcome-based relationships had universal similarities that were not obvious to the companies that were studied: they all had created a blended approach of outcome-based thinking and shared value thinking. The University of Tennessee researchers named this new methodology *Vested Outsourcing* because the term conveyed the essence of these successful relationships: how the companies and service providers were committed to each other's mutual success and worked toward shared outcomes by jointly leveraging their capabilities to innovate, lower costs, and improve service. Based on this research and continuing field study the university created a new standard for successful outsourcing agreements.

NEW METHODOLOGY—NEW BUSINESS MODEL

In chapter 3, we explore three sourcing business models and explain in detail how Vested Outsouring is built on a fourth model: a hybrid business model. Vested Outsourcing is a hybrid sourcing model that combines approaches to yield a greater value proposition than previously known using each business model separately. Vested Outsourcing leverages components of an out-come-based model with the Nobel award-winning concepts of behavioral economics and the principles of shared value.

Behavioral economics is the study of the quantified impact of individual behavior or of the decision-makers within an organization. The study of behavioral economics is evolving more broadly into the concept of relational economics, which proposes that economic value can be expanded through positive relationship (win-win) thinking rather than adversarial relationships (win-lose or lose-lose). Using this concept, entities can work together to expand their reward position.

Shared value principles are concepts of creating economic value in a way that creates such value for all parties involved. In essence, shared value thinking involves entities working together to bring innovations that benefit the parties—with a conscious effort that the parties gain (or share) in the rewards. This shared value thinking is what the University of Tennessee researchers have coined "what's in it for we" (WIIFWe). Shared value principles are starting to gain traction. Two advocates are Harvard Business School's Michael Porter and Mark Kramer, who profiled their "big idea" in the January–February 2011 *Harvard Business Review Magazine*. The article states that shared value creation will drive the next wave of innovation and productivity growth in the global economy.[5] Porter is renowned for his Five Forces model of competitive advantage. Due to his prominence, it is likely that his take on shared value, although focused on society, likely will cause practitioners to embrace the philosophy of WIIFWe.

The heart of each of these progressive approaches forms the thinking behind the Vested Outsourcing business model, which

Figure 1.1   Vested Outsourcing's Hybrid Business Model

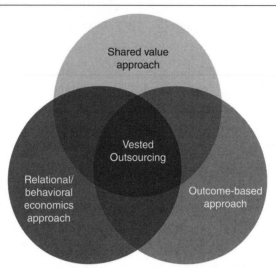

can provide your company with the fluidity, give-and-take, and collective behavior that can deliver transformational results.

Figure 1.1 illustrates Vested Outsourcing's hybrid business model approach.

PERFORMANCE PYRAMID: OPTIMIZING FOR RESULTS

By their very nature, no two Vested Outsourcing relationships are alike, nor should they be. However, all good ones achieve mutual success based on optimizing three key goals:

1. Innovation and improved service
2. Reducing cost to the company outsourcing
3. Improving profits to the service provider

Conventional wisdom says that there typically is a trade-off among these three goals. For example, achieving higher service levels often costs more money. Or allowing the service provider to double its profit margin may raise costs for the company that is outsourcing. We call an emphasis that focuses on optimizing—versus trade-offs—the Performance Pyramid (as depicted in Figure 1.2) because it forces a company and its service provider to strategically drive innovation aimed at achieving what appears to be conflicting objectives.

Many progressive companies are reinventing their outsourcing practice by developing collaborative Vested Outsourcing solutions designed to create incentives for service providers that deliver value as they achieve the company's cost and service objectives. Thus, the company and the service provider are *vested* in each other's success by creating ways to optimize for the three goals, instead of accepting the conventional and one-dimensional trade-off wisdom.

A Vested Outsourcing agreement is based on specific Desired Outcomes that form the basis of the agreement. A Desired Outcome is a *measurable business objective* that focuses on what will be accomplished as a result of the work performed. Desired Outcomes must have supporting metrics that, as much as possible, objectively indicate whether the outcomes are achieved. A Desired Outcome is *not* a task-oriented service-level agreement (SLA) that often is mentioned in a conventional statement of work for a service provider. Rather it is a mutually agreed upon, objective, and measurable deliverable for which

Figure 1.2   Performance Pyramid

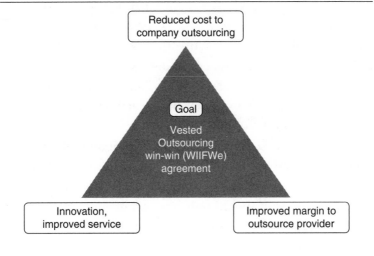

the service provider will be accountable. It is generally categorized as an improvement to cost, schedule, market share, revenue, customer service levels, or performance.

Desired Outcomes are beacons—the guiding light posts along your path that keep the parties in an agreement moving forward in the same direction as business changes.

ARE YOU REALLY READY?

Although this manual will help you to develop a Vested agreement, we recommend that you challenge your readiness. Doing due diligence at the outset will ensure that you are ready for the journey and that you get to your destination—a completed agreement and governance structure—in the most efficient manner. We recommend that all parties involved in the agreement take the time to complete three readiness tasks, summarized next and then discussed in detail.

1. Complete the deliverables in Steps 1 to 3 of *Vested Outsourcing.*
2. Complete a readiness assessment.
3. Complete a Vested Outsourcing knowledge base assessment.

First, we recommend a review of Chapters 6 to 8 of *Vested Outsourcing: Five Rules that Will Transform Outsourcing.* These chapters outline in detail the first three steps for implementing a Vested Outsourcing business model.

Chapter 6, "Lay the Foundation," establishes an essential precondition: You must determine whether the outsource scope of work under consideration is suitable for a Vested relationship or if it is better accomplished under a simpler transactional outsource model. Simply put, you must understand the opportunity. Vested Outsourcing is not easy and can take time to implement, so it should only be done in situations that will have a large payoff or impact on the company. It is important to get buy-in from internal corporate stakeholders and approval to pursue a Vested approach. It is also crucial to understand your company's decision-making framework and any guardrails you may need to adhere to as you develop the Vested agreement.

Chapter 7, "Understand the Business," explains that you must establish a baseline that documents the as-is state of the existing process planned for outsourcing. Doing this will help clarify and establish Desired Outcomes. It is the starting point for making the business case that justifies the pending financial and operational changes that go into the development of the new Vested agreement.

In Chapter 8, "Align Interests," you will transition from due diligence and research to action by jointly planning on ways to create value by implementing the change to the Vested process and realigning workloads. This is basically the first pass at envisioning how the parties will interact to achieve desired results.

If you accomplish the essential work and deliverables from Steps 1 to 3, you are likely ready for Step 4: Establish the Contract. This manual is the perfect resource to help you develop and document the Ten Elements and the master services agreement that together comprise your Vested Outsourcing agreement. If you have not completed some of the suggested deliverables, this manual provides homework assignments for the ten essential elements that must be included in any Vested agreement. For example, in Chapter 7 of *Vested Outsourcing*, "Understand the Business," we explain the need to create a requirements roadmap and share a process and a tool to do this.[6] If you have not yet created the roadmap, you can complete the homework that is an essential component to crafting your agreement.

Our second recommendation is to take a *readiness assessment*, which ensures that you have laid the proper foundation and are ready to establish a Vested agreement (Step 4). Understanding whether you are ready will greatly reduce the amount of time you need to create and document your formal Vested agreement.

Begin your readiness assessment by evaluating the following key attributes and behaviors of your joint company and service provider team that is chartered to develop the actual Vested agreement.

- Vested Outsourcing knowledge base
- Vested center of competency
- Champions
- Stakeholder analysis
- Organizational alignment
- Dynamic mandate or guardrails

Each attribute is discussed in detail, and you can take the readiness self-assessment at the end of the chapter. We advise that everyone complete a Vested readiness assessment before beginning to develop an agreement. A readiness assessment tool is available for download at the Vested Outsourcing website, www. vestedoutsourcing.com/resources/tools. This step will allow you to develop an action plan to close gaps in capabilities and competencies before they become an issue. It is important to address these gaps early.

Vested Outsourcing Knowledge Base

Success starts with knowledge. The participating organizations need to demonstrate competency in Vested concepts across multiple levels of the organizations, not just at the top. Developing a Vested agreement involves many people from different parts of each organization. Companies should ensure that the key people involved in establishing the Vested agreement, as well as all the major stakeholders, understand and embrace the overall concept of Vested Outsourcing. Take the time to educate all participants in the process.

A company is ready to move forward when it can demonstrate competency in Vested Outsourcing concepts across multiple levels of the organization and show that it has gained comprehensive knowledge and experience in Vested concepts and tenets across participating companies.

Vested Center of Competency

In an ideal situation, a company already will have implemented one or more Vested Outsourcing agreements. Individuals can leverage the wisdom and advice from those who have blazed the trail. This is particularly true for progressive service providers that have multiple clients. For example, Jones Lang Lasalle and Grubb & Ellis—both facilities management service providers—each have multiple Vested Outsourcing agreements.

For organizations without prior expertise, there are two ways to ensure that at least one person has significant experience developing and governing Vested Outsourcing agreements. The University of Tennessee offers a comprehensive training program in Vested Outsourcing; participants attend ten days of classroom training and are assigned a faculty member who will provide mentoring guidance and advice as they implement a deal. Upon successfully developing a Vested Outsourcing agreement, individuals are awarded a Certified Deal Architect certification.

The Certified Deal Architect program is much like the Six Sigma Black Belt programs where companies send individuals to train as champions to lead Six Sigma implementations. University of Tennessee acts as the certifying agency for Vested Outsourcing deal architects.

Investing in a Certified Deal Architect is a great option for companies that know they would like to have more than one Vested Outsourcing agreement; it may not be prudent for companies that have small or simpler agreements, or a limited number of Vested agreements. In such cases, we recommend that companies consider working with a neutral third party who is already a Certified Deal Architect to provide field-based coaching to your team. We also recommend that companies consider using a deal architect for deals of more than $10 million. A Certified Deal Architect will act as a sounding board and provide insight and advice on constructing your Vested agreement. A secondary benefit is that deal architects can play a role of win-win coaches and provide neutral feedback to ensure that the parties reach a fair and equitable Vested agreement that has the most likelihood of success.

Champions

One of the most critical factors for success in any project is senior leadership commitment to the project. This high-level commitment is even more important in a Vested project because the goal of Vested Outsourcing is a fundamental change of the outsourcing business model. Proceeding without such support is a mistake. Senior leadership from the company and the service provider must engage fully with their respective organizations to drive toward a true win-win Vested business model. Their commitment to the project, support in getting stakeholder buy-in, and willingness to remove roadblocks as they occur is vital for success.

Before starting on the agreement, be sure that champions are in place in each organization and are strong advocates—to the point of evangelism—for the need to change from the existing course of action to a cooperative, what's-in-it-for-we (WIIFWe) approach to the partnership. Champions keep the organizations on track during the ups and downs of the process and keep all participants focused on the expected benefits of a Vested relationship.

Stakeholder Analysis

A Vested Outsourcing project will impact many individuals; each one has a stake in the project's outcome. It is important to know who the stakeholders are and to have them fully onboard and engaged in the Vested process. Addressing stakeholder concerns is essential to building a strong consensus and participation toward common objectives. Senior leadership involvement in the agreement process will keep stakeholders engaged and also help keep the organizations aligned as they work toward a Vested agreement.

Organizational Alignment

It is not enough for the team creating the Vested Agreement to be aligned. The alignment must extend to both the company and the service provider's organization. Leadership champions should engage fully with their respective organizations and project teams to drive the organizations to the best possible agreement to achieve the Desired Outcomes. Alignment across departments and teams (horizontal) and from the top to bottom (vertical) of the management structure will provide full visibility and coordination to achieve top-level outcomes while driving lower-level performance metrics in the most efficient manner.

Dynamic Mandate or Guardrails

The sixth readiness checkpoint is to establish guardrails for your Vested agreement. While getting formal stakeholder buy-in ideally is done in Step 1, many teams get to Step 4 of developing their agreement only to find that corporate roadblocks prevent the parties from developing a formal agreement to frame the Vested business relationship. For example, one team completed their agreement only to find that the outsourcing company had a corporate policy stating that no business agreements could last more than one year. The service provider was going to invest millions of dollars in process efficiencies; a one-year contract term was a deal breaker.

If they have not already done so, both parties will need to set up formal checkpoints with internal stakeholders using a formal decision-making framework that ensures proper buy-in from authorities within each company. By design, Vested agreements discuss and optimize for risk and reward structures. For that reason, Vested agreements almost never use standardized corporate contract templates and instead require formal endorsement from corporate authorities.

The parties should clearly understand any formal boundaries—guardrails—for conducting external business agreements. Vested agreements trade risk and mutual gain at the highest levels and are at the heart of contributing to the business bottom line, or earnings before interest, taxes, depreciation, and amortization (EBITDA). Vested agreements are also dynamic in nature and typically have high visibility internally. It is crucial that the parties involved in the agreement set up a formal gate review, or a process for providing measures and project authority for the teams, before implementing Step 4. This formal review will ensure a no-surprises policy.

As you proceed with your Vested agreement using this manual, you will use the gate review process frequently and concurrently as you establish your agreement in order to avoid surprises. After completing each element of your Vested agreement, use the formal gate review process and ensure complete buy-in from authorities at the companies involved. For example, after your joint team has created the Shared Vision and Statement of Intent (see chapter 3), review and compare them with the gate review process before proceeding to Element 2—developing your statement of objectives (see chapter 4).

In some cases, companies grant their Vested project teams a blanket negotiation strategy approval with wide degrees of flexibility to collaborate on a win-win agreement. In this case, we highly recommend that the company outsourcing set some boundary Desired Outcomes and least-acceptable-alternative outcomes.

MIND-SET CHANGE

Human relationships are fundamental to successful Vested Outsourcing. Almost by definition, effective business relationships evolve over time as the parties learn to operate under a collaborative, win-win philosophy. As stated, a collaborative win-win approach is unnatural for many individuals and companies; the company and the service provider may need to unlearn conventional patterns and ways of thinking. In addition, they must make sure they are comfortable in their new roles. The service provider must be comfortable signing up to take the risk to deliver the "how." Organizations constantly must seek to anticipate and overcome roadblocks in the processes, infrastructure, technology, and people that prevent mutual success.

Vested implies that there are not two sides staring across the table at each other, weighing the angles for individual self-interest. A Vested agreement focuses on creating a culture where the parties work together to ensure their ultimate success: A Vested mentality should shift from an us-versus-them to a "we" philosophy. Only by working together can everyone succeed. A Vested Outsourcing relationship focuses on identifying Desired Outcomes and then aligns the interests of all the players so that all benefit once those outcomes are reached. As the relationship grows and matures, it becomes more collaborative and intuitive, expanding beyond simply meeting the requirements of the original outsourcing agreement.

We will jump-start your journey with a reminder that Vested Outsourcing is not for the faint of heart; it often challenges senior executives, middle managers, and especially procurement specialists. It takes people out of their traditional comfort zones and often requires leaving easy money on the table by walking away from an immediate price savings that could be gained by exercising procurement muscle. Instead, it forces long-term thinking on how to enlarge the proverbial pie. Committed executive leadership from each organization is required from the very outset to nurture the required long-term thinking.

If you feel you are ready, this manual will guide you through your journey to establish a Vested Outsourcing agreement designed to help you take your outsourcing relationship to the next level. Do the self-assessment shown in Figure 1.3, then turn to chapter 2 to see how to develop an outsourcing agreement that applies the Five Rules of Vested Outsourcing.

Let us get started on your Vested journey.

Figure 1.3   Self-Assessment: Vested Outsourcing Readiness Assessment

Vested Outsourcing Foundation Benchmarks	Level 1 Inadequate	Level 2 Common	Level 3 Good
Organizational Readiness			
Stakeholder Analysis: Strong consensus and participation across all stakeholders toward common support strategy objectives. Strong top-down support to align stakeholders for optimal solutions.	• Little need or effort to recognize or reconcile stakeholders needs.	• Recognition and accommodation of stakeholder interests, short of strong integrated consensus. • Little top level support to align stakeholders.	• Senior leadership from both company and participating suppliers are fully engaged with their respective organizations to drive towards a true win-win Vested philosophy. • Strong consensus across all stakeholders toward common support strategy objectives. • Strong top-down support to align stakeholders for optimal solutions.
Vested Knowledge Base: Comprehensive knowledge and experience in performance based concepts, tenets, business model, and implementation of Vested type strategies.	• Vested not used— knowledge level not applicable.	• Limited understanding of the Vested business model. • Knowledge of basic Vested concepts and tenets, with minimal experience in Vested implementation.	• Comprehensive knowledge and experience in Vested concepts, tenets, business model, and implementation of Vested strategies across participating organizations. • Participating organizations show demonstrated competency in Vested concepts across multiple levels of the organizations (this is not a top only initiative).

Vested Center of Competency: Organization has a Vested Center of Competency. A formal process exists where knowledge is collected and leveraged across all Vested programs. A formal Vested benchmarking of programs exists and a Vested readiness assessment has been completed with an action plan to close gaps in capabilities/ competencies associated with Vested program implementations.	• Vested not used— knowledge level not applicable.	• Vested or "Vested-like" programs may exist—but no centralized knowledge base is in place to leverage learning's and improve implementation and effectiveness. • No internal benchmarking of Vested programs.	• Organization has a Vested Center of Competency. • A formal process exists where knowledge is collected and leveraged across all Vested programs. • A formal Vested benchmarking process exists and is used to assess and improve Vested programs. • A Vested readiness assessment has been completed and an action plan has been developed to close gaps in capabilities/competencies associated with Vested.
Champions: Senior leadership from both the Customer and the Supplier are fully engaged with their respective organizations to drive towards a true win-win Vested business model. Champions in both organizations are strong advocates "to the point of evangelism" for the need to change from the existing course of action to a cooperative, 'What's In It For We' (WIIFWe)' approach to the partnership.	• Vested not used—no Vested champions.	• Focused advocacy with limited cross team advocacy.	• Senior leadership from both company and participating suppliers fully engaged with respective organizations to drive towards a true win-win Vested philosophy.

CHAPTER 2

PLAYING
BY THE RULES

*Classical law views cooperation as being "of little interest" and
external to the contract. In part this is because it assumes a
common base of presumed rules by the parties.*

—Ian Macneil, contract scholar

As you begin the journey to a Vested agreement, you should
heed the advice of the legal scholar Ian R. Macneil, who
observed that most contracts are ill-equipped to address
the reality of business needs. In his 1968 work, *Contracts:
Instruments for Social Cooperation,*[1] Macneil wrote, "Somewhere
along the line of increasing duration and complexity [the con-
tract] escapes the traditional legal model." He argued further
that contracts are rooted in the classical approach to contract
law and thus crafted to address transactions and legal protections such as pricing and price changes, service levels, limitation of liability, indemnification and liquidated damages.[2]

Macneil was instrumental in developing a wider view of
the contract, a view that is called relational contract theory.
He contended that business-to-business contracts should be
"instruments for social cooperation," and he taught that contracts can be "governed efficiently only if the parties adopt a

consciously cooperative attitude." His idea was that contracts are rooted in relationships and activities that have a large context, rather than as the discrete transactions prescribed in a contract. Macneil challenged lawyers to rethink their approach to business-to-business agreements and chastised classic approaches to contract law, stating: "Classical law views cooperation as being 'of little interest' and external to the contract. In part this is because it assumes a common base of presumed rules by the parties."[3]

But what exactly *are* the rules? Macneil's work directs companies to look at their relationships well beyond that of a legal contract document and encourages cooperation and dialogue based on mutual interest and trust. This book addresses how to develop business-to-business agreements that create a set of working rules that have the power to facilitate successful and long-lasting business relationships based on mutual Desired Outcomes. It shows companies and their service providers how to craft business agreements that not only recognize that the business world is a dynamic environment but also embrace changes and alter how they work to adapt to those changes in a way that is both fair and logical.

BUSINESS HAPPENS—EMBRACE IT, DO NOT FIGHT IT

Although Macneil advocated business agreements should be based on collaboration, Oliver E. Williamson established the concept with the study of transaction cost economics (TCE) and was awarded the 2009 Nobel Prize. In its simplest form, TCE is the study of the economics of hidden costs associated with the transactions that companies perform. Williamson maintains that businesses should collaborate for mutual interest or face hidden transaction costs. The University of Tennessee's applied research augments the work of Macneil and Williamson with evidence of hidden transaction costs in the form of the Ten Ailments of outsourcing. (See Appendix A.)

To reduce hidden transaction costs, Williamson says companies should create a flexible framework for managing their business, not a rigid contract that serves as a legal weapon or protective device. In fact, he states that because the business world is dynamic and constantly changing, "all complex contracts will be incomplete" with gaps, errors, and omissions. For this reason, he suggests businesses create agreements that include a process for understanding and documenting the parties' relationship while achieving their mutual goals.[4]

Williamson suggests using a flexible framework, which is highly adjustable or adaptable, rather than one that prescriptively outlines detailed transaction, rigid terms and conditions, statements of work, and working relations. This is quite logical. Practitioners realize that the world of business is not static; it changes and evolves over time. Think of a Vested agreement as a framework for developing a deal that not only allows business to happen but actually allows companies to have a formal set of rules on how to manage business changes in a dynamic manner.

A common mistake companies make in outsourcing today is that they create detailed statements of work (SOWs) and then try to define too tightly the work to be done. Williamson advises that the contract should have "the effect of which is to facilitate adaptation, preserve continuity and realize mutual gain during contract implementation." Business agreements and their associated contracts should be structured with flexibility that can deal with unanticipated problems, innovations or business changes as they arise.

Also involved with the need for a flexible framework is the ease of the contracting process, which, according to Williamson, "varies with the attributes of the transaction, with special emphasis on whether preserving continuity between a particular buyer–seller pair is the source of added value."

Moreover, the scope of today's outsourcing relationships makes it necessary to have governance structures that align and "vary with the nature of the transaction"[5] and that span not just checking for the integrity of a discrete activity or transaction (e.g., was that product shipped in the 48-hour service level?) but rather how a company and its service providers work together effectively to achieve Desired Outcomes.

What makes it hard for today's practitioners is the statement that governance structures "vary with the nature of the transaction." It is difficult to determine precisely what *should* be in a good governance structure because, by design, that structure is supposed to change with the nature of the work.

In a 2002 paper, Williamson observed that while a contract is an exercise in organization or structure, economists "have been skeptical that organization matters and that it is susceptible to analysis."[6] He continued: "The surprise is that a concept as important as governance should have been so long neglected."

TIME FOR A CHANGE

Unfortunately, not much has changed since the conclusions of Williamson and Macneil were written: An April 2010 study (see Appendix B) by the International Association of Contracting and Commercial Management (IACCM) concluded—sadly— that contract terms remain deeply rooted in the classical legal approach of contract law, which focuses almost exclusively and hierarchically on pricing, limiting liability, indemnification, service and transaction levels, risk mitigation, and liquidated damages.[7] Figure 2.1 presents a complete list of the top ten terms that were negotiated in 2010.

The IACCM findings show that today's practitioners are firmly rooted in old-school contract principles of shifting risk and focusing on price instead of value. The survey states: "Contracts (and the professionals charged with their creation) are frequently seen as obstacles to value creation and are viewed by many as an unfortunate pre-requisite to doing business, rather than as a fundamental asset to successful relationships."[8] Far too many companies are using contracting practices that are mired in protective legalese rather than

Figure 2.1   Terms for which Internal and External Concern Increased in
2010

Terms where internal and external concern increased during 2010
Price / Charge / Price Changes
Payment
Limitation of Liability
Invoices / Late Payment
Indemnification
Service Withdrawal or Termination (cause / convenience)
Service Levels and Warranties
Business Continuity / Disaster Recovery
Confidential Information / Data Protection
Liquidated Damages

Source: IACCM Top Terms Report

building a more legal-easy way of achieving trusting, collaborative relationships.

The IACCM report also says the vast majority of the contracting community understands this problem and acknowledges that current practice does not result in the best outcome.[9]
But the road from that understanding to a solution is difficult,
mostly unpaved, and full of potholes.

Rather than contract terms that start with pricing, price protections, and payment, why not collaborate on terms that begin
instead with scope and goals, change management, and communication *before* worrying about price? According to IACCM
survey respondents, in order to set the stage for developing a
successful relationship, a more beneficial focus would be on the
areas outlined in Figure 2.2.

It is exciting that the contracting community is starting to
respect the lessons of Macneil and Williamson and beginning
to realize the benefits of focusing agreements on the business,

Figure 2.2   Terms that Would Be More Productive in Supporting Successful Relationships

Terms which would be more productive in supporting successful relationships
Scope and Goals
Change Management
Communications and Reporting
Responsibilities of the Parties
Service Levels and Warranties
Price / Charge / Price Changes
Limitation of Liability
Delivery / Acceptance
Dispute Resolution
Indemnification

Source: IACCM Top Terms Report

not on finger pointing. Why not develop an agreement that is based on what IACCM members believe is most important?

The University of Tennessee's applied research with companies such as Microsoft validate that some firms are indeed making an effort to change their approach.

Progressive chief procurement officers such as Tim McBride from Microsoft explain why:

Most procurement professionals are hard-wired to win, which means if Microsoft wins, the supplier loses. For Microsoft, this means we need to work hard to build trust with our supply base and business units that outsource to educate them that there really is a better way where both Microsoft and the suppliers can both win. As such, we have been exploring innovative approaches like Vested Outsourcing to help us not only say partnership—but to also contract for partnership.[10]

Macneil advised companies to look beyond the agreement document and build an agreement based on mutual interest and trust. Unfortunately, this does not come easy for most organizations; exactly how does one document and prioritize "mutual interest" and "trust" in a meaningful, non-subjective way?

What really is needed is a practical and useful process to develop the most appropriate collaborative commercial agreements for specific types of transactions that can remain aligned through the lifecycle of that relationship. This manual provides that practical and useful process to work out those often-nebulous presumed rules as parties embark on a business agreement. It provides guidelines for what we believe are the most critical components that should go into any commercial agreement.

Companies that elect to use this manual as a guiding beacon on their journey to a dynamic and multidimensional business-to-business Vested agreement will evolve from a culture of oversight and control to one of mutual respect and trust. Getting to a true win-win relationship takes time, patience, and practice.

We provide destination checkpoints along the way that will help ensure that you stay on the right path. Ultimately, that path will lead you to a successful business agreement that addresses and clarifies those nebulous rules that Macneil refers to while also showing you how to come to agreement and document them in a flexible framework. This framework will allow your Vested agreement and relationship to travel beyond the standard scope of work outline to a place that embraces and charts the course for transforming the work to be quantifiably more efficient and effective.

Macneil advised that companies should have a "common base of presumed rules." By working through this manual, you will develop an agreement that follows the Five Rules of Vested Outsourcing and a set of working rules, or elements, that have the power to create successful and long-lasting business relationships based on mutual Desired Outcomes.

Let us explore the rules before embarking on your journey.

THE FIVE RULES OF VESTED OUTSOURCING

As shown in Figure 2.3, the University of Tennessee has identified five key rules that should be used when crafting business-to-business agreements that require more than basic market-based exchanges.[11] Although these rules originally were created for outsourcing deals, they are applicable to any business agreement where both parties want to create a shared value relationship to jointly leverage capabilities to innovate, lower costs and improve service.

Figure 2.3   Five Rules of Vested Outsourcing

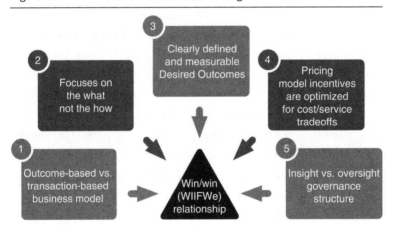

These Five Rules work together to create a framework that follows Macneil's advice to create agreements that are "an instrument for social cooperation." We prefer to think of Macneil's advice as creating an embedded, interrelated what's-in-it-for-we (WIIFWe) philosophy, as seen in Figure 2.4.

1. Focus on outcomes, not transactions.
2. Focus on the *what*, not the *how*.
3. Agree on clearly defined and measurable outcomes.

4. Optimize pricing model incentives for cost/service trade-offs.
5. Governance structure provides insight, not merely oversight.

The Five Rules and their implementation elements are examined in detail in part II of this book, "Creating the Rules of Engagement." Each chapter in part II is devoted to one of the Five Rules, and for each rule, your Vested agreement must include critical components. Think of these elements as signposts directing you along the right road to the desired destination. Part II also details ten of these elements; each one is essential and should not be skipped.

Appendix B presents an outline summary of each element. Chapters 3 through 7 go into greater detail regarding each one.

Figure 2.4   Ten Elements of a Vested Agreement

10 Elements of a Vested Agreement	
Rule 1: Outcome-Based vs. Transaction-Based Business Model	
Element 1	Business Model Map
Element 2	Shared Vision Statement and Statement of Intent
Rule 2: Focus on the WHAT, not the HOW	
Element 3	Statement of Objectives/Workload Allocation
Rule 3: Clearly Defined and Measurable Desired Outcomes	
Element 4	Clearly Defined and Measurable Desired Outcomes
Element 5	Performance Management
Rule 4: Pricing Model Incentives are Optimized for Cost/Service Tradeoffs	
Element 6	Pricing Model and Incentives
Rule 5: Insight vs. Oversight Governance Structure	
Element 7	Relationship Management
Element 8	Transformation Management
Element 9	Exit Management
Element 10	Special Concerns and External Requirements

More details and tools on the Ten Elements are available for
download on the Vested Outsourcing website (www.vestedout-
sourcing.com/resources/tools).

RULE #1: FOCUS ON OUTCOMES, NOT TRANSACTIONS

Element 1: Business Model Map

This section is designed to help you understand and document
your outsourcing business model. The first step in the journey
is to take the time and map potential outcomes and see how
well the parties are aligned to each other's goals. In this section you map out a model where transactions of value between
the parties lead logically and inexorably to collaboration, loyalty and mutual satisfaction, market share, and sustainable
profit. Once you have the model, use it reciprocally to compare
results. Element 1 also raises awareness and agreement around
creating a culture where the company and the service provider
can maximize profits by working together more efficiently, no
matter who is doing the activity.

Element 2: Shared Vision and Statement of Intent

This section outlines the parties' joint vision that guides them
for the duration of their Vested journey. A cooperative and
collaborative mind-set opens a conversation between the parties: They share what is needed, admit to gaps in capability,
and aim to focus on the benefits that the other party can bring
to enhance capability gaps. That vision and alignment form
the basis of a Statement of Intent drafted by the outsourcing
teams.

RULE #2: FOCUS ON THE *WHAT*, NOT THE *HOW*

Element 3: Statement of Objectives/Workload Allocation

This element enables the parties in the Vested partnership to do
what they do best. Depending on the scope of the partnership,

the company transfers some or all of the activities needed to accomplish agreement goals to the service provider. Together they develop a Statement of Objectives (SOO), which is very different from a standard statement of work (SOW). Simply put, a SOO describes intended results, not tasks. Based on the SOO, a service provider will draft a performance work statement that defines in more detail the work to be performed and the results expected from that work.

RULE #3: CLEARLY DEFINED AND MEASURABLE OUTCOMES

Element 4: Top-Level Desired Outcomes

To have an effective, successful Vested Outsourcing relationship, the parties must work together to define and quantify Desired Outcomes. This element is a centerpiece of the whole enterprise and must not be skipped or downplayed. Outcomes must be expressed in terms of a limited set of high-level metrics. It is imperative that the parties spend time—jointly and collaboratively—during the outsourcing transition and particularly during agreement negotiations to define exactly how relationship success will be measured. Once the Desired Outcomes are agreed upon and explicitly defined, the service provider will propose a solution that will deliver the required level of performance at a predetermined price.

Element 5: Performance Management

Once Desired Outcomes, Statements of Intent (SOI), and SOOs are in place and the agreement is implemented, the parties will measure performance to determine if the Desired Outcomes are being met. Of necessity, these statements will include high-level performance management measures that are easily understood by business stakeholders and all parties involved in the process. The metrics will help align performance to strategy.

RULE #4: PRICING MODEL INCENTIVES THAT OPTIMIZE COST/SERVICE TRADE-OFFS

Element 6: Pricing Model and Incentives

In order to attain Desired Outcomes, the parties must have a properly structured pricing model that incorporates incentives for the best cost and service trade-off. The approach of many procurement professionals to outsourcing remains stuck in the Dark Ages: Their focus remains on getting the lowest possible service and labor pricing. The strategic bet—and paradigm shift—of Vested Outsourcing is that the service provider's profitably is directly tied to meeting the mutually agreed upon Desired Outcomes. Inherent in this model is a reward for service providers to invest in process, service, or associated products that will generate returns in excess of agreement requirements. Higher profits are not guaranteed—what business model can claim that?—but this element provides service providers with the authority and autonomy to make strategic investments in processes and product reliability that can generate a greater return on investment than a conventional cost-plus or fixed-price-per-transaction agreement might yield. Incentives are a key element of this mix: Service providers are taking on risk to generate larger returns on investment. An incentives package delivers the most commercially efficient method of maintaining equitable margins for all parties for the duration of the relationship. Principles such as margin matching, which is discussed in detail in chapter 6, should be embedded into the pricing model.

RULE #5: INSIGHT VERSUS OVERSIGHT GOVERNANCE STRUCTURE

Element 7: Relationship Management

Vested Outsourcing is a new hybrid business model resulting in a new type of relationship. Elements 7 through 10 provide the tools for the parties to manage and operate the agreement. The parties monitor the agreement within the framework of a flexible governance structure that provides top-to-bottom insights into what is happening. The Vested agreement is not based on transaction counting! A relationship management structure creates joint policies that emphasize the importance of building collaborative working relationships, attitudes, and behaviors.

Element 8: Transformation Management
We stress again that the Vested approach is a new way—people and company ecosystems are changing. This section acknowledges that the parties are doing things differently and probably not operating in familiar comfort zones. Managing this transformation, including transitioning from old to new—along with change management once the new agreement is up and running—often are difficult and complex to implement. It is imperative to preserve as much continuity as possible among personnel and teams as the transition progresses into day-to-day implementation and operation. The focus here is on end-to-end business metrics, mutual accountability for Desired Outcomes, and the creation of an ecosystem that rewards innovation and of an agile culture of continuous improvement.

Element 9: Exit Management
Sometimes the best plan simply does not work out or is trumped by unexpected events: Business happens, and companies should have a plan when assumptions change. This section explains how an exit management strategy can provide a template to handle future unknowns. The goal is to establish a fair plan and to keep the parties whole in the event of a separation that is not a result of poor performance.

Element 10: Special Concerns and External Requirements
Governance frameworks are not one-size-fits-all, especially in more technical or complex relationships. For instance, in supplier and supply chain relationships involving information technology and intellectual property, security concerns may

necessitate special governance provisions outside of the normal manufacturer-supplier relationship. Supply chain finance and transportation management are other areas that often require special handling under the governance framework. For some practitioners, completing each of the Ten Elements will feel like an exercise or a required homework assignment. However, the most successful companies treat completing them as a way to take the time to change their mind-set—to challenge conventional approaches to establishing a dynamic business-to-business agreement.

By working through each chapter and following the Five Rules and their component elements, firms learn by doing and transition their thinking from adversarial to *truly collaborative*. They move beyond simply saying "collaboration" and "partnership" to actually creating an agreement and a working environment that drives transformative change.

Getting into the Mind-set

Developing a business agreement using Vested Outsourcing's Five Rules is much more than delivering a higher level of service on a given activity, a blur of metrics, or simply counting transactions or filling seats more cheaply.

This is a *fundamental business model shift* in how a company and its service providers work together.

A Vested agreement embeds a true win-win mentality between a company and the service provider. As mentioned earlier, we call this WIIFWe, or what's-in-it-for-we, thinking. A WIIFWe approach always trumps the more usual self-interested what's-in-it-for-me (WIIFMe) approach. You will examine this thinking in much more detail in Part II as you develop a shared vision and intent statement.

A true win-win approach requires effort and commitment by all parties. Outsourcing is never an abdication: It must be a partnership with regular, frequent communication to manage the expectations of everyone as well as the work. Although the most pernicious problems that affect outsource arrangements usually are brought on by micromanagement, a different set of problems can emerge when a company hands over a process or multiple processes completely to the outsource provider.

Once the decision is made to outsource the work, the work definitely is not done: "Do what you do best and outsource the rest!" as Peter Drucker and Tom Peters famously said—a natural temptation in upper leadership echelons might be to disengage and let the service provider worry about it. Guess again!

Some disengagement is healthy and necessary: let the experts exercise their expertise without continuous micromanagement. But there is just as much danger in becoming too disengaged, too complacent, too unaware.

The real work at each end of the outsourcing spectrum is just beginning, particularly in a Vested Outsourcing relationship. Establishing a credible, flexible governance framework; setting systems for communicating, monitoring, and measuring Desired Outcomes; and keeping the right people in place all take on vital significance.

We stress that the latter point applies from the top down.

Human relationships are fundamental to successful Vested Outsourcing. Almost by definition, effective partnerships must evolve over time as the parties learn to operate under a win-win philosophy. As we have said, this approach is unnatural for many individuals and companies and must be learned. But they also have to unlearn conventional patterns and ways of thinking. In addition, the company and the service provider must make sure they are comfortable in their new roles. The service provider must be comfortable signing up to take the risk to deliver the "how." Organizations constantly must seek to anticipate and overcome roadblocks in the processes, infrastructure, technology, and people that prevent mutual success.

The word *partner* implies that there are not two sides staring across the table at each other, weighing the angles for individual self-interest. A Vested agreement focuses on creating a culture where parties are working together to ensure the ultimate success of both. A Vested mentality should shift from an us-versus-them to a we philosophy. Only by working together can everyone succeed. A Vested Outsourcing partnership focuses on identifying Desired Outcomes and then aligns the interests of all players so that all benefit once those outcomes are reached. As the relationship grows and matures, it becomes more collaborative and intuitive, expanding beyond simply meeting the requirements of the original outsourcing agreement.

It bears repeating that Vested Outsourcing is a commitment; it challenges senior executives, middle managers, and especially procurement specialists. It takes them out of their traditional comfort zones and often requires the willpower to leave money on the table by walking away from an immediate price savings gained from exercising procurement muscle in order to save more money or increase revenue by enlarging the pie in the future.[12] Committed executive leadership from each organization is required from the very outset.

Vested Outsourcing demands a willingness to transcend the conventional win-lose approach most companies take in procuring goods and services.

Yes, it is different; yes, it is not easy. That is why the Five Rules and the Ten Elements we outline is this manual are so useful in devising and implementing a flexible, Vested agreement to manage your business.

Move to Part II to begin your journey!

PART II

CREATING THE RULES OF ENGAGEMENT

CHAPTER 3

RULE #1: FOCUS ON OUTCOMES, NOT TRANSACTIONS

A dam Smith, an eccentric Scottish academician at Glasgow University, observed human propensity for self-interest and formulated the law of supply and demand in 1776 with the publication of *An Enquiry into the Nature and Causes of the Wealth of Nations*. His theory said that society benefits as a whole from a multiplicity of trading transactions because humans seek what is best for them, resulting in fairness and honesty among equals. As demand for repeat transactions emerged, trading preferences evolved and modern transaction-based business models were born. These transaction-based business models have been the cornerstone of conventional business relationships ever since.

Transaction-based thinking is widely adopted in today's outsourcing business practices. Conventional outsourcing agreements typically focus on negotiating agreements at a detailed per-transaction level, by paying either for a business task (cost per pick, cost per minute of call) or on a per-headcount basis. Unfortunately, many business professionals wrongly assume that a transaction-based business model is the most cost-efficient model. *For simple transactions with abundant supply and low complexity, a transaction-based business model is likely the most efficient model.* But real weakness in transaction-based approaches emerges when any level of added complexity, variability, and mutual dependency is part of the transaction. A transactional approach cannot produce perfect market-based price equilibrium in variable or multidimensional business agreements.

To make matters worse, procurement philosophies introduced in the 1980s, such as the Kraljic model,[1] encouraged businesses to selfishly use buying *power* to condition the supply chain and force a change in the demand curve to lower dependency on service providers. The ultimate objective of the buying approach is to trigger lower-cost entrants into the market and force reductions in price and, by default, validate the make/buy decision. The more companies applied dominant win-lose behaviors, the more service providers hunkered down to protect their margins. These heavy-handed transaction-based approaches lead to perverse incentives and missed opportunities to innovate that were outlined in *Vested Outsourcing.*[2]

A heavy-handed transaction-based approach can be lucrative in the short term if the buyer gets away with it; however, it is completely inefficient over the long term, especially where a service provider will need to make investments in business infrastructure that require trust and cooperation to deliver results. For this reason, organizations have been exploring other types of sourcing business models that challenge the Kraljic model.

This chapter has two purposes. First, it ensures that you fully understand what an outcome-based business model is so you can determine if it is right for your organization. As you work through this chapter, be prepared to document your business model to ensure that all parties fully understand its nature and agree that Vested Outsourcing is the right choice for your business. Second, this chapter helps you take the first step in crafting your agreement by providing direction to help you create a Shared Vision statement and the associated Statement of Intent.

ELEMENT 1: DOCUMENTING YOUR BUSINESS MODEL

If the core purpose of outsourcing is to enable the most efficient delivery of business outcomes, the company and the service provider must spend the necessary time to ensure that the selected business model rewards positive outcomes. Continuous improvement results from continuous innovation. The typical transaction-based business model does not afford service providers the ability to innovate. By focusing attention on outcomes and not transactions, service providers—recognized experts in their field—have the proper incentives and are highly motivated to innovate.

Research by the International Association for Contract and Commercial Management shows that most companies operate in a conventional transaction-based model that is constrained by a formal, legally oriented, risk-averse, and liability-based culture.[3] There is growing awareness that this approach is lacking and does not always give each party the intended result. University of Tennessee research and the authors' industry-specific experiences applying new approaches to complex contracting demonstrate that outcome-based business models are a viable alternative to the conventional transactional methods. They are gathering momentum as a preferred approach because senior leaders see real results from carefully crafted collaborative agreements.

A number of Vested Outsourcing programs have been recognized for their outstanding achievements.

- Microsoft won three industry awards for its innovative agreement with Accenture for back-office procure-to-pay.
- Jaguar moved from number 9 in the J. D. Power customer satisfaction rankings to number 1 in its partnership with Unipart for worldwide supply chain management services.

- The U.S. Department of Energy won the Project Management Institute's prestigious "Project of the Year" Award for its work with Kaiser-Hill on the Rocky Flats nuclear site environmental clean-up project.

When improvements and cooperation occur, the trust that exists between the parties enables them to unlock far more innovation and value than outdated power-based transactional approaches. Vested Outsourcing takes outcome-based approaches a significant step further; it represents a change in how outsourcing is approached. The good news is that there are proven success stories across multiple industries and types of outsourced services.

Map the Trading Relationship to the Best Business Model Type

Understanding the Types of Transactions

Because we recommend alternatives to the transaction-based business approaches in all but the most basic transactions where no mutual dependency exists, a deeper understanding of *what* you actually trade is a necessary first step as you start your Vested Outsourcing journey. The starting point is to understand your *type* of transaction. There are three primary types of transactions: goods, goods and services, and pure services. Each type has different attributes that define the multifaceted relationship. It is vital to understand the unique attributes of your firm's transaction types and your Desired Outcomes. Then you can map each attribute into the appropriate business transaction model.

Transaction of Goods

The buying and selling of goods is fairly easy to define. Goods are tangible, and there is a defined point in time where title passes to the goods, thus denoting a finite boundary to the transaction. With wide availability, goods can be replicated over time with little deviation and little or no additional effort or interdependence on the part of the customer or service provider. Common examples of goods transactions are paper, food products, televisions, cars, and washing machines.

Transactions of abundant, uncomplicated goods can remain very simple even for large volumes and for high spend values. For example, often a simple purchase order is used for buying 1 unit or 1 million units. Generic legal terms and conditions are acceptable, and little negotiation is necessary as long as the terms are fair and reasonable.

The difference between the terms *commodity* and *transaction* is worth noting. A commodity is a highly valuable asset, uniform in style, undifferentiated, easy to trade, generally abundant, and usually natural or organic in nature, requiring either farming or extracting from the earth. Soybeans, coal, and copper are commodities. Commodities are dependable, certain, and traded on every stock exchange in the world. Modern procurement practice often uses the term *commodity* to refer to goods that are abundant and uniform and therefore easy to switch from one supplier to another. It is preferable to not use the term *commodity,* as we believe that many procurement professionals often confuse it with the "simple transaction-based" business model.

Goods that have increasing complexity (e.g., safety issues involved in the production of the goods or customization) or require more dependence on third parties to bring them to market often need more advanced business models and contracting vehicles. Examples include petroleum, titanium, and palladium, which are highly valuable "commodities" that require significant investment and complex trading relationships to bring to market.

Transaction of Goods and Services
Unlike the simple transaction of goods that happens at one defined moment, goods and services are delivered over a longer time period; the buyer does not actually "own" a service. For

example, Jaguar Platinum Coverage on new Jaguar cars offers consumers complimentary scheduled maintenance, no-cost replacement of wear-and-tear items, and 24/7 roadside assistance for five years or 50,000 miles.[4]

Goods and services transactions are more complex in nature and entail a mutual dependency for the buyer and seller to work together to enable the service component of the transaction. Trading agreements that involve both a good and service component should take into account the way service providers deliver the service, the risk of changes in the business environment, and the behaviors contributing to service satisfaction. In most cases, buyers and service providers set out success criteria in the form of performance metrics. The more complex and integrated the delivery of the service is to a company's core purpose, the higher the level of interdependency.

Transaction of Pure Services
Some organizations have acquired specific skills in service delivery and market this expertise as a highly differentiated "asset" (or capability) to firms that need their expertise. Because not all businesses have that asset or capability, they find it more efficient to outsource the asset to a service provider. In simple service transactions, such as domestic service house cleaning, people find it more efficient to outsource on a transactional basis and spend the time doing something more valuable.

In complex business service transactions, the outsourced service may directly impact the outsourcing company's reputation. This type of agreement denotes a high level of interdependence of the parties. A common example might be outsourcing a company's call center functions. If the service provider hires customer service representatives who speak in accents that are unfamiliar to a company's customers, it may reflect poorly on the company's reputation and in turn reduce customer satisfaction.

In a pure services transaction, consumers' impressions of the company often are established by the service provider's action or inactions. The service provider goes beyond providing a service to actually becoming the connection between the consumer or end customer and the outsourcing company. In highly strategic or complex business ecosystems, a company could not operate effectively or efficiently without its most strategic service providers.

Understanding Sourcing Business Models

Once you understand your type of transaction, you must determine the sourcing business model that is best suited for your business. A business model mapping analysis will help you make an informed decision about the suitability of using a Vested approach for the services you are outsourcing. Such an analysis also will help you determine if your culture and the relationship with your service provider are good fits for a Vested agreement.

The exercise will help set the foundation for deriving the most mutually advantageous agreement for the parties. It also will help service providers consider how to offer added value that is more closely related to the Desired Outcomes of the parties.[5] Our intention is to help you understand the difference between outcome-based and transaction-based thinking, which will enable the company and the service provider to mutually agree that a Vested agreement is the right approach.

Figure 3.1 illustrates the four types of sourcing business models.

Next we discuss each sourcing business model type in detail. We begin by reviewing the three most used business models: transaction-based, outcome-based, and investment-based.

Transaction-Based Model

Most companies use transaction-based business models for all of their commercial agreements when they make a "buy" decision.

Figure 3.1   Business Mapping Framework

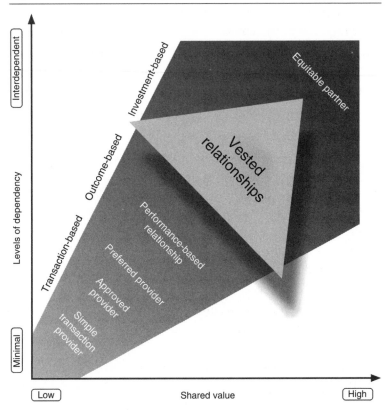

Conventional approaches to transaction-based models keep service providers at arm's length. Three types of transaction-based sourcing relationships have evolved over time as businesses wrestle with how to create service provider relationships that are better suited for more complex business requirements. The three types are simple transaction providers, approved providers, and preferred providers.

Each of these types is discussed in more detail later.

Outcome-Based Business Model

Rolls-Royce PLC was the first known organization to explore outcome-based approaches in the 1960s. However, outcome-based business models did not gain traction until around the

year 2000, and their use still is limited. An outcome-based
business model pays a service provider for the realization of a
defined set of business outcomes, business results, or achievement of agreed-on key performance indicators. A good example
is when an airline pays its outsourced ground crew for achieving
a 20-minute turnaround time after the plane is parked at the
gate. In the simplest form, service providers do not get paid if
they do not deliver results. An outcome-based business model
typically shifts risk for achieving the outcome to the service provider. A well-structured agreement compensates a service provider's higher risk with a higher reward. Many deals are structured
around "all risk, no reward"; in such cases, a supplier or service
provider that does not meet the desired results is penalized.

Outcome-based approaches are used most widely in the
aerospace and defense industries. Often they are referred to as
performance-based logistics because they couple maintenance
and support to the procurement of a product. An example is
Rolls-Royce's Power by the Hour solution (discussed in the next
case study), where its clients pay a fixed-fee charge for engine
logistics and maintenance support based on flight hours.
Outcome-based business models have gained in popularity in
the last few years as more companies outside of the aerospace
industry have adopted the concepts and have expanded the
thinking to pure outsourced service deals.

Investment-Based Model

Companies that struggle to meet complex business requirements using conventional transaction-based or outcome-based
approaches typically adopt an investment-based business model
as the solution. With an investment-based business model, the
company returns to a single balance sheet entity (merged in-
source solution). These equity partnerships can take different
legal forms, from buying a service provider, to becoming a subsidiary, to equity-sharing joint ventures. Equity-based partnerships
often are born out of a company's need to acquire mission-critical goods and services. Also, these partnerships often require the

strategic interweaving of infrastructure and heavy coinvestment. Equity partnerships, by default, bring costs "in house" and create a fixed cost burden. As a result, equity partnerships often conflict with the desires of many organizations to create more variable and flexible cost structures on their balance sheets.

The Catch-22

Although each sourcing business model offers advantages, a real catch-22[6] has emerged for companies that want to work more closely with suppliers to drive innovation and create a competitive advantage.

At the lowest transactional level, competition is normally high and prices for services often are driven to the lowest common denominator. Companies may choose to switch service providers if doing so makes it more efficient for customers to get goods or services. Given the low complexity at this transactional level, there is generally a lack of dependence and quite a bit of freedom of choice. As complexity and dependency increase, however, companies tend to migrate to an approved provider or a preferred provider sourcing relationship.

An investment-based business model is at the highest transactional level. Under this model, a company determines that coinvestment is the best approach to ensure continuity of supply due to extreme mutual dependency. Companies embarking on this model turn to joint ventures or create other legally binding business partnerships.

In a transaction-based environment, there is a tension between getting the lowest cost and developing a deeper business relationship. Procurement teams have a natural desire to reduce dependency and prices of goods or services; the contribution to the company's bottom line is greater if all providers have uniformly available goods and services that can be procured as simple transactions. Yet in most cases companies are finding that their service providers are not making business investments on their behalf and driving innovations and efficiencies at the pace they would like to see. The struggle is that the vast majority of companies want to avoid investment-based business models where they have joint ownership in service delivery operations.

On the flip side, service providers have a natural desire to increase interdependence through specialization and technical expertise. If a service provider can embed its processes in the company, it can create mutual dependency and complexity, making the processes difficult to "untangle." This approach may be good for the service provider, but many companies do not like the idea of feeling trapped if they become too dependent on a service provider.

The result is a catch-22. How can a company create sustainable value with a service provider yet still maintain a buyer-service provider relationship? Many companies want the benefit of an investment-based model without the investments. Progressive companies have addressed this by creating a new Vested Outsourcing hybrid business model.

A New Hybrid Business Model: Vested Outsourcing

Progressive companies are striving to achieve the benefit of an investment-based model, sans investments, by leveraging a Vested Outsourcing hybrid business model that enables success in an outsourcing environment while still allowing a company to remain a separate entity through outsourcing. These companies achieve mutual advantage and gain by working in a completely integrated and mutually beneficial manner where the parties have a vested interest in each other's success.

As we discussed in chapter 1, the Vested Outsourcing business model is a hybrid of outcome-based and shared-value principles best used when a company wants to move beyond having a service provider perform a set of directed tasks and wants to develop a solution based on mutual advantage to achieve the company's Desired Outcomes.

Vested Outsourcing's hybrid model requires the parties to build a solid, cooperative foundation for sharing value—together. Highly integrated outcome-based business models use value incentives to maintain mutual advantage. In the purest cases, a service provider is paid only when it is successful in achieving the mutually agreed Desired Outcomes. However, some Vested agreements skillfully combine fees per transaction with a sophisticated version of value-based incentives. This mix of fee-for-transaction and value exchange and commercial incentives creates agility and opportunities for organizations to deliver value efficiencies instead of merely trading on price.

Rolls-Royce PLC provides a good example to help get you thinking about outcomes.

Case Study

Vested in Success:
Rolls-Royce PLC's *Power by the Hour* Solution

Rolls-Royce PLC[7] was the first company known to use an outcome-based business model. Its groundbreaking Power by the Hour outcome-based agreements with civil aviation airlines changed the way Rolls-Royce and its airline customers do business. The business model has matured over time as Rolls-Royce has deployed the approach with more of its customers.

The business model is designed to achieve the airlines' desired outcome: to have planes continuously flying passengers from destination to destination, resulting in a steady revenue stream. Any unexpected maintenance downtime disrupts the system and results in high levels of unplanned expenditure for airlines. Under a conventional approach, airlines would pay Rolls-Royce a transaction fee for every single engine maintenance event and service request on a spare parts and labor basis to restore equipment to a serviceable condition. Simple guarantees were offered for replacement parts, and these evolved into maintenance guarantees for labor as well as parts for single aircraft or entire fleets, based on the total anticipated cost per flight hour (time in flight) and cycle of flight (wheels up and wheels down). The result was a true perverse incentive. Airplane downtime for maintenance, either planned or unplanned, meant revenue for Rolls-Royce under the conventional transaction-based business model.

Rolls-Royce began working with airlines to create an outcome-based "TotalCare" approach and decided to flip the conventional transaction-based approach on its head. The premise? Build a long-term relationship with customers based on aligning Rolls-Royce's goals to the airlines' goals of keeping the aircraft flying. Under the new outcome-based approach, Rolls-Royce would get paid for "continuous uptime" rather than deriving revenue from turning wrenches during downtime. Rolls-Royce now guarantees serviceable equipment availability and takes care of all maintenance in the chosen service plan.[8] The outcome-based business model gave Rolls-Royce an inherent incentive to drastically increase engine reliability and preventive maintenance that would increase engine on-wing life, reducing unplanned engine downtime and allowing airlines to focus on their core business.

Rolls-Royce's Power by the Hour customers were able to smooth out the total cost of aircraft ownership and pay only for utilization of flying power according to the use of that power. Rolls-Royce and its customers achieve success through a long-term and transparent Vested agreement based on performance metrics geared to deliver Desired Outcomes.

Mapping Business Attributes to the Appropriate Business Model

Figure 3.2 summarizes the typical attributes for each sourcing relationship type.

Mapping Attributes of Your Business to a Business Model

Now that you understand the difference between the types of sourcing business models, the next step is to ensure that your business is suited for a Vested Outsourcing business model. Mapping your business agreement will ensure that the type of transaction and type of sourcing relationship is a good fit for a Vested agreement. For example, Microsoft has hundreds of fee-based service agreements but only a very limited number of commercial agreements that use a Vested Outsourcing business model.

Figure 3.3 presents a business model mapping framework that maps the potential outcomes your company could achieve through external relationships. Conducting such an analysis will show how well each party is aligned to the other's goals. The framework should be used by companies and service providers to ensure that the thinking of both parties is aligned.

Using the business model mapping framework, start by asking yourself what you buy in terms of Desired Outcomes. Figure 3.3 lists some of the most commonly cited Desired Outcomes in corporate business plans. Decide on your own specific outcomes. Remember that outcomes are benefit-based and therefore last longer and do not change as often as tasks, which may be deployed to deliver outcomes. Plot the results on a simple axis and overlay it onto the relationship map to create a visual of the most appropriate relationship business model and sourcing relationship type for a given service provider. Repeat the exercise for a complete outcome-based segmentation map for each of the key services that are in scope.

The final output of the modeling exercise is the business model relationship map. To maximize the real value of the mapping framework, companies and their service providers should

Figure 3.2 Summary of Sourcing Relationship Types

Sourcing Relationship	Focus	Interaction	Cooperation Level	Required Trust Level	Characterized by
Transaction Based Business Model					
Simple Transaction Provider	Cost and Efficiency	PO, Standard Terms, Fixed Price	Low-Automated where possible	Minimal – single transaction	Abundant and easy to resource, no need for a relationship
Approved Provider	Economies of Scale, Ease of transactions	Blanket PO, Negotiated Terms, Pricing Agreements	Medium – based on pricing or specifications	Medium – common terms and price agreement	Managed by category locally and cross business sector and bundled for economies of scale
Preferred Provider	Capability, Capacity, and Technology transactions	Contract, SOW, Pricing Agreement, Possible Gain Sharing SLAs	High – Set out in long term service contract	High – defined by contract, high spend zone	Integral supply across business units, delivering added value and capability, not so abundant, a pain to re-source
Outcome Based Business Model					
Outcome-Based/ Performance-Based Relationship	Outcomes or Performance	SRM Governance, Performance Incentives, Fees at Risk	Integrated	Integrated	Longer term relationship
Vested Outsourcing Relationship	Mutual Gain, Shared Outcomes	Vested Agreement, Vested Governance Framework, Performance Incentives, Margin Matching	Integrated – cooperative, Win-Win	Integrated – behave as single entity	Interdependent outcomes, aligned, mutual gain, managed performance, long term relationship
Investment Based Business Model					
Equity Partner	Equity Sharing	Joint Venture, Asset Based, Governance Framework	Integrated – cooperative, interrelated structure	Integrated – dictated by equity sharing	Legally bound, formal strategic partnerships, mergers and acquisitions, asset sharing/ holding

Figure 3.3   Business Model Mapping Framework

| Mapping Attributes | Transaction Based | | Preferred Provider | Outcome Based | Hybrid | Investment Based |
| | Simple Transaction Provider | Approved Provider | | Outcome/ Performance Relationship | Vested Outsourcing Relationship | Equitable Partner |
	Zone 1	Zone 2	Zone 3	Zone 4	Zone 5	Zone 6
Vital to core business purpose	Minimal	Low	Medium	Medium to High	High	Critical
Enhances brand image	None	Low	Medium	High	High	Critical
Impact on customer experience	None	Low	Medium	High	High	Critical
Maintains customer experience	None	Low	Medium	High	High	Critical
Opportunities for efficiency gains	None	Low	Medium	High	Very High	Critical
Contributes to Innovation	None	Low	Medium	High	Very High	Critical
Consistently safe and reliable	Not capable	Semi-skilled	Skilled	Professional	Professional	Expert
Impact on operational safety	Minimal	Low	Medium	High	High	Critical

Business Model →

	None	Low	Medium	High	Very High	Constant
Organic growth capability	None	Low	Medium	High	Very High	Constant
Access to critical systems and processes	None	Low	Medium	High	High	Critical
Availability of required technology	Universal	Limited	Restricted	Scarce	Scarce	Unique
Impact of supplier loss or failure	None	Low	Medium	High	High	Critical
Cost to switch supplier	None	Low	Medium	High	High	Very High
Dependence on assets/capabilities	None	Low	Medium	High	High	Critical
Lean supply cost	Low	Medium	High	High to Invest	Invest	Capital
Cost of Staff	Minimal	Low	Medium	High	High	Very High
Availability of qualified personnel	High	High	Medium	Low	Low	Low
Skill level of predominant personnel	Unskilled	Semi-skilled	Skilled	Professional	Professional	Expert

complete an analysis and then compare results. Doing this will begin a dialogue, encourage questions, and highlight compatibility gaps in the relationship, along with potential opportunities to demonstrate added value and further alignment. The process also will make visible capabilities that you had not previously considered. In some circumstances, mismatches will become transparent and thus able to be addressed in a positive, constructive manner.

If you are a service provider, start by mapping your capabilities against your client's Desired Outcomes detailed in the framework. If 80 percent of your capabilities fall within a particular sourcing relationship type, aim to establish a new relationship or reposition an existing relationship in accordance with the predominant sourcing relationship type.

Case Study

Getting It Right: How Ryanair and Swissport Managed a Business Model Mismatch

In our academic research and years of operational practice, we have seen many outsourcing agreements that operate under a business model mismatch, which often creates tension and conflict between the parties. Mismatches most certainly lead to one or more of the ten ailments of outsourcing (see Appendix A) and can even lead to complete failure, changing service providers midstream, or a decision to bring the work back in-house.

Ryanair, a low-cost European airline, is widely known for its adversarial and domineering transaction-based approach toward its service providers. It operates on a low-cost commodity mind-set. For example, customers must choose and pay for extra services beyond a seat.[9] Service providers do not typically associate Ryanair with collaboration, and the company has a reputation for having little time for rapport building.

Ryanair's relationship with Swissport is an example of a business model mismatch. Swissport, an outsourced service provider for aviation ground-handling services, was struggling to meet Ryanair's Desired Outcomes. Simply put, Swissport reportedly was locked in a ruinous outsourcing deal with Ryanair.[10] Deregulation and intense market competition in the United Kingdom had created a price war that drove prices spiraling down. The Ryanair-Swissport outsourcing service agreement triggered payments on the completion of administrative tasks unrelated to the aircraft actually being dispatched from the airport. Swissport staff members felt that the rewards and penalties associated with the agreement were unbalanced; they were tired of Ryanair's constant on-site supervision of Swissport supervisors and wrote about it frequently on blogs.

Swissport needed a solution fast. Its executives called a meeting with Ryanair at Ryanair's European hub airport at Stansted, in the United Kingdom. The meeting had a make-it-or-break-it atmosphere. The Ryanair team members, typically adversarial, might have been thinking "Don't talk to us about collaboration." What they said was "We just want our aircraft out on time!"

Surprisingly, that statement was the beginning of an opportunity to talk about service outcomes. With awareness of the benefits of the outcome-based approach, the parties restructured their agreement and made the relationship more transparent.[11] In the new spirit of "low-cost efficiency," Ryanair offered to have its own staff work with local teams as integrated team members, not supervisors. Not only did an outcome-based solution save the contract, it improved the relationship.

Ryanair was satisfied with the new agreement. Adrian Dunne, the deputy ground operations director, said, "Our collaboration with Swissport has already proved its worth. And this latest agreement puts us in an excellent position to face tomorrow's challenges in cost terms, too."[12] More important, from a Vested point of view, the relationship shifted to a collaborative outcome-based business model and delivered a more sustainable commercial model.

Is a Vested Business Model Right for You?

During discussions, the company and the service provider should agree on and align each of the attributes of their joint business model. Once you have agreed on the attributes of your business model, you will reach a point in the journey where you will formally agree that a Vested agreement is the right relationship fit and make a joint commitment to stick together for the journey.

But what if you discover that you are not a good fit? As stated in the *Vested Outsourcing* book, creating an outcome-based business model is often challenging and may not be appropriate for everyone. Vested Outsourcing requires significant mind-set adjustments and a shift from conventional transaction-based approaches to a collaborative and transparent relationship with service providers. There are risks in partnering with a service provider. However, done properly, the rewards far outweigh the risks.

If your company has entrenched cultural and ecosystems that may be averse to some of the key attributes of Vested Outsourcing (transparency, trust, mutual gain, collaboration), the method is likely a difficult leap. Even if a true Vested agreement is not a perfect fit right now, every organization can aspire to achieve a more transparent collaborative relationship with its service providers and evolve over time to build a number of Vested agreements into its portfolio. Therefore, you can still benefit from the process. For example, what business agreement would not benefit from having a Shared Vision, a Statement of Intent, and a sound governance structure?

For service providers, there is also enormous value in having a structured process to articulate how aligned your services are to clients' business objectives. It is not the customers' job to tell you how great you are. Keep in mind that if you choose to embark on a Vested journey, the probability of success in reaching a fully optimal agreement will depend on the time and effort the parties invest in completing the exercises in this manual.

The key message is that while it is not always appropriate to invest time setting up a Vested agreement, adopting a collaborative approach and being open to suggestions about how the other party can add value to your operation is *always* the wisest approach. It is a key to competitive advantage.

Once you have confidence that Vested Outsourcing is the right business model, you can feel comfortable moving to Element 2 of your Vested agreement, where you proceed to develop a Shared Vision and share your intentions with your business partner.

HOMEWORK

Element 1

Mapping Your Business Model

Getting Started

At the end of each homework section there are Tips of the Trade tables that provide important summary points and take-aways for each element.

Using the business mapping template from Figure 3.4, map the potential outcomes your company could achieve through external relationships. This analysis will visually establish how well each of you is aligned to one another's goals. The model can be used by companies and suppliers.

If you are the outsourcing company, map your attributes against the business model criteria. Your analysis will give an indication of where you are. If a majority of your service provider's capabilities fall within a particular zone, aim to base a new relationship or reposition an existing one in accordance with the predominant zone.

If you are a service provider, start with a target customer and map your own capabilities against the Desired Outcomes. These outcomes are generic in nature and can be tailored to specific customers. If the majority of your capabilities fall within a particular zone, aim to base a new relationship or reposition an existing relationship in accordance with the predominant zone.

To maximize the real value in this exercise, the parties should complete it and then compare results. Doing this will begin a dialogue about the gaps between the views. Encourage questions and double-check assumptions about compatibility gaps in the relationship, potential opportunities to demonstrate added value, and further alignment. The process also will highlight each party's capabilities, if they were not previously visible. In some circumstances, mismatches will become obvious and can be addressed in a positive, constructive manner.

A bilateral approach affords the greatest opportunity for transparency. Your discussions should result in a consensus view of capabilities. With a consensus view, you can determine if Vested is the right model for your relationship. You can even map the business model and relationship over an extended period of time to keep a running record.

> *Tools of the Trade*
> Use the template from Figure 3.4 to assess company fit and compatibility. Once you have your own view, find out how your supplier or client views your organization. Then compare the gaps.

✓ *Check Your Work*

1. Have you completed the model? How do you compare?
2. In which zone did you place your relationships?
3. How did this compare with your original expectations?
4. How does this knowledge change your perception of where your relationships should fit?
5. What information do you need to make a conscious, committed decision to focus on agreed outcomes?
6. Have you asked your provider/customer to score your relationship?
7. Were there mismatches between the views of each party? What conversations will you have to resolve mismatches?

Templates, tools, and other resources are available for download at the Vested Outsourcing website, www.vestedoutsourcing.com/resources/tools/. (Also see Appendixes C and D.)

Figure 3.4 Mapping Business Model Template

Mapping Attributes	Zone 1	Zone 2	Zone 3	Zone 4	Zone 5	Zone 6
Vital to core business purpose	Minimal	Low	Medium	Medium to High	High	Critical
Enhances brand image	None	Low	Medium	High	High	Critical
Impact on customer experience	None	Low	Medium	High	High	Critical
Maintains customer experience	None	Low	Medium	High	High	Critical
Opportunities for efficiency gains	None	Low	Medium	High	Very High	Critical
Contributes to Innovation	None	Low	Medium	High	Very High	Critical
Consistently safe and reliable	Not capable	Semi-skilled	Skilled	Professional	Professional	Expert
Impact on operational safety	Minimal	Low	Medium	High	High	Critical
Organic growth capability	None	Low	Medium	High	Very High	Constant
Access to critical systems and processes	None	Low	Medium	High	High	Critical
Availability of required technology	Universal	Limited	Restricted	Scarce	Scarce	Unique
Impact of supplier loss or failure	None	Low	Medium	High	High	Critical
Cost to switch supplier	None	Low	Medium	High	High	Very High
Dependence on assets/capabilities	None	Low	Medium	High	High	Critical
Lean supply cost	Low	Medium	High	High to Invest	Invest	Capital
Cost of Staff	Minimal	Low	Medium	High	High	Very High
Availability of qualified personnel	High	High	Medium	Low	Low	Low
Skill level of predominant personnel	Unskilled	Semi-skilled	Skilled	Professional	Professional	Expert

Figure 3.5   Tips of the Trade

Tips of the Trade – ELEMENT 1 – Business Model	
Tip 1	Use a bilateral approach to Business Model Mapping companies outsourcing and their service provider should both complete an analysis and then compare results.
Tip 2	Open a dialogue, encourage questions and highlight compatibility gaps in the relationship, work together to resolve gaps
Tip 3	Develop a consensus view of the capabilities
Tip 4	It is always a wise to adopt a collaborative approach to your outsourcing relationship

ELEMENT 2: GETTING TO WE—CREATING A SHARED DESTINY BY STATING YOUR INTENTIONS

If you have chosen to adopt a Vested agreement, you should already be a firm believer in what's-in-it-for-we (WIIFWe) thinking. Most people who choose the Vested model have experienced firsthand how the all-too-prevalent what's-in-it-for-me (WIIFMe) thinking can cause relationships and commercial agreements to deteriorate. When creating a Vested agreement, all parties are striving together for the win-win outcome.

Getting to We is the essential precondition, the philosophical mantra, if you will, that forms the architecture for a collaborative, trusting endeavor while keeping narrow, win-at-all-costs urges at bay. It is really not possible to have a successful Vested ecosystem in place without first committing to the WIIFWe approach.

The problem is that businesspeople often have a blind spot when it comes time to collaborate. Many organizations *believe,* and even boast, that they have solid partnerships in place. People expound about "partnership" and "win-win," but our experience and research has found that individuals and companies often revert to selfish WIIFMe behaviors. This is a natural instinct. You see it all the time in almost every human endeavor. We are taught to win from early childhood; most institutions, universities, and sports teams—even at an amateur level—focus on winning. Many organizations formally train procurement and sales professionals in the art of negotiation tactics designed to give their organization leverage and a winning edge. At the same time, it is easy to stay entrenched in WIIFMe thinking. It is tough to change a mind-set to WIIFWe. (Specific WIIFWe negotiation and collaboration techniques are outlined in chapter 9.) As parties progress toward a Vested Outsourcing agreement, they should focus on creating a culture and ecosystem where they are working together to ensure mutual success.

There is a significant difference between engaging a service provider and establishing a Vested Outsourcing agreement. To be a true Vested partner, the service provider must have a vested interest in being a competent and efficient collaborator in the company's success. The mentality *must* shift from an us-versus-them to a we philosophy, or WIIFWe. Our experience and the case studies we have researched show that companies that recognize their service providers as partners to their success can achieve transformational results. Outsourcing companies cannot expect partnership and transparency from service providers while withholding information or manipulating situations to their own benefit. The WIIFWe mentality is a two-way street.

Shift in Thinking

Before proceeding further, let us examine a real example of WIIFMe versus WIIFWe thinking. An outsourced contract manufacturer touched a box 12 times to assemble a package for its customer. Under a conventional transaction-based (non-Vested) outsourcing agreement, the service provider got paid for each touch. Let us say the parties negotiated 2 cents per touch. In that case, the provider would make 24 cents per assembled box.

After an hour of building boxes, one of the service provider's employees told the line supervisor that the boxes were poorly designed. He felt that with simple design modifications, a box could be fashioned that would require only seven touches. Under the conventional agreement, the supervisor would have said, "Go back to work, buddy. We get paid by the touch! If we tell the customer we could do it in seven touches, then not only would we have to pay for the modification ourselves, we'd also lose 10 cents labor per box and another 5 cents in material charges! At 5 million boxes, this would reduce our revenue by $750,000!"

Because the conventional model was a fee per unit of activity, or transaction-based business model, the service provider would be penalized by a reduction in revenue for a significant process improvement. It is easy to see why service providers would have no motivation to suggest a change like this: It reduces revenue. After all, isn't the goal to make as much money as possible? Cutting the service provider's revenue stream does not seem like a way to accomplish this goal.

But when you apply the WIIFWe thinking strategy, the parties would create a culture and an incentive program to encourage employees to bring ideas forward to enhance innovation and efficiencies. In this scenario, when the line worker brings the idea to the supervisor, she immediately says, "Hey, good thinking! Let's take a look at how much it will cost to redesign the box to see if your idea will save money. If it works, we can offer better lead times and delivery targets making our customer more competitive. We can save inventory costs, earn a service performance bonus, save the costs of production, and can offer a better volume reduction. The customer gets a better overall total cost of ownership—and you get a bonus for your idea. Everyone's a winner!" Using a Vested approach, the service provider would have substantial incentives to help the customer redesign this package to reduce the total cost.

Figure 3.6 shows the costs and revenue for the 12- versus 7-touch box. Making a change to the box has the potential annual savings of $750,000, but it also impacts the service provider's profit margin, reducing it from $300,000 to $75,000, a

Figure 3.6   Box Costs and Revenue Detail—Example

	12 Touch Box	7 Touch Box	Difference	% Change
Supplier revenue				
Box cost	$0.50	$0.45	$(0.05)	–10%
Supplier fee per touch	$0.02	$0.02		
Supplier touch fee revenue	$0.24	$0.14	$(0.10)	–42%
Total cost per unit	$0.74	$0.59	$(0.15)	–20%
Total units/year	5,000,000	5,000,000		
Supplier total revenue	$3,700,000	$2,950,000	$(750,000)	–20%
Supplier costs				
Material cost	$2,500,000	$2,250,000	$(250,000)	–10%
Inventory carrying	$250,000	$225,000	$(25,000)	–10%
Labor	$600,000	$350,000	$(250,000)	–42%
Overhead	$50,000	$45,000	$(5,000)	–10%
Cost to modify	N/A	$5,000	$5,000	
Total supplier cost	$3,400,000	$2,875,000	$(525,000)	–15%
Supplier margin	$300,000	$75,000	$(225,000)	–75%
Build cycle time	48 sec	28 sec	–10 sec	–42%

loss of $225,000. Because there is no incentive for the supplier to bring this innovation to the company, the company would lose out on any savings from the improvement.

Let us look at this case under a Vested agreement where the parties have agreed to these points:

- The service provider is reimbursed for the cost to implement improvements.
- The service provider is reimbursed for lost margin.

- There is an incentive bonus to the supplier of 20 percent of the savings (after reimbursements for costs and margin).

(See Figure 3.7.)

It is clear that under a Vested agreement, implementing the improvement is beneficial to both parties: the company receives an 11 percent savings of $416,000, and the service provider improves its margin by 36 percent, or $109,000. The $750,000 savings is used to cover the cost of the improvement and to make the supplier's margin whole. The additional margin the service provider receives ensures that it has an incentive to make the processes better. There is an added benefit in the form of improved productivity; by reducing the number of touches, each box now takes 20 seconds less to assemble, a 42 percent reduction (over 1,000 person-days of labor).

Within the Vested Outsourcing philosophy, service providers are more apt to achieve clients' Desired Outcomes, because

Figure 3.7   Box Cost/Savings and Margin—Example

Non-Vested	Company Cost/ Savings	Supplier Margin
Original $	$3,700,000	$300,000
$ After improvement	$2,950,000	$75,000
Change $	$75,000	$(225,000)
% Change	20%	–75%
Vested Model		
Base savings/margin	$750,000	$75,000
Reimburse implementation cost	$(5,000)	$5,000
Reimburse lost supplier margin	$(225,000)	$225,000
20% of savings incentive	$(104,000)	$104,000
Vested savings & margin	$416,000	$409,000
% Change	11%	36%

they also will be rewarded with sustainable margins and perhaps an increasing portfolio in other areas. In essence, service providers are rewarded for applying brainpower to solve the company's business problems, not just for executing an activity. This is a classic win-win example where the company and the service provider apply WIIFWe thinking to achieve innovative commercial solutions.

Admittedly, developing a WIIFWe relationship is easier to describe than to implement. Moving from a culture of oversight and control to one of mutual respect, cooperation, and trust is a very different and difficult transition for most companies. Adversarial relationships often persist if the conditions to pursue self-interest rather than collaboration prevail. Getting to a true win-win relationship can take time and practice.

Companies that use a Vested Outsourcing approach do not spend much time talking about how a business model can give their service providers the opportunity to make more money. The parties focus instead on how the model delivers better value or better performance at the same or lower total overall lifecycle cost. Nevertheless, service providers that work under Vested Outsourcing partnerships often focus on its higher profit potential. Interestingly enough, successfully designed Vested Outsourcing partnerships create happier clients despite service providers' opportunities to generate greater profit potential.

Because both organizations are working together to achieve a common set of results, Vested Outsourcing works based on the mutual-relationship philosophy, which is what partnership is all about. Each organization may have different motivations, but both share the same set of Desired Outcomes. They are vested in each other's success.

Shared Vision, Shared Success

There are two steps to take as parties create a Shared Vision. The first is to develop that Shared Vision. The second is to distill the Shared Vision into a joint Statement of Intent.

The Shared Vision statement is the cornerstone of the Vested agreement. It sets forth the larger, guiding principles for the business relationship and the purposes for going on the Vested journey together. Many complex transactions have recitals, or statements explaining the reasons upon which the agreement is established, at the beginning of the contract. The Shared Vision is more comprehensive than recitals.

A Shared Vision might follow this template:

[Enter the name of the Parties] mutually agree that we will jointly deliver [enter the defined service or outcome that the agreement is accountable for delivering] for our mutual customer(s) and we agree that this cannot be achieved without the care, dedication and commitment of our integrated teams operating always with the same voice and with complete focus on the [enter outcome]

The lesson here is to ask questions until you find the words that represent the link between the core purpose of the agreement and the paradigm shift that occurs through collaboration.

The parties will then use the Shared Vision to set the foundation for their Vested agreement. The Shared Vision should be *included* in the agreement itself; this is not optional. The parties should review it at the start of each meeting during the life of the agreement as a reminder of the raison d'etre for the collaborative effort and the principle of reciprocity embedded within the agreement. The homework section assists the parties in developing their Shared Vision and joint Statement of Intent.

We highly recommend that you start working with a neutral party at this point in the process, much like an executive business coach, to act as a "deal architect."[13] A deal architect acts as a mediator or facilitator, encouraging the parties to look for the mutual gain by helping both parties see the opportunities that are obscured by win-lose thinking. A deal architect helps both teams define goals and unlock the positive behaviors that will help them achieve those goals. Therefore, a deal architect should not be an employee of either company. The point is that a neutral party helps the parties learn to work collaboratively during all phases of the agreement.[14]

C a s e   S t u d y

Jaguar and Unipart: Vested for Success

The Importance of a Shared Vision

Companies should enlist senior leadership, including chief executive officers (CEOs), if possible, to participate in creating the Shared Vision. The reason is simple: when two leaders help set the vision, it is much easier for the teams implementing the project to create an agreement that will embody the strategic direction of both firms. Also, if you are crafting a Vested agreement, it is likely because the relationship is strategic in nature and warrants executive-level support.

Jaguar and Unipart are a great example of the power of CEO vision to get a Vested agreement jump-started. Jaguar began working with Unipart almost 25 years ago. The initial focus of the outsourcing effort was aftermarket parts fulfillment in the United Kingdom. When Sir Nick Scheele took over at the helm as CEO of Jaguar in 1992, the two companies had an established track record. But after recognizing that the relationship was not working as well as it could, he had an informal dinner discussion with Unipart's CEO, John Neill. The goal was to discuss how the companies could improve the business model while also driving more positive benefits for both Jaguar and Unipart. These discussions ultimately led to the creation of this Shared Vision statement.

To support Jaguar dealers in delivering a Unique Personal Ownership Experience to Jaguar Drivers

*worldwide, ensuring industry leading owner loyalty
through partnership and world-class logistics*[15]

This Shared Vision statement embodies a key tenet of
Vested Outsourcing: WIIFWe. The Shared Vision not
only strengthened the personal relationship between
two leaders; it led to a deeper understanding of each
other's business model and how to leverage the other
for maximum gain. It led to discussions on such topics
as who the real customer is, who defines the success of
both companies and how to measure success.

There are two key takeaways from this example.
The first important point is that a Shared Vision statement aligns the companies toward a common goal and
also transcends the self-interests of each individual
company. "Our destinies are linked," explained Neill.
He elaborated: "If Jaguar's sales increase, our profits
increase, and if their sales go down, we make less money.
But we also have the ability to influence sales through
the investments we make to innovate and improve our
processes."[16]

The second takeaway is that a Shared Vision and a
flexible Vested business model allow companies to adjust
as economics and markets change. As all business professionals know, business is dynamic. A Shared Vision
statement keeps the companies focused on how to drive
the business forward as markets evolve. Open dialogues
build trust, allowing the partners to look beyond the
documented statement of work and tactical measures
that typify most outsourcing agreements. Trust further
enables Unipart to take independent action in pursuit
of the Shared Vision statement—ultimately driving
value for Jaguar and Jaguar's customers.

The Shared Vision statement has become embedded in each company's culture, surviving many organizational changes. Neill noted, "There have been

personnel changes at Jaguar and Unipart over the years. This sometimes has led to changes in the way we work together, but the Shared Vision statement helps keep our relationship pointed in the right direction." The Shared Vision, coupled with a strong governance structure, helps to keep the relationship on track when senior leadership changes occur.

Bottom-Line Benefits

Jaguar and Unipart's Shared Vision focusing on delivering "industry leading owner loyalty" has paid off handsomely as the companies work together to deliver real value for Jaguar dealers and car owners. When Unipart entered into the contract more than 20 years ago, Jaguar ranked ninth in the J. D. Power and Associates survey for Customer Satisfaction. In 2008, it moved to number 1—passing Lexus, BMW, and Mercedes Benz. Jaguar has maintained that spot ever since.[17]

Customer satisfaction comes from other improvements, such as:

- Increased parts availability from 92.3 percent to 97.5 percent
- Reduced call center wait from 10 minutes 10 seconds to 20 seconds
- Increased U.K. to U.S. container fill to 46 percent
- Reduced inventory by 30 percent
- Reduced backorders by 76 percent
- Improved warranty parts processing from seven days to same day

The end result? The Shared Vision led to true collaboration and WIIFWe thinking between Jaguar and Unipart. Collaboration has led to further transformational improvements in getting Jaguar's service parts logistics to best in class. The companies' Shared Vision, supported by active collaboration, can certainly enhance business prospects as Jaguar aggressively launches its new XJ luxury model.

As the Ryanair and Jaguar examples demonstrate, for true collaboration to occur, it is necessary to shift mind-sets and approaches from the pursuit of independent goals to the joint attainment of a mutually expressed vision.

Getting to We: Stating Intentions

Establishing shared intentions is the second step in the Vested process. For any business agreement to succeed, the parties must establish the right kind of relationship dynamics. The Shared Vision sets the stage, but it also is important to ensure that each company aligns its intentions with that vision. More important, the relationship must be based on integrity, trust, and respect. Our experience proves that once companies make a commitment to move forward, there are often periods of uncertainty, and mistakes are bound to occur. There should be enough trust in the stability and foundation of the relationship to allow open communication about shortcomings when a mutual adjustment is needed.

As stated earlier, business happens. Events occur that can destabilize relationships. The parties must have clearly stated intentions that describe how they will align the business relationship if and when it gets out of sync. In short, how will each company behave? Ground rules are necessary for the business relationships in order to avoid miscommunication and misalignment.

If the Vested journey is beginning with a new partner, it is important to discuss intentions as early as possible. We can assure you there is no downside to early engagement, whether the partner is new or existing.

Sharing intentions builds the foundation for the entire agreement. Not only does it set out how you will work together to achieve your agreement, it establishes how the parties will behave once the agreement is documented in a written contract. Consider the time you spend together to develop your agreement as a trial period—an expressway that allows you to get to know the other party and test your intentions and behavior.

During this early stage, parties should work to establish trust and openness and to build this trust at every opportunity prior to a formal commitment. As the relationship grows, each company will seek to maintain that trust and openness in a manner consistent with the Shared Vision and Joint Statement of Intentions.

Sharing intentions is not easy. Companies with a selfish mind-set almost always will focus only on what is *required* of them. A cooperative and collaborative attitude encourages conversations to explore what is needed to deliver unambiguous business outcomes. Some companies may even admit to a gap in their own capability; however, by focusing on the vision and business outcomes, gaps in capability easily can be rectified.

In order to achieve this level of openness, the other party must be equally open-minded and collaborative. Only complete candor can clarify intentions and achieve agreement on the best possible path forward. Candor makes it easier to do business with each other and removes the need for scoring points because the effort required to reach the goal is fair and equitable. If the secret intention is to win and you only make public statements about collaboration, the underlying disconnect between your words and your deeds inevitably will spill over into the relationship, causing clarification questions. Eventually it will erode trust and confidence. You should be in sync on your joint intentions right from the get-go, and you must stay in sync. This is where behavioral economics meets conventional economics, proving to be the most powerful and long-lasting joint relationship statement you will make as you begin your Vested journey. The statement does not have to be big, but it does need to have teeth, and it needs to matter.

Creating the Joint Statement of Intent

We believe it is most appropriate to develop the Statement of Intent jointly. Consider your Statement of Intent as working principles under which the parties commit to operate. Intentions are not metrics. Some companies directly link service provider behavior to the performance of deliverables in exchange for the negotiated price per widget. Outlining metrics should come much later in the Vested journey. Here the parties need to decide whether to include a clause stating that a failure to behave as expressly intended can be a trigger that potentially leads to a breach of the agreement.

At a minimum, a joint Statement of Intent should include these seven elements:

1. Shared Vision and purpose
2. Communication
3. Perspective
4. Trust and confidence
5. Flexibility
6. Focus
7. Feedback

Each of these elements is explained in more detail next.

Shared Vision and Purpose
The Shared Vision and purpose statement is reiterated in its entirety at the beginning of the joint Statement of Intent. It sets the big picture for the operation of the joint business endeavor throughout its existence.

Communication
The communication section outlines the parties' expected communications program. In a Vested relationship, having a performance governance structure is not enough, as it often focuses on maximizing the successful implementation of the agreement's finite provisions within defined targets. (This is

discussed in more detail in chapter 7.) A strategic communication statement is the bold, visible, joint commitment of mutual trust and integrity. The companies' leaders promise to nurture and maintain their relationship at the highest organizational level. When building the rest of the Vested agreement, team members will rely on the leadership mandate to improve cooperation and explore new transformational programs.

Perspective

In the perspective section, the parties openly acknowledge that each brings its own opinions and perspectives to the relationship. Neither is right or wrong. The opinions are just that—opinions. During the course of the relationship, there will likely be points of contention and disagreement. Issues will arise that will not be covered under the terms of the agreement. Setting an intention to respect perspectives creates the boundaries and guidance for the team members executing the agreement. It further encourages team members to listen actively by asking clarifying questions. (Clarifying questions seek to understand the facts and appreciate the other party's perspective about those facts.)

Trust and Confidence

Mutual trust and confidence are built over time. We consider this part of the joint Statement of Intent to be the spirit of the agreement. It is also the broad context of agreed-upon ethical behavior. Each party demonstrates trust by appreciating the specific skills and capabilities of the other party. Trust is enhanced when each party delivers the Desired Outcomes without unnecessary interference or additional input. With trust, each company can do its job without micromanaging the other.

Flexibility

The flexibility section provides stability. Because Vested agreements are long term, and markets change over time, some market changes may disrupt a Vested agreement. The parties will be required to convene quickly in order to adjust the business model. At the outset of the agreement, both parties should agree on their flexibility tolerance level. Each company also will commit to reciprocal flexibility. We suggest you set up a nominal "flexibility fund"—a mutually agreed collection of resources designed to smooth out little issues or variations that people forgot to include in the statement of work and are needed to keep the agreement on the right track before the formal contractual change process kicks in. It also sets a psychological boundary around small variations and encourages good behavior when small changes happen. Don't sweat the small stuff!

Focus

The focus section determines the order of priorities in pursuit of the Desired Outcomes. By establishing focus at this stage of the journey, the companies maintain a positive outlook in unfamiliar situations. It is important to set forth effective techniques to ensure an equitable balance within the relationship.

Feedback

The feedback section details the process the parties will use to give each other advice. This section creates the vision that will guide you in creating the governance section of your agreement. The goal is to establish a profitable relationship over the course of many years. Therefore, it is better to use a collaborative process to create the joint feedback procedure. Decide now how to keep in touch with each other's thoughts and opinions about the health of the relationship and how often you will informally and formally give each other feedback.

The amount of time devoted to addressing each of these points is entirely a matter of choice. What is important is to discuss each element jointly. The meeting to do so may be the first time each party candidly expresses its perspectives to the other. It also may reveal some unpleasant attitudes that are actually very easy to rectify. No one likes to hear tough or negative feedback; however, bad news does not age well, and it is much better to get it all out in the open so you can clear the path to better performance.

There is absolutely no value in spending time and effort building a close working relationship with a service provider that simply wants to get the basic job done, get paid, and keep the relationship at arm's length. Likewise, if companies want to shop around for cut-rate prices and terminate short-term relationships to save a few pennies, there is no reason to go to the effort of creating a Vested agreement. The parties owe it to one another to be honest about their intentions. As mentioned several times, Vested agreements openly address risks and rewards. You do not want to enter uncharted waters with a company that is not committed to making the journey focused and determined to meet the joint goals and outcomes.

Getting It Right

As we have said, Vested Outsourcing is not for the faint of heart; it challenges the mind-set of senior executives, middle managers, and especially procurement specialists.

Unfortunately, a culture of adversarial intentions exists in most stakeholder professions that are involved in getting to a Vested agreement, such as legal, sales, and commercial and procurement professionals. Vested Outsourcing often requires people to have the willpower to walk away from an immediate price savings in order to build relationships that really work, unlock untapped value, and save total transactional costs in the future.

Vested Outsourcing demands a willingness to throw out the Kraljic models of the 1980s and transcend the ingrained win-lose approach. Many senior executives have adhered to conventional transaction-based approaches for their entire careers.

They may be reluctant to change their business style and their company's culture. The most successful Vested Outsourcing agreements garner top-level executive support from both the company outsourcing and the service provider involved in the agreement.

Executives such as Sir Nick Scheele of Jaguar and Unipart's CEO John Neill have challenged conventional transaction-based approaches and charted the course, proving that a Vested Outsourcing business model can and does enable companies to drive business transformations spanning the boundaries of what either party could achieve on its own. (See Appendix B.)

Vested Outsourcing is no different from other transformational business improvement initiatives, such as Total Quality Management, Lean, or Six Sigma, in that the more executive support and buy-in there is, the more the likelihood for success. The most important support top-level executives can provide is ensuring that Vested agreement team members have sufficiently broad corporate guardrails, or boundaries, to achieve success in the development of creative risk and reward structures. Ultimately, among the parties involved in a Vested agreement, it is the senior leaders who must take an active role shaping a WIIFWe culture and guide teams on the right kind of behavioral competencies.

A note of caution: even when senior leadership commits to the Vested Outsourcing approach, middle-level managers can succumb to what we refer to as the "junkyard dog factor"—one of the ten ailments of outsourcing. (See Appendix A.) We have witnessed employees going to great lengths to maintain what they consider their territorial claim to certain processes, insisting that these processes must stay in-house to protect themselves and their turf, or simply to make them feel more comfortable with a known way of doing things. This ailment can afflict some companies so severely that they have to restructure entire departments or bring in new senior-level people to challenge conventional thinking and defensive behavior and lead change management programs by coaching employees to get beyond conventional win-lose thinking and move to more effective behavior.

In a Vested agreement, it is critical for the company and the service provider to ensure a combined professional community and understand the need to shift away from the conventional I-win-you-lose adversarial thinking and work together to deliver the best results. A deal architect can play an important role in helping teams unlock their abilities to balance all stakeholder requirements and remain agile and focused on making sure the Vested agreement works for all parties involved. Deal architects are also well suited to play a neutral third-party role to temper the position of certain stakeholder groups, such as sales, legal, and procurement, which often adversely impact potential deal outcomes by taking extreme positions.

Vested Outsourcing demands a WIIFWe mind-set, which stresses benefits to the company, the service provider, and the consumer over the long haul. Using the Vested approach everyone reaps the mutual gains promised when creating the Vested business model. With a new mind-set and cultural shift, Vested Outsourcing will work. We have seen it work!

And even better news? The partnership is stronger because the parties have explored the limits and expectations of the relationship, everyone involved has a clearer understanding of expectations, and ground rules for behavior are set at the highest leadership levels and will be measured. A new level of cooperation and trust will occur, and firms will identify and avoid the typical outsourcing ailments.

HOMEWORK

Element 2

Shared Vision and Statement of Intent

Getting Started

Putting a joint Statement of Intent at the beginning of the agreement makes sense; it establishes the ground rules and framework for mutual behavioral expectations. Expressing your intentions is the second step in developing your agreement, and it is often done simultaneously with developing your Shared Vision. These two exercises, Shared Vision and joint Statement of Intent, set the stage for the entire relationship and determine how the companies will strive to make the agreement work.

For your homework on this element, outline major points you would include in a Shared Vision statement and Statement of Intent with a prospective company or service provider:

- Shared Vision and purpose
- Communication
- Perspective
- Trust and confidence
- Flexibility
- Focus
- Feedback

To do this, go back and review each required section of the Statement of Intent and create your own statement of intentions for each section. Be honest about your intentions for the relationship, and test whether your initial intentions are aligned with the Vested approach or if you must close some gaps before you proceed. There is no easy blueprint or checklist to this homework section. It requires deep self-awareness, a gap analysis, and an action plan to rectify any gaps. This process will be entirely personal and business specific. What we can offer is a template of a Statement of Intent that embodies all the Vested principles at the highest levels of cooperation. The real home-work is not just to copy it but to test your own ability to live it and behave in the way it suggests.

> ### Tools of the Trade
>
> Here is a simple template that can be used as a format for each section of the Statement of Intent.
>
> ### Sample Joint Statement of Intent
>
> #### 1. Shared Vision
>
> *Option 1:*
>
> The Parties will work together for the Term, in good faith and with the overall mutually desired intention, to achieve [ENTER THE SHARED VISION]. The Parties agree that the Shared Vision will be achieved only by the continuing cooperation, combined mutual efforts, and good relations among and between the Parties and in accordance with the principles set out in this Statement of Intent.
>
> *Option 2:*
>
> Example text>The Parties will work together in good faith for the Term to achieve transformational business solutions that are mutually beneficial to the Parties ("Shared Vision"). The Parties agree that the Shared Vision will be achieved only through continuing cooperation, trust, and commitment. In order to achieve the vision and foster good relations, the Parties recognize the importance of adhering to the principles set forth in the Statement of Intent.
>
> #### 2. Communication
>
> The Parties will, at their mutual convenience, begin regular and frequent dialogue and, where applicable, organize a

schedule of working initiatives including but not limited to face-to-face meetings with key senior leaders, and embark on employee exchanges, joint working-level forums. and relevant company events in the furtherance of deeper mutual understanding to assist attainment of the Shared Vision. The precise method and manner for these and other meetings will be detailed in the Governance section of the agreement. The Parties may, at their own election, nominate suitable representatives for the purpose of enhancing understanding and communication between the Parties and will make known to the other Party any relevant and appropriate matters that would assist and enable the other Party to further succeed in the delivery of their specific obligations in this Agreement.

3. Perspective

During the Term, the Parties will seek to build on the good relations between the Parties through careful consideration and mutual appreciation of the perspective of the other Party on all matters and questions that arise during the lifetime of the Agreement. The Parties appreciate and respect that there may be occasions where they have differing views and perspectives. Notwithstanding the terms of the Agreement, the Parties desire to have a harmonious working-together relationship and will counsel all contributors to the performance of this Agreement to be courteous and respectful at all times.

4. Trust and Confidence

The Company appreciates the Service Provider's skills and capabilities. The Company has confidence in the Service Provider's ability to deliver work without undue interference. The Service Provider trusts that the Company will provide

88

it with all necessary, timely, and accurate information and feedback throughout the duration of the agreement. The Parties will create and focus on metrics that matter (as set out in clause XX) to the Shared Vision.

5. Flexibility

The Parties have mutually agreed on the Scope of Work for this agreement. The Parties further agree that there may from time to time be occasions when unforeseeable events occur not anticipated in the Scope of Work that require small amounts of additional resources or effort not previously anticipated. If and when such an event(s) occurs, the Parties will in good haste seek to agree a course of action to ensure that the Shared Vision remains achievable within the price. This flexibility shall be achieved by the creation of a defined "fund" comprising XX USD from Party 1 and XX USD from Party 2. This fund shall be used to [insert decide use here] and called upon in exceptional circumstances only, recorded and logged in accordance with the Change Order Process.

6. Focus

The Parties agree that in setting out priorities in respect of delivery of the work, pursuit of the Shared Vision is the primary focus of achievement. The Parties agree that in their plans to deliver the work, the Shared Vision will be visible to those performing work associated with this Agreement so that their contribution is clearly and directly relevant to the work being performed. All contributors to the delivery of covered services will be encouraged to express thoughts and observations on the best approach to deliver the best possible achievable results.

7. Feedback

In pursuit of continuing good relations, the Parties will create a formal feedback process to assess the health and fitness of the relationship and will seek contributions from all employees, affiliates, and subcontractors involved in delivering the work. The feedback will be presented in the communication forum to the joint leadership team and will be utilized to guide any necessary adjustments to support continued good relations between the Parties.

✓ *Check Your Work*

1. Review your Shared Vision statement; does it reflect the collaborative effort and principle of reciprocity you desire in the agreement?
2. Did you develop the Statement of Intent jointly? Is there agreement? Have you received top-level buy-in from both companies?
3. The Statement of Intent is a working guideline of principles under which the parties commit to operate. Have you decided whether to include a clause stating that "a failure to behave as expressly intended" can be a trigger leading to a breach of the agreement?
4. Have the parties been clear about their intentions for the relationship?
5. Did you test if your intentions are aligned to the Vested approach? If there were gaps, have you closed them?
6. Are you ready to accept your intentions and, more important, live by them?

Figure 3.8   Tips of the Trade

Tips of the Trade – ELEMENT 2 – Shared Vision and Statement of Intent	
Tip 1	The Shared Vision statement is the cornerstone of the Vested Agreement. It sets forth the larger, guiding principles for the business relationship
Tip 2	Be honest about your intentions for the relationship and test if your initial intentions are aligned to the Vested approach
Tip 3	If you identify gaps, close them before you proceed in developing your agreement
Tip 4	Living up to your intentions is more difficult than stating, however you must accept your intentions in order to have a successful Vested agreement
Tip 5	The parties should review it at the start of each meeting during the life of the agreement to keep parties aligned

CHAPTER 4

RULE #2: FOCUS ON THE *WHAT*, NOT THE *HOW*

A ll business agreements include some form of workscope. The purpose of Rule #2 is to understand and document outsourcing workscope between the company and the service provider. Adopting a Vested Outsourcing business model does not change this need. What does change is the level of detail and documentation.

The main difference between a conventional approach and the Vested Outsourcing approach is that under the Vested approach, the company that is outsourcing specifies *what* it wants and moves the responsibility of determining *how* the work gets delivered to the service provider.

Following the Vested Outsourcing approach for documenting workscope avoids a common trap from the ten ailments of outsourcing (see Appendix A) that we call the "outsourcing paradox." The "outsourcing paradox" occurs when a company outsources to a service provider because it knows the service provider can do a better job, yet the agreement is written as if the company is the expert, strictly defining how the work is to be done.[1] If you are reading this book, you have chosen to outsource and want to use a Vested Outsourcing approach. Do not constrain or undermine your service provider by telling it how to do its business!

To follow Rule #2, your Vested Outsourcing agreement should include documentation of the Desired Outcomes and the associated Statement of Objectives (SOO). Desired Outcomes set the high-level outcomes, and the SOO establishes the required objectives that the parties will strive to accomplish under the agreement. Under a Vested agreement, the company outsourcing must be willing to allow and enable the service provider to make significant changes to improve overall processes and flow within the workscope it is assigned.

Workload allocation plays a vital role in this process. A good Vested agreement ensures that the company and the service provider work together to optimize the end-to-end process rather than focusing on process effectiveness specific to the internal company. The parties focus on maximum integration (management and visibility) of the entire business process effectiveness. Workload allocation goes hand in hand with an SOO because it allows the service provider the flexibility to change current processes significantly to improve performance and meet the Desired Outcomes. For this reason, it is vital that the parties have a clear understanding of the end-to-end process and which party is accountable for which processes.

The aspects of Element 3 are discussed in detail in this chapter. As you work through your Vested agreement, you will complete homework assignments on each facet of Element 3. By the time you complete this chapter and its homework, you will have documented the Desired Outcomes for your agreement, along with the SOO. The deal's workscope is defined by allocating key processes to the party that provides the best value to the overall agreement.

ELEMENT 3: DESIRED OUTCOMES, STATEMENT OF OBJECTIVES, WORKLOAD ALLOCATION

Starting Point: Documenting Desired Outcomes

Baseball great Yogi Berra is often quoted for his folksy wit and funny but oddly apt takes on leadership and life. One of his notable quotes says, "You've got to be very careful if you don't know where you're going, because you might not get there."[2]

It is important to ask yourself (and then make yourself answer) the question about where you are headed or, more concretely, what you hope to achieve by developing a Vested agreement. The most effective Vested Outsourcing agreements focus on enterprise-wide performance expectations. We refer to these high-level expectations as Desired Outcomes. We start with a definition from the Macmillan Dictionary of the words *desire* and *outcomes* to help form a solid understanding of what we mean when we combine them to form the term *Desired Outcomes.*

Desire: Strong feeling of wanting to have or to do something.

Outcome: (1) The final result of a process, meeting, activity, and so on; (2) the possible or likely result of something.

Using these definitions, we can conclude that a Desired Outcome is a result that someone or some company strongly wants to achieve. Typically, Desired Outcomes include system-wide, high-level results for items such as lowered cost structures, higher service levels, higher market share, faster speed to market, reduced cycle time, more loyal customers, or more revenues. Desired Outcomes typically are boundary spanning—requiring that the company and the service provider work together to achieve success. Most important, Desired Outcomes are *not* the task-oriented service-level agreements (SLAs) typically found in conventional outsourcing agreements.

Many companies find it hard to identify and develop Desired Outcomes. This is especially true for organizations that suffer from the "outsourcing paradox," because they are so used to dictating how service providers should do the work. Companies that dictate how service providers should do work in an area where they have already decided they are deficient or simply do not want to work anymore are shortsighted, because dictating the "how" prevents the service provider from bringing its expertise to the relationship.

Companies should heed the advice of management gurus Tom Peters and Peter Drucker to "do what you do best and outsource the rest."[3] If a process is "core," do not outsource it; if it is not core to the business, leave it up to the service provider to understand how to put the supporting processes and resources in place to achieve the Desired Outcomes.

Consider information technology (IT) outsourcing arrangements, such as outsourcing help desk processes. Under a conventional approach, the company outsourcing would specify the hardware and software to use. It also likely would establish the level of staffing and staff-to-management ratios. Some companies dictate the skills required and insist on interviewing candidates.

This scenario diminishes or ignores the service provider's role as the expert. The service provider is the one that is constantly in the marketplace and keeping tabs on the latest developments that are core to its business. Unless the company has the skills and the resources to keep up with the latest innovations in the service it is outsourcing, it should leave the details to the experts. Vested Outsourcing relationships leverage what each firm does best. A Vested agreement challenges the service provider to deploy resources and assets needed to solve client problems and achieve the agreed upon Desired Outcomes.

One example of how a service provider can help solve a company's problems by aligning its efforts with the company's Desired Outcomes is Fujitsu. Fujitsu, an IT service provider, worked with one of its airline customers to cut IT expenditures. The costs were not aligned with the business processes, and it was almost impossible to tell how IT spend related sales, seats, or profits—all important Desired Outcomes—to the airline. Fujitsu and the airline restructured IT so that it related to the business and developed an agreement that linked IT costs to business performance. One example related to rescheduling missed takeoffs. If the airline missed a takeoff slot, rescheduling cost a lot of money. If Fujitsu caused the failure, it bore the cost of rescheduling. Under the agreement, the successes of the airline and of Fujitsu are intertwined—both are vested in each other's success.[4]

Determine Desired Outcomes before proceeding to the rest of your agreement. This is a must because Desired Outcomes are critical to Vested Outsourcing; they are the focal point for the Vested agreement and the primary message communicated to the service provider and to stakeholders. Service providers must agree on the Desired Outcomes because financial incentives are allocated when they achieve the company's Desired Outcomes. Stakeholders should agree on the Desired Outcomes because they reflect success for the organization.

Figure 4.1 is an example of the Desired Outcomes for a company that outsourced the facilities management and maintenance of its office campus.

You will develop Desired Outcomes as part of the homework for this chapter.

Creating the Statement of Objectives

Once you have jointly identified your Desired Outcomes, create a correlating statement of objectives (SOO). The SOO describes

Figure 4.1   Example Desired Outcomes

Example Desired Outcomes

- Facility management (ongoing operations and maintenance) that provide fully functioning facilities that are free from interruption outside of scheduled and approved maintenance activities
- Energy conservation efforts that reduce the campus carbon footprint by 20%
- Cost management practices that reduce planned total campus operations costs by 20%
- Standardized processes that achieve consistent service levels across all locations

and clarifies the Desired Outcomes in more detail, helping to define what success looks like. People often confuse a SOO with other tools for documenting the workscope. As a result, they often fall into the trap of defining *how* to perform the work. To prevent this common mistake, we outline the three tools for documenting workscope and show how they vary in nature. These tools are:

SOW: Statement of work
SOO: Statement of objectives
PWS: Performance work statement

Defining a Statement of Work

The SOW is the tool usually used by practitioners to document business requirements. Typically, a company outsourcing defines the tasks it wants the service provider to accomplish and documents those tasks. Most SOWs go to great lengths and detail to document the work. Many firms hire outside consultants and subject matter experts to help them write their SOWs. Frequently, SOWs dictate how to do the work, often detailing specifics such as staffing ratios of management to employees, the type of hardware to use, or the process steps to deploy.

There are two real weaknesses in using a SOW to document requirements. The first is that SOWs often let the service provider avoid accountability for results. If the service provider has performed the stated work under the SOW, it can state that it has met SOW requirements simply by doing the work. This is particularly true for companies that use a time and material approach for pricing the work. The second weakness is that when the company defines the work in detail, it limits innovation on the part of the service provider.

In summary, SOWs are best suited for transaction-based models, not for outcome-based or Vested Outsourcing business models. SOWs should be avoided in favor of SOOs.

Defining a Statement of Objectives

A SOO is drastically different from a SOW. A SOO specifies Desired Outcomes in terms of high-level objective statements and metrics with minimal detailed or prescriptive direction. Clearly stated objective statements clarify the meaning of a company's Desired Outcomes, helping to pinpoint what is strategically important to the company. The SOO also aligns and documents the key objectives that a company is trying to accomplish to achieve its Desired Outcomes.

Under a SOO, the service provider provides the know-how, innovation, and solutions to meet the company's objectives. A properly written SOO allows the service provider the flexibility to change current processes significantly by giving it flexibility regarding *how* to achieve the Desired Outcomes. A SOO expresses *what* the customer wants done (outcome); it does not focus on *how*. For that reason, the SOO does not specify any tasks.

It is important to remember that different companies engaged in outsourcing likely will have differing objectives and associated definitions of success for their Desired Outcomes. Take, for example, two companies considering the outsourcing of foodservice operations. Both might have a stated objective to reduce the cost of foodservice operations, so they might share a common Desired Outcome statement, say, "foodservice that reduces subsidized costs to the company."

However, let us dig a little more into each company. One company is a high-tech company located in a major industrial park. Meal cost and healthy menu options are important to the employees. Many leave the company's campus and go offsite for lunch. Because the company is located in an industrial park, most restaurants are at least a ten-minute drive from the company's campus, and it is common for employees to take a one-hour (or more) lunch break when they go off campus. As a result, the high-tech company has an additional objective of getting employees to eat on campus, which in turn will increase employee productivity by keeping employees from leaving the facility. This high-tech company's Desired Outcome may be stated as "foodservice that eliminates subsidized costs to the company and increases cafeteria utilization by employees." Reduced costs and improving utilization would be measures of success.

The second company has its corporate office in a large city and has a diverse workforce. The firm struggles with recruiting and maintaining highly talented employees and wants to differentiate itself from other nearby companies as a "good place to work." Because of the company's urban location, many of its employees are interested in trendy, gourmet-quality foods. Company executives believe that providing on-site high-end foodservice will give their company a competitive advantage when recruiting. The company's Desired Outcome is thus expanded to: "foodservice that reduces subsidized costs to the company and supports an image of company as the best place to work." This company would want to measure costs as well as recruiting success and employee retention, even though the service provider is not directly accountable for recruiting success and employee retention.

When determining Desired Outcomes and SOOs that are boundary-spanning, as in the last examples, it is understandable that a service provider may be hesitant to enter into an agreement that holds it accountable for success for objectives outside its control. The proper approach is to capture the high-level, end-to-end Desired Outcomes and associated objectives but to hold the service provider accountable for its specific roles and metrics. This is addressed in the workload allocation, discussed later in this chapter, and in chapter 5, which addresses establishing metrics.

Defining a Performance Work Statement

A PWS resides between a SOO and SOW in terms of specificity. When using a PWS, the company defines the expected results in the SOO and solicits solutions from service providers. The selected service provider then develops a PWS. Many companies that are first starting down the Vested Outsourcing road find it hard to move away from a conventional SOW. A PWS is often a good approach when a company wants to see how a service provider will perform the work while still allowing the service provider the flexibility to determine how to do it. Companies therefore often use a combination of SOOs and PWSs when developing SOWs and defining expectations for their Vested agreements.

A PWS still expects the service provider to drive innovation to fulfill the company's SOO—but it goes into more detail than a SOO. A PWS allows for input and innovation from the service provider in *how* it meets the Desired Outcomes and associated SOO. Using this approach allows the service provider to develop the best solution to solve the problem, including how to apply labor, processes, and capital. The PWS holds the service provider accountable for delivering solutions that meet the Desired Outcomes. For this reason, a PWS can and often does list tasks to be accomplished by the service provider. The requirements are always clearly stated and are measurable in a PWS, but the service provider has the flexibility and the freedom to change the PWS as needed.

It is important to note that using a PWS is *not* a requirement in a Vested agreement. If a PWS is used, it is not part of the formal agreement; rather, it is an additional resource that helps the companies to establish trust as they learn to work together effectively.

Comparing SOWs, SOOs, and PWSs
When comparing the level of service provider input to the tasks that are specified, the SOW has the lowest level of service provider input—often none at all—and is the most detailed in specifying the tasks to be performed. The SOO has the most service provider input and should not specify tasks at all, only outcomes, as illustrated in Figure 4.2.

Figure 4.2   SOW, PWS, and SOO

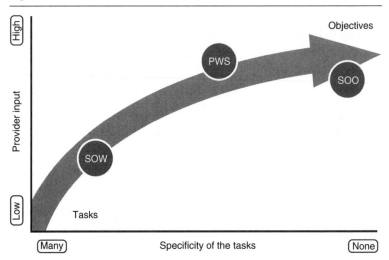

How the workscope is written either allows innovative solutions or limits the service provider's ability to propose them, so getting this right is important. Collaboration and flexibility are at the heart of a Vested Outsourcing agreement. Your agreement should contain a SOO and, if desired, a PWS—but, as we have said, never a SOW.

The process starts by determining how the company and the service provider will work together to document the workscope. It is important to envision how the two will interact to best achieve results because Vested Outsourcing is dependent on *cooperation* and *communication*. Understanding the cultures within the different organizations is imperative. In documenting the Desired Outcomes and workscope, the company must understand that it is giving control to the service provider to overcome the inherent risks that come with ensuring the Desired Outcomes are met.

Learning by Example
Requirements Roadmap—Foodservice

The next example helps illustrate how to document Desired Outcomes and objective statements. Objective statements are aligned to the Desired Outcomes in the SOO. Each outcome may be further refined with a few specific statements of objectives.

For example, a company that is outsourcing its foodservice developed this Desired Outcome statement: "A foodservice program that eliminates subsidized costs and increases the utilization by employees." Because the Desired Outcome is broad, a service provider is not likely to fully understand what success in reaching the Desired Outcome entails. The next step in the process is to develop objectives for each outcome that further defines *what*, not how. Remember, a good SOO has minimal prescriptive direction and allows the service provider to define the how.

In this case, the Desired Outcome is split into three SOOs:

1. Eliminate the company subsidy immediately.
2. Increase employee use of the cafeteria at lunchtime.
3. Pricing to the employees should remain at or below the current benchmark.

The resulting requirements roadmap is shown in Figure 4.3.

Figure 4.3   Requirements Roadmap Example

Desired Outcome	Performance		
	Statement of Objective	Standard	Tolerance/ AQL
Food service that eliminates subsidized costs to the company, and increases utilization by employees	Eliminate company subsidy immediately		
	Increase utilization rate of employees that eat in the cafeteria at lunchtime		
	Pricing to employees should remain at or below established benchmark		

The requirements roadmap allows objectives to have a measurable standard, or metric, which is defined in the "standard" and "tolerance/acceptable quality level (AQL)" columns of the roadmap. (See Appendixes C and D for additional tools and resources.) We explore how to make each objective measurable in chapter 5.

Workload Allocation

With the outcomes defined and the SOO quantified, it is time to make clear decisions about who does what. We call this *workload allocation*.

Workload allocation involves two key steps. The first step is creating an inventory—or taxonomy—of all the work that is performed. The taxonomy is a simple grouping or classification of the processes the company and the service provider will perform. The second step involves determining who is accountable for each of the processes identified in the taxonomy. This is often referred to as *best value assessment*.

Taxonomy

The workload allocation process begins by identifying the processes and sub-processes with the workscope. Process taxonomy describes the processes of interest to form a common language the parties use to understand the work. The taxonomy includes a brief identification of each process performed. By *brief*, we mean a one-to-three-word description or name that can be assigned to that process. Typically top-level and sub-processes are identified, as seen in Figure 4.4. As a rule of thumb, processes are cataloged to a level where only one party is responsible for the entire process.

Properly cataloging current processes often is a tedious challenge, and many times it is met with stiff resistance. Some will view this as a complete waste of time: "Why should we do this? We know we want to change our processes." The answer? The purpose of the taxonomy is to gain clarity about the work

Figure 4.4   Taxonomy Process

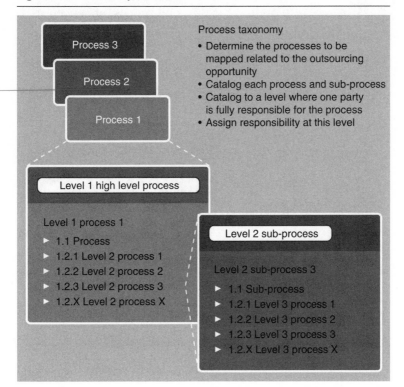

and who does what. This is why we recommend that companies document processes at a high level by creating the taxonomy rather than merely detailing work instructions. If a company has work instructions, great. But do not spend the time doing detailed as-is work instructions when the goal is to transform the process; focus your efforts on cataloging the processes rather than documenting how work currently is done. (See Appendix D for a list of tools and resources, and the Vested Outsourcing website, www.vestedoutsourcing.com/resources/tools.)

Best Value Assessment

Once the taxonomy is completed and there is an inventory of all the processes, the parties should determine how they will allocate the processes. Success almost always depends on both organizations performing processes in support of the objectives. The aim here is to optimize end-to-end process effectiveness. It is important to find the right mix of work by using a best value assessment, which is the process of reviewing each party's capabilities, skills, infrastructure, affordability, and compliance by determining where the best value resides. In essence, deciding *who* does *what* is based on the best value. The service provider is a key participant in this process; both it and the company together should agree on what is the best allocation of work.

Unfortunately, stakeholders often disagree on the extent of what should be outsourced. Usually debate exists not only within the company that is outsourcing; often there is a big difference between what the company and the service provider feel is the proper mix of work to outsource. One reason is that employees fear job loss. Simply put, the more processes that are outsourced, the more employees will fear potential job loss. A better way to look at this is to think of it not as jobs lost but as jobs *allocated to the right organization to perform that work.* Over time, the overall solution is improved so that jobs are reduced (possibly through attrition) until the right number of people are performing at an optimal level.

A common misconception about Vested Outsourcing is that companies should outsource all aspects of a particular function; of course, service providers love this thinking, but it is simply not true. We have seen successful Vested Outsourcing agreements that range from narrow in scope to entire functions. A key point to remember is that the broader the scope of the program, typically the more risks the service provider is challenged to take on. In addition, the core Desired Outcomes and metrics used to define the service provider's success will change as the workscope responsibility increases or decreases. Depending on the scope of the relationship, the company transfers some or all of the activities needed to accomplish agreement goals to the service provider. For example, when outsourcing cleaning services, a company could outsource all aspects of maintaining restroom facilities, which might then expand the service provider's scope to include managing plumbing needs, performing maintenance, or procuring supplies.

We challenge the notion that companies prefer to outsource all activities associated with a particular function or process. It is important to review each activity and determine the proper workload allocation to define the right place to do the work. It is also important that neither party discount the best value potential of the people currently working for the company. There may be significant business opportunities associated with the utilization of an in-house facility and people.

Companies often have infrastructure, test equipment, facilities, and experienced workforces. In some cases, they may have necessary training or certificates and permits that can be difficult or costly for a service provider to obtain. The required capabilities and the costs make up the total cost of ownership—not just the initial price. People who have worked for the company often are hired by the service provider and continue doing a version of their old job for a new employer. An example of this occurred when Procter and Gamble (P&G) shifted hundreds of existing employees to a service provider. P&G had talented people on its staff and wanted to avoid unnecessary layoffs when it outsourced global real estate facilities management services to Jones Lang Lasalle. Under the agreement, P&G shifted roughly 600 people to Jones Lang Lasalle in January 2004. William Reeves, one of the P&G executives who helped mastermind the deal, was pleased with the effort. "From a real estate standpoint, this is clearly the largest relationship that we have ever established with a single supplier in our history as a company. They (Jones Lang Lasalle) have met or exceeded our expectations and the objectives we had in place."[5] Reeves's words are an understatement because Jones Lang Lasalle went on to win P&G's supplier of the year award for two years in a row. This is no small achievement as the award is given to only seven firms out of P&G's 80,000 suppliers.[6] Collaboration is at the heart of Vested Outsourcing. Thus, transparency between company and service provider involvement is required in order to truly determine best value. Transparency is critical for two reasons.

1. Best value determination often requires developing a business case and scenarios when establishing the pricing model to evaluate and compare costs structures and effectiveness. Therefore, workload allocation may change as the economics of the agreement are refined.

2. Often a service provider agrees to additional risk under a Vested Outsourcing agreement. The service provider is accountable for delivering results and no longer has the option to throw up its hands and say "Not my fault!" Service providers need to be involved in candid discussions about what workload they are best suited for and what risks are associated with certain workload allocations.

Case Study

Workload Allocation: Microsoft OneFinance

When a company outsources, it is usually difficult for many of its employees to accept one key fact: the company is outsourcing for a reason, often because it has decided it is not the expert. The OneFinance core team internalized this early on. In order to achieve its Desired Outcomes, it had to have faith that its partner would help transform the work.

> "It would be incorrect to say Microsoft did not think of cost–but what became a core driver for the team was to create an outsourcing model aimed at improving the efficiency and effectiveness of executing Microsoft's financial processes."
>
> Srinivas Krishna
> Microsoft Director of Global Vendor Management

This was a hard concept for Microsoft (and many companies) to accept; Microsoft employees are not used to admitting they are not the smartest people around. But the team realized a trap that the University of Tennessee calls "the outsourcing paradox" (see Appendix A), which is what happens when a company decides to outsource yet insists on telling the service provider how to do the work.

A key component for Microsoft was to focus on the *what*, not the *how*. Microsoft set this tone by creating a formal taxonomy, or framework for cataloging the work *and thus achieve a clear understanding of roles and standard global processes.*

Microsoft purposely did not dictate to Accenture (its outsource partner) how to do the work. Instead, it focused on creating the taxonomy for each of the three areas that were outsourced (record, accounts payable, and buy centers). Creating the taxonomy would lead to a mutual learning journey used to identify and communicate improvement efforts. The taxonomy was designed around four "levels," with each high-level process being segmented into more discrete lower-level processes. For example, for the "record" process, a high-level process was general ledger accounting, which in turn had three Level 4 processes: journal entries, payroll accounting, and local billing. A sample can be seen in Figure 4.5.

As part of the taxonomy, Microsoft and Accenture jointly spent three months developing a global standard process and controls. Each step in the process was documented, and roles and responsibilities were agreed to. (See the example in Figure 4.6 of the employee setup and maintenance process.) Once this high-level standardized process was determined, and each party had agreed to *who* would do what, Accenture then worked to

Figure 4.5   Level 4 Standard Global Processes

High Level Process	Level 4 Process	High Level Process	Level 4 Process
Fixed assets accounting services	Acquisitions	General ledger accounting	Journal entries
	Depreciation		Payroll accounting
	Transfers (intra-co)		Local billing
	Transfers (inter-co)	Close accounting	Close management services
	Asset disposal		Open PO accruals
	Physical audit		Open PO fixed assets accrual
	Adjustments		Standard and one time accruals
Inter-company accounting	Intercompany account reconciliation		Prepayment and deferred expenses
	Intercompany commissions		Account reconciliations
	Non in house cash center (IHCC) foreign exchange		Balance sheet and profit & loss review
	Intercompany dividends		Business rule violations
	Intercompany cross charges		Allocated cost pools
	Intercompany interest & loans	Statutory & report preparation accounting	Financial filling preparation
	Netting & settlement		Statutory fixed assets register

	Microsoft global resources—locally paid interns (MGR-LPI)
	MGR—subsidiary leasing fee
Treasury accounting	Cash forecasting
	Bank administration
	Posting bank transactions
SOX & SODA	User access & segregation of duties
	SOX 302
	SOX 404

	Direct tax
	Indirect tax
	Other taxes
	Statistical reporting
	Audit support

Figure 4.6   Process Steps for Employee Setup and Maintenance

Process Steps	Accenture	Microsoft
Microsoft initiates employee add/change request according to Microsoft procedure and policy.		✓
Business Process Outsourcing (BPO) Vendor validates that request is complete and in accordance with Microsoft procedures and policy and takes action to set up record.	✓	
If the request is not complete and is missing required information, BPO Vendor returns the request to the request originator. The request originator will provide the missing information and send back to BPO Vendor for processing.		✓
BPO Vendor will perform reviews/reconciliation of data between SAP and Microsoft HR solutions to ensure discharged employee's payee records are blocked/ deleted on a timely basis per Microsoft procedures and policy.	✓	
End Process		

determine the detailed *how.* (Additional tools and resources are listed in Appendix D and on the Vested Outsourcing website: www.vestedoutsourcing.com /resources/tools.)

This approach saved Microsoft a tremendous amount of time in its outsourcing ramp-up. Accenture employees worked with Microsoft to learn the existing processes and migrate them to the standardized global process as quickly as possible. Rather than documenting the existing as-is state at a detailed level, the focus was on getting the work to Accenture as quickly as possible. The taxonomy of the global standard process provided the basis to move work

over rapidly. Accenture would evaluate the work and
identify ways it could be done more efficiently. This
was essential because Microsoft has 95 subsidiaries,
and each subsidiary did things differently. Special
requirements of local law sometimes required a deviation from the global standard, but these were treated
as exceptions and special permission was required to
grant any exceptions. The OneFinance team evaluated each of these to see if it was really needed. Once
Accenture knew the roles of the processes it was managing, it developed desktop procedures outlining the
"how."

A key point to note about this approach is that
the jointly developed standardized process became
the intellectual property of Microsoft. This was an
important aspect of the agreement because at the
expiration of the agreement (it spanned 12 years),
Microsoft would own the standardized process, which
it could then keep and use if it ever changed service
providers.

Learn By Example
Workload Allocation—Foodservice

In our foodservice example, we developed a SOO that
included three objective statements: (1) eliminate the company subsidy immediately; (2) increase employee use of the
cafeteria at lunchtime; (3) pricing to the employees should
remain at or below the current benchmark. To meet these
objectives, the service provider and the company have to perform a number of processes, each of which can be identified
and mapped.

Some processes that would support the objectives might
include menu development, maintenance, food management, and staffing. Each of these high-level processes may be

comprised of subprocesses. All these processes and subprocesses are mapped, and each is assigned to the company or the service provider. Figure 4.7 maps our simple example.

Figure 4.7   Responsibility Matrix: Foodservice Example

High Level Process	Sub Process	Responsibility	
		Company	Provider
Menu development	Menu board		x
	Post to company web	x	
	Recipes		x
Maintenance	Cleaning		x
	Equipment maintenance		x
	Facility repairs	x	
	Installation	x	
Food management	Order food		x
	Inventory		x
	Waste disposal	x	
	Receiving and storage		x
Staffing	Training		x
	Food safety and sanitation		x
	Schedules		x

HOMEWORK

Element 3

Statement of Objectives

Part 1. Document Desired Outcomes and Statement of Objectives

Getting Started

In Chapter 3, Element 2, you developed a Shared Vision and statement of intent. It is now time to use the Shared Vision and Statement of Intent to develop Desired Outcomes and a SOO for your Vested agreement.

The requirements roadmap helps to capture the Desired Outcomes and objective statements; you will populate the roadmap as you progress through this manual. At the end of the homework section there are Tips of the Trade tables (Figures 4.9 and 4.11) that provide important summary points and takeaways for Element 3.

Start by reviewing your Vision Statement. Develop a limited number of Desired Outcome statements (five or less) that describe outcomes. Remember these are *what*, not *how*, statements. Keep the statements short and to the point. Think ahead, because outcomes must be measurable, and start to think about how the outcomes are linked to key strategies and key performance measures. More is done with establishing performance metrics in chapter 5.

Desired Outcomes support the Vision Statement. Because each Desired Outcome is rather broad, it can be further refined by writing a SOO for each one. Specific objectives further define the various facets of each outcome. Characteristics of a good SOO include:

- Avoid "how" words.
- Limit the number of words used. (Aim for fewer than five words for each.)

- Because metrics will be tied to objectives, results should be measurable.

In this exercise, you will be completing the first two columns of the requirements roadmap. Place your Desired Outcomes and any associated SOOs into the roadmap document.

> **Tools of the Trade**
> Figure 4.8 presents the complete requirements roadmap template. The template is also in Appendix C, and an Excel version of the template can be downloaded from the Vested Outsourcing website: www.vestedoutsourcing.com /resources/tools.

Figure 4.8   Charting Your Desired Outcomes

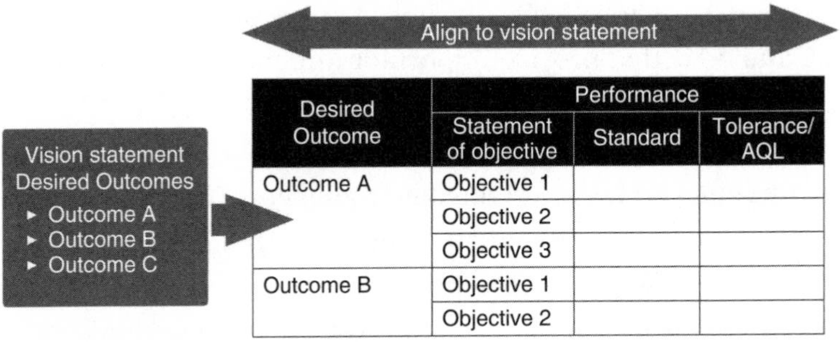

✓ *Check Your Work*

Before you move on to the second part of this homework, sense-check and validate your progress against the following questions:.

1. Do your Desired Outcomes support your Vision Statement?
2. Do your Desired Outcomes support the scope of the agreement?
3. Are the objectives statements clear and do they clarify the Desired Outcome?

Figure 4.9   Tips of the Trade: Element 3: Desired Outcomes and
Statement of Objectives (Part 1)

Tips of the Trade – ELEMENT 3 - Desired Outcomes and Statement of Objectives (Part 1)	
Tip 1	Avoid the Easy Path. Teams should be very careful that the "easy path" does not lead straight to the Outsourcing Paradox, the Junkyard Dog Factor, and/or the Zero-Sum Game. (See Appendix A, Ten Ailments of Traditional Outsource Relationships). The easy path is typically defined as taking the existing statement of work or process documentation and dusting it off and putting it into this agreement.
Tip 2	Support your Vision Statement; the vision is the guiding light, aligning to the vision will ensure that all efforts by both parties are focused.
Tip 3	In drafting the SOO, let the service provider solve the problem. Follow these guidelines: • Do not write the objectives too tightly or too narrowly. • Allow for and encourage creativity from the service provider. • Be open to new solutions and new approaches. • Allow the provider to accept risks for work scope that is not core to the company and not essential for the company to perform. • Gather information from the service provider on what you don't need to do any longer to meet the objective
Tip 4	Do not try to write the perfect SOO or the perfect PWS; it does not exist. Do not sacrifice "good" while waiting for "best."

Part 2. Document Workload Allocation

Getting Started

In this exercise, you will be mapping the processes and subprocesses that support the Desired Outcomes and SOOs you documented in Part 1. You will need to identify processes to a level that is sufficient to assign responsibility for each one. Start with an end-to-end view of the processes, and assign the work to the party best suited to do it. Challenge your thinking and use the talents and knowledge of your service provider. Recognize that processes will change as they are improved.

> **Tools in Your Toolkit**
> Figure 4.10 (and Appendix C) provides a simple template to help you assign responsibilities. You can use any format to accomplish this work as long as each process that supports your Desired Outcomes is identified and responsibility is clearly assigned. Remember: The task here is not to document work instructions but to develop the taxonomy or inventory of the processes and to assign each process to the party that provides best value.

Figure 4.10   Responsibility Matrix

High Level Process	Sub Process	Responsibility	
		Company	Provider
Process 1	Sub-process 1		
	Sub-process 2		
	Sub-process 3		
Process 2	Sub-process 1		
	Sub-process 2		
Process 3	Sub-process 1		
	Sub-process 2		
	Sub-process 3		
	Sub-process 4		
Process ...	Sub-process 1		
	Sub-process 2		

✓ **Check Your Work**

Before you move to chapter 5, sense-check and validate your progress against the following questions:

1. Is work assigned to the party that provides the best value?

2. Did you review all processes that support the Desired Outcomes?

3. Is only one party responsible for the entire process you are cataloging?

Figure 4.11   Tips of the Trade: Element 3: Desired Outcomes and Statement of Objectives (Part 2)

Tips of the Trade – ELEMENT 3 - Desired Outcomes and Statement of Objectives (Part 2)	
Tip 1	Do the work where it will provide the best value
Tip 2	Focus on the processes that support the Statement of objectives
Tip 3	Involve the service provider in creating the taxonomy and determining who will perform the process
Tip 4	Don't attempt to document 100% of the process detail

CHAPTER 5

RULE #3: AGREE ON CLEARLY DEFINED AND MEASURABLE OUTCOMES

S uccess in your outsourcing and business relationships depends mainly on knowing the answers to two seemingly simple questions: What results do I need? How will I know when I get them? As is often the case in business and in life, trying to answer a simple question or two often is quite complex. Reflection, clear thinking, and resources usually are needed.

In chapter 4, you answered the first question by establishing your Desired Outcomes and statement of objectives (SOO). The purpose of Rule #3 is to help you answer the second question. In this chapter, you will establish a crystal clear understanding of how to measure and monitor success.

A Vested agreement always contains performance metrics that clearly define and measure success against the Desired Outcomes. Establishing Key Performance Indicators (KPIs) help avoid the ailment we call "driving blind disease" (see Appendix A). Organizations must spend the time collaboratively to establish the definitions that describe success. Investing time at this stage is critical to ensure that neither party spends time or resources measuring the wrong things.

Once the measures for the Desired Outcomes are agreed upon, the parties can create the quality assurance plan (QASP), which outlines how the KPIs will be reported and validated for accuracy. The QASP lays the foundation for performance management and reporting. To follow Rule #3, your agreement should include two Vested Outsourcing agreement elements:

- *Element 4: Top-Level Desired Outcomes.* Performance metrics are established at three levels. The broadest sets of metrics are end to end in nature and determine overall success against the Desired Outcomes, regardless of whether the company or the service provider is accountable for discrete activities. The next level of metrics includes specific service provider metrics, often known as service-level agreements (SLAs). The third measurement level should include capturing detail and data that help drive *root cause analysis.* Each of the metrics levels is discussed in this chapter.
- *Element 5: Performance Management.* Success is measured against the established metrics that are reported on regularly and frequently. A formal performance reporting process should be embedded into the governance structure.[1] We refer to this formal process as a QASP. Metrics reports should be used as part of regular review meetings across all functions/ all levels (e.g., linking strategy to shop floor metrics to ensure all parties are marching to the beat of one drum). When possible and cost effective, companies should strive to have in place automated dashboards with drill-down functionality for root cause analysis.

Elements 4 and 5 are discussed in detail in this chapter. As you work through your Vested agreement, you will need to complete the homework for both. Once you complete this chapter, you

will have a definition and method for measuring, documenting, and reporting success.

ELEMENT 4: MEASURE TOP-LEVEL DESIRED OUTCOMES

Defining Success and Setting the Target

In chapter 4, you documented the Desired Outcomes and
developed a SOO. Now it is time to define how to measure and
report success. Each of the objectives should be further defined
by a *performance statement*, which is the targeted level of performance for each objective. The performance statement includes
both a standard and a tolerance. To illustrate, let us use the
Wright brothers' first contract for an airplane to demonstrate
the standard and tolerance to standard concept. In 1909, the
Wright brothers signed a contract with the United States Army
with these terms:[2]

> Target price: $25,000
> Minimum speed requirement: 36 mph
> Target speed: 40 mph
> Incentive: For every mph over the 40 mph target, the Army
> would pay an additional $2,500; for every mph under
> the target, the Army would deduct $2,500, down to the
> 36 mph minimum, below which point the contract was
> void.

The results: The final delivered speed was 42 mph, and the
Wright brothers earned an additional $5,000. This target
statement becomes the measure of success, or metric, for that
objective.

   In this example, the standard is 40 mph and the tolerance is a minimum of 36 MPH with no maximums. Success
against the Desired Outcomes is defined by the performance
statement standards; the service provider is measured against

those standards. This is logical, yet most practitioners find it easier said than done. One common mistake companies make is creating service provider SLAs rather than establishing metrics that are used appropriately to manage the business and drive it toward success against the Desired Outcomes. A second common mistake is what we call "measurement minutiae" (see Appendix A). The hallmark of "measurement minutiae" is trying to measure *everything*; few companies have the diligence and time to monitor every measurement they create.

Getting Grounded—from Top to Bottom

One common mistake companies make is focusing on service provider SLAs as opposed to end-to-end KPIs. It is important to establish metrics that can be used appropriately to measure achievement of overall Desired Outcomes as well as drive root cause analysis. The overarching agreement should focus on the critical few metrics that are linked to the Desired Outcomes. However, many other process and operational measures are needed to track day-to-day performance. Thinking about metrics in terms of a metrics hierarchy (see Figure 5.1) can help ensure that companies properly establish both KPIs and SLAs.

KPIs

At the top of the hierarchy are KPIs. These are the critical few metrics in the agreement that reflect performance against the overall Desired Outcomes. In most cases, both the company and the service provider must work together to achieve the KPIs.

A good example comes from the Jaguar-Unipart Vested Outsourcing agreement. Under the agreement, Unipart provides supply chain management services for Jaguar. A key Desired Outcome is customer loyalty. Success against customer loyalty is defined by the J.D. Power customer satisfaction, sales satisfaction, and dependability rankings. Historically, Jaguar ranked poorly on the J. D. Power ranking list for customer loyalty and reliability, with rankings as low as number 9 for

Figure 5.1   Metrics Hierarchy

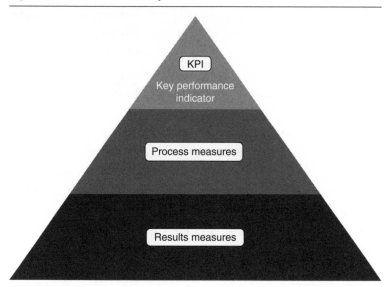

customer loyalty and number 11 for dependability.[3] Jaguar and Unipart created a Shared Vision to improve customer loyalty under their Vested agreement. They worked together, leveraging each entity's core competency, and moved to the number 1 position in 2008 in sales satisfaction and have remained in the top spot ever since.[4]

A key point to remember is that often KPIs are end-to-end in nature and are *achieved only when the parties work together toward the same Desired Outcome.* Many service providers balk at using end-to-end metrics to measure relationship success, claiming they should not be held accountable for overall performance outside of their control. This is especially true in complex situations with many success factors where the service provider does not have 100 percent control of the outcome. For example, Unipart could easily claim that it is accountable only for an on-time shipment of parts to dealers. However, by working together and measuring end-to-end effectiveness, both parties can better determine where a process is failing, and they can work together to make adjustments to drive success. It is critical that KPIs are measured and tracked by both parties, because the Desired Outcomes are mutually dependent. Accountability can be established at the workload allocation level.

We encourage tying incentives to KPIs; they motivate the service provider to invest in processes and innovations where it can help the company achieve Desired Outcomes.[5]

Process Measures and SLAs

The second level of metrics in the hierarchy is process metrics and service-level agreements. A process metric measures the success of a process. SLAs are specific metrics that a service provider must meet. Often there are incentives for exceeding SLA targets or penalties associated with missing them.[6]

Companies often assume that they are measuring a process based on an SLA they have established with the service provider. All too often this is flawed logic because processes frequently go beyond a service provider's control. It is wise, therefore, to measure process effectiveness. It is not fair—or collaborative—to hold a service provider accountable for a process when part of that process is out of its control.

Let us use cycle time from customer order to delivery as an example. A company may have a target for customers to receive their shipment within five business days after they place an order. Order to delivery cycle time is a process metric because it spans multiple processes. Figure 5.2 demonstrates three distinct processes to achieve the company's goal of getting orders to customers within five business days.

A common mistake is to try to hold a service provider accountable for a process when part of the process is not their responsibility. The following is a real-world instance where this happened.

Brand X sold its product through a retail channel that included customers such as Wal-Mart, Best Buy, and hundreds of smaller regional and local retailers. Brand X had its own in-house customer service representatives who dealt with each of the retailer chains. Brand X was responsible for the order

Figure 5.2   Order Cycle Time

Customer Order to Delivery Cycle Time = Target Five Days					
Order Management Process		Distribution Process		Transportation Process	
Customer Order to Release		Released Order to Shipped Order		Shipped Order to Delivered Order	
Cycle time from Order to Credit Check	Cycle time from Credit Check to Release	Cycle time from Order Release to Order Pick	Cycle time from Order Pick to Order Ship (Ready for Pickup)	Cycle time from Order Ship to Pickup	Pickup to Delivery

management process and had an agreement with Fulfillment House Y to pick, pack, and ship its product. Brand X provided all customer support and would release the orders to Fulfillment House Y once a customer order was approved and passed a credit check. A process was designed where orders would be released to the service provider every two hours. Under the agreement Fulfillment House Y had a 48-hour cycle time to ship product. The "cycle time clock" started when Brand X's customer service representative entered the retailer's order into the order management system, and the clock stopped when Fulfillment House Y "shipped" the product.

This situation created three fatal flaws:

Flaw 1: Brand X could not release an order until its customer, a major retailer, passed a credit check. In most cases this was done within a matter of minutes. However, when a retailer placed an order that exceeded its credit limit, Brand X would hold an order for hours or even days waiting for payment from the retailer or approval to exceed credit limits. Any orders not approved for release to Fulfillment House Y within 2 hours virtually always meant the 48-hour SLA for Fulfillment House Y would be missed. In fact, Fulfillment House Y never even realized the orders were on credit hold and assumed it had 48 hours to fulfill the order from the time it received the order.

Flaw 2: Brand X owned the inventory and managed the forecast and inventory levels at Fulfillment House Y. The marketing team was notorious for its poor forecasting, and Fulfillment House Y frequently had stock-outs on at least one or two of Brand X's stock-keeping units (SKUs). Fulfillment House Y was "dinged" on its performance for any SKU that was out of stock because the order would go into backorder and add cycle time days until stock was received.

Over time, the sales representative for Fulfillment House Y and the contract manager for Brand X changed the definition of success so that Fulfillment House Y would start the clock on the 48-hour SLA when it received the order. All credit holds and backorders were "subtracted" from the calculation. Fulfillment House Y began reporting near-flawless performance—yet it might take days to get a product shipped. The problem? No one measured the complete end-to-end order-to-ship cycle time. Everyone thought they were doing well (even reporting green on their scorecards), but the overall system failed to deliver the Desired Outcome, which was to meet the retailer's on-time and complete requirements

Flaw 3: This flaw centered on the definition of *ship*. Under the agreement, Brand X worked with three national transportation carriers to pick up its products from Fulfillment House Y and deliver them to hundreds of retail stores across the country. These carriers were known for top-notch performance. When Brand X and Fulfillment House Y originally designed the cycle time SLA, Fulfillment House Y was quick to point out that as a distribution provider, it was not responsible for transportation to the retailer. This made sense, and the agreement was written to say that Fulfillment House Y was accountable only for a 48-hour cycle time, and the clock would stop once the product was shipped in their system. Under the agreement, Fulfillment House Y would call the carrier and schedule a pickup time. The problem? Brand X's shipments could sit on the dock for up to 2 days waiting for the carrier to pick up the product. To make matters worse, the transportation providers did not start their own SLA clock until they had picked up Brand X's product!

Failing to look at process measures led Fulfillment House Y and the carriers to claim success and report green scorecards on their SLAs when in reality Brand X's retailers might wait days to get their product. No one was looking at overall performance. The focus instead was on narrowly defining success in terms of span of control.

This example clearly illustrates the need to measure process metrics as well as SLAs. If a process is important to measure, we recommend splitting a process metric into discrete SLAs that map to each party's span of control. Doing this means having SLAs not only for the service provider but for the company's internal business groups that may have impactful inputs on the service provider (such as an order that needs to drop to a fulfillment house).

Operational Metrics

The lowest level in the metrics hierarchy is operational metrics, which measure results at the task level. The service provider should manage these; they should not be part of the Vested agreement. If a service provider is achieving the SLAs and Desired Outcomes, why spend the time reviewing reports providing operational metrics that are collected often but reviewed only on an as-needed basis? For example, if a service provider is not performing against a particular SLA, it is appropriate to ask it to share operational data in order to explore the root cause of the failure.

Creating Performance Statements

There are two rules of thumb for creating performance statements.

1. *Use metrics that are quantifiable and measurable.* If you do not, you might well find yourself chasing that

proverbial pot of gold at the end of the rainbow that keeps mysteriously changing location. This is particularly frustrating (and unfair) for service providers that invest their time and resources into solving client problems without reaping any reward.

2. *Ensure that stakeholders—including end customers—will value the outcome if success is achieved against a specific metric.* Why bother to measure something if it is not supporting the outcome?

In chapter 4, we introduced the requirements roadmap (see Appendix D) as a tool to help you document your Desired Outcomes and performance objectives. You will continue to use the requirements roadmap in this chapter as you more specifically document how you define success and report success.

Learning by Example:
Setting the Standard—Foodservice

Let us continue to build the requirements roadmap we used in the example in chapter 4. At this point, we have developed Desired Outcomes and a SOO. Now it is time to document specifically how you define success.

The Desired Outcome statement: A foodservice program that eliminates subsidized costs and increases the utilization by employees.

This Desired Outcome was refined into three SOOs:

1. *Eliminate the company subsidy immediately.* The standard for this objective is to eliminate the subsidy— there is no tolerance; the subsidy must be zero for regular cafeteria service (employee purchased breakfast and lunch) and for any catering services.

2. *Increase employee use of the cafeteria at lunchtime.* For this objective, the parties agreed that increasing utilization will take time, so increasing targets were set for multiple years. Target utilization levels were set

as: Year 1—57%; Year 2—62%; Year 3—64%; Year 4—66%. This target is also tied to an incentive, which will be documented later. It was agreed up front that the incentive will be based on the targets and the targets will not change even if they were exceeded in the prior year.

3. *Pricing to the employees should remain at or below the current benchmark.* The benchmark value still needs to be established for food types, but, once established, is added to the requirements roadmap. Because food costs and labor costs will change over the life of the agreement, the parties agree up front to adjust the benchmark value semiannually for changes to the consumer price index.

As you can see from this example, setting the performance standard and the tolerance requires some thought and some

Figure 5.3   Performance Statement Example

Desired Outcome	Performance		
	Statement of Objective	Standard	Tolerance/ AQL
Food service that eliminates subsidized costs to the company, and increases utilization by employees	Eliminate company subsidy immediately	For standard cafeteria (6am–2pm)	None
		For catering services	None
	Increase utilization rate of employees that eat in the cafeteria at lunchtime	Target levels: • Yr 1—57% • Yr 2—62% • Yr 3—64% • Yr 4—66%	Target level must be achieved to earn incentive. Targets do not change even if exceeded in prior year
	Pricing to employees should remain at or below established benchmark	Benchmarks (values to be established): • Hot entrée • Sandwich • Salad bar • Pizza	Benchmark value can be adjusted semi-annually for changes to consumer price index

flexibility. After the standard and tolerance for each objective are established, they are entered into the requirements roadmap.

A Word about Baselines

Having a good baseline of the business being outsourced makes it easier to establish performance statements. If you have followed the Vested Outsourcing implementation framework, you should have completed a baseline as part of Step 2, Understand the Business.[7] A baseline provides the starting point for each performance statement and should provide the true status of the process being outsourced. Once performance statements are defined, the baseline also will help show the gaps between the current state and the desired state and help the service provider gauge the size of the gap and estimate the level of effort and investment needed to close the gap.

The company and the service provider can and should participate in the baseline effort equally. Here the role of the service provider is to push for an objective, comprehensive, fact-based description of the current process and performance against each of the established metrics. Many Vested agreements have been written without a baseline. In these cases, the service provider took on risk by committing to performance targets without fully knowing the existing performance and the associated gaps. Although this approach is doable, it is not advisable because service providers will most likely have to increase pricing to cover the risk—especially if the pricing model is a fixed-price contract type.

In some cases, it is not physically possible (or cost effective) to do a baseline prior to writing the contract. In that event, we advise companies to establish a cost-plus contract that includes a formal baseline as part of the initial scope of work, preferably to be completed within the first six months. Using an interim approach allows the service provider to begin work but prevents it from padding the price due to the risk associated with unknowns.

HOMEWORK

Element 4

Clearly Defined Performance Metrics for Desired Outcomes

Getting Started

In chapter 4, you developed your Desired Outcomes and SOO for your agreement. Here you will continue to complete the requirements roadmap by establishing performance statements that include setting standards and an acceptable tolerance.

As you set standards, ensure that you are establishing metrics that appropriately manage the business and drive it toward success against the Desired Outcomes. Remember to use metrics that are quantifiable and measurable and ensure that stakeholders will value the change if success is achieved. Performance statements can take a number of forms; this chapter presents several examples, but it is not possible to anticipate all the potential configurations a performance statement can take. Our advice is that you keep yours clear and concise. At the end of each homework section there are Tips of the Trade tables that provide important summary points and takeaways for each element.

At this point, you may be unsure of the correct target for some objectives, or some work may be needed to establish a baseline. If so, put a placeholder in the requirements roadmap. It is important to agree on how and when placeholders will be finalized and to document this information on the requirements roadmap. Remember that you will need to update the roadmap once your targets and/or baselines are finalized.

Tools of the Trade

Figure 5.4 is the template for this section of the homework. A complete template is in Appendix C. An Excel version

of the template also is available for downloading from the
Vested Outsourcing website: www.vestedoutsourcing.com/
resources/tools. (Also see Appendix D for information on
additional tools and resources.)

Figure 5.4   Template Requirements Roadmap: Performance Statement

Desired Outcome	Performance		
	Statement of Objective	Standard	Tolerance/AQL

✓ *Check Your Work*

Before moving on to the next element, validate the Requirements
Roadmap by sense- checking against the following questions.

1. Have you established performance standards and
    tolerances for each SOO? If you still have work to
    do, have you included a placeholder in the require-
    ments roadmap?
2. Are you measuring what the service provider can
    influence and control?
3. Is the standard clear? Are the tolerances clear and
    fair?
4. Do you have too many or too few metrics?
5. Can you clearly link the standard back to the desired
    outcome?
6. Have you determined which of the objectives and
    associated performance standards the service pro-
    vider will be accountable for and which the com-
    pany will be responsible for?

Figure 5.5   Tips of the Trade: Element 4

Tips of the Trade – ELEMENT 4 – Clearly Defined Performance Metrics for Desired Outcomes	
Tip 1	Metrics are clearly aligned to Desired Outcomes, ideally focused on achieving end-customer requirements and support the vision statement
Tip 2	Accountability is aligned with the scope of service provider's authority
Tip 3	Metrics are tracked at the Statement of Objectives level (entire process level) not at the task level (operational level)
Tip 4	Baseline data will assist in the development of performance statements

ELEMENT 5: PERFORMANCE MANAGEMENT

So far you have determined your SOO and set a performance standard by which success will be measured. But setting the performance standard is not enough. As we show in the example of Brand X and Fulfillment House Y, metrics must have clear definitions; also, all parties must agree on how to collect the data and monitor success. To this end, the requirements roadmap includes a quality assurance plan. For each performance statement tied to an objective, the plan defines four things:

1. Who is responsible for the data related to the metric?
2. What is the source of the data?
3. How is the metric calculated?
4. How often is the data collected?

Learning by Example: Requirements Roadmap—Quality Assurance Plan

We will continue to complete the requirements roadmap from the earlier foodservice example. There we developed Desired

Outcomes and SOOs and set a performance standard objective. Setting the performance standard alone is not sufficient; all parties must agree who is responsible for the data related to the metric, the source of the data, how the metric is calculated, and how often the data will be collected.

In Figure 5.6, the quality assurance plan is completed for each objective. Let us take a closer look at the objective "*increase employee use of the cafeteria at lunchtime*"

1. *Who is responsible for the data related to the metric?* Corp. HR and service provider. Two groups are responsible because the data comes from both the company and the service provider.
2. *What is the source of the data?* Cash register transactions for the time period 11 AM to 2 PM and HR employee records.
3. *How is the metric calculated?* Average weekly transactions (by service provider) divided by average weekly full-time employees (by HR). This formula is clearly stated.
4. *How often will the data be collected?* Collected weekly, posted quarterly, evaluated annually.

You can see from this simple example that the performance management requirements are clearly stated in the requirements roadmap.

Reporting and Scorecards

In Vested agreements, performance reporting is necessary for governance. It is important that top-level metrics reports are distributed regularly and frequently. Metrics are posted and communicated companywide, and the reports are seen and used by all levels to proactively manage performance. Typically, formal metrics reports are distributed monthly with

Figure 5.6 Performance Management Example

Desired Outcome	Performance			Inspection			
	Statement of Objective	Standard	Tolerance/AQL	Who	Data Source	Calculation	How Often Collected
Foodservice that eliminates subsidized costs to the company, and	Eliminate company subsidy immediately	For standard cafeteria (6am–2pm)	None	Corp acct'g dept	Invoicing system	No subsidy to be charged on monthly invoice	Monthly
		For catering services	None	Corp acct'g dept	Invoicing system	No subsidy to be charged on monthly invoice	Monthly
increases utilization by employees	Increase utilization rate of employees that eat in the cafeteria at lunchtime	Target levels: • Yr 1—57% • Yr 2—62% • Yr 3—64% • Yr 4—66%	Target level must be achieved to earn incentive. Targets do not change even if exceeded in prior year	Corp HR & supplier	Cash register transactions for time period 11am–2pm HR records	Average weekly transactions (by supplier) divided by average weekly full time employees (by HR)	Collected weekly, posted quarterly, evaluated annually
	Pricing to employees should remain at or below established benchmark	Benchmarks (values to be established) • Hot entrée • Sandwich • Salad bar • Pizza	Benchmark value can be adjusted semi-annually for changes to consumer price index	Corp program manager	Posted menu in cafeteria	Compare current pricing against benchmarks and record variance	Collected monthly, reviewed in QBR (quarterly business review)

working-level reports for critical operational metrics distributed more frequently.

The overall performance management plan should include regular review meetings across all functions and all levels (e.g., linking strategy to shop floor metrics to ensure all parties are marching to the beat of one drum). The most successful Vested agreements require accurate and timely performance information. In large deals, we find it is common to incorporate the top-level metrics into automated dashboards with drill-down functionality into process-level metrics for root cause analysis. In some cases, establishing precise measures is difficult using existing systems and methods of data collection. In those cases, weigh the expense of gathering the information against its potential value.

HOMEWORK

Element 5

Performance Management

Getting Started

Continue to develop your requirements roadmap by completing the quality assurance plan. For each SOO, answer these
questions.

1. *Who is responsible for the data related to the metric?* List
    the department responsible.
2. *What is source of the data?* Be specific so that it is clear
    what data is used and where it is located.
3. *How is the metric calculated?* Clearly document the
    formula used to calculate the metric. If the metric
    relies on other reported metrics, take the time to
    validate and document these calculations.
4. *How often is the data collected?* Clearly establish how
    frequently the data is collected, the metric calcu-
    lated and when is it reported and reviewed.

Complete Your Requirements Roadmap

This is also a good time to discuss performance reporting in
general. When will metrics reports be distributed? How will
metrics be posted and communicated companywide so that all
levels can manage performance proactively?

Tools of the Trade
Figure 5.7 is the template for this section of the homework.
A complete template of the Requirements Roadmap is in
Appendix C. An Excel version of the template is available for
download on the Vested Outsourcing website: www.vested
outsourcing.com/resources/tools.

Figure 5.7   Requirements Roadmap Template—Performance Management

Desired Outcome	Performance			Inspection			
	Statement of Objective	Standard	Tolerance/ AQL	Who	Data Source	Calculation	How Often Collected

✓ *Check Your Work*

Before you move on to the next chapter, sense-check and validate your work against the following questions:

1. Have you clearly documented the quality assurance plan for each SOW?
2. Are all parties in agreement?
3. Is the frequency of collection and reporting sufficient to manage performance?

Figure 5.8   Tips of the Trade: Element 5

Tips of the Trade – Element 5: Performance Management	
Tip 1	Clearly document who is responsible for each metric, its source, calculation and frequency that it will be collected and reported.
Tip 2	Get agreement from all parties.

CHAPTER 6

RULE #4: OPTIMIZE PRICING MODEL INCENTIVES FOR COST/ SERVICE TRADE-OFFS

O ne of the most frequent questions companies ask us when embarking on a Vested Outsourcing agreement is: How exactly do we establish pricing to foster a win-win relationship with our service provider? In many respects, getting to a win-win pricing relationship is the heart of the matter. Pricing is likely among the very first questions the parties will consider because getting pricing and the pricing relationship right speaks directly to the bottom line of the enterprise and its ultimate success.

Establishing the right pricing and incentive mix is complicated for outsourcing agreements. It is also technical. There is no one-size-fits-all pricing model in Vested Outsourcing, but you do not have to be an accountant, a mathematics professor, or an economic scientist to recognize the benefits of a fair pricing structure, reached through cooperation, flexibility, and innovative thinking. The purpose of this chapter is to help you get past the jargon and offer some practical guidance to use when establishing the pricing model for your Vested agreement.

As you work through this chapter, remember that there are no quick and easy answers when it comes to creating a Vested pricing model. Yet pricing is not a guessing game. We have customized many different pricing model approaches for companies. There is no generic template or standard spreadsheet to help you get the correct pricing "answer." We understand that the goal is to make sense of the financial drivers forming the foundation of your enterprise. This chapter provides sound advice on 12 steps that will help you increase the prospect of achieving a pricing win-win. We also address the questions you should ask (and then answer) as you develop your pricing model and incentives.

This chapter is structured around the 12 steps that you will need to work through as you develop your Vested pricing model:

Step 1.   Form the team.

Step 2.   Establish guardrails.

Step 3.   Document input assumptions.

Step 4.   Identify total ownership costs and perform best value assessment.

Step 5.   Perform risk assessment and allocate risks.

Step 6.   Agree on the compensation model.

Step 7.   Determine target contract duration.

Step 8.   Complete the pricing model and establish prices.

Step 9.   Test the model and agree on the baseline.

Step 10. Define margin-matching triggers and techniques.

Step 11. Agree on incentives.

Step 12. Document deployment processes.

If you do the homework at the end of this chapter for each step, you will create a Vested pricing model for your agreement.

ELEMENT 6: PRICING MODEL AND INCENTIVES
Pricing Model Primer

Throughout this chapter, we use many terms that may be unfamiliar to individuals who participate in Vested agreements. Before we move ahead, we want to establish definitions for several key terms. Understanding these terms and concepts will help you establish the correct pricing model for your agreement.

Pricing model. The mechanism that companies use to determine the optimum price between the company and the service provider. In some cases the pricing model consists of nothing more than an estimate of total cost, volume of sales, market price, and desired return on sales. Most pricing models are expressed in a simple spreadsheet; however, some are more like small customized software packages or macro-based Excel spreadsheets.[1] We use the term *model* because a good pricing model enables the parties to manipulate the underlying pricing assumptions, which allows them to "model" the outputs relative to the input components. Common pricing model components include:

- The total cost build-up and best value assessment
- Underlying financial and operational assumptions
- Risk factors and allocations
- The desired compensation method (e.g., fixed price, cost plus, hybrid)
- Margin-matching triggers and techniques
- Contract duration
- Incentives

Vested pricing model. A pricing model that is designed to reward the company and the service provider for achieving mutually agreed upon Desired Outcomes. When properly structured, the pricing model should generate returns in excess of target margins for both parties when the parties achieve the Desired Outcomes.

Margin matching. A technique used to adjust prices fairly based on movements in defined underlying pricing model assumptions. The pricing adjustment is based on trigger points that, when activated, reset prices as fluctuations occur. The goal of using margin matching is to maintain economic alignment in the relationship as the business environment changes, ensuring fairness in prices. We strongly recommend the inclusion of a margin matching technique in your Vested pricing model.

Incentive. A type of award for the company or the service provider. Incentives can be monetary or nonmonetary. In a Vested pricing model, incentives are based on achievement of incremental performance of the Desired Outcomes. In a Vested Outsourcing agreement, incentives motivate companies that outsource and their service providers to make decisions that ultimately meet the companies' Desired Outcomes.

Incentives framework. The mechanism the parties use to measure performance and trigger incentive awards or payments. Typically, the value of the incentive is calculated using a mathematical formula. We recommend that you keep incentives as simple as possible.

Gainshare. A monetary incentive where the company and the service provider share cost savings. The purpose of gainsharing is to encourage the parties to drive out non–value-added activities and reduce costs.

Valueshare. The practice of allocating to the parties a share of the total value that is derived from an improvement or innovation by achieving a Desired Outcome. The value is based on the realizable value benefit to all defined stakeholders, not just the party with the idea or that takes the action. Valuesharing encourages service providers to innovate for total overall value. Because some Desired Outcomes are not easily quantifiable, valuesharing sometimes uses nonmonetary incentives to reward the parties.

Best value. Best value bases pricing decisions on the value associated with the benefits received and not on the actual prices or cost. A best value assessment uses decision criteria that go beyond costs and include decisions on workscope and pricing based on intangibles such as market risks, social responsibility, responsiveness, and flexibility.

Later we define more important terms, but the ones just listed are the essential terms that everyone must understand and agree on before moving forward with your discussions.

You might think that moving to a Vested pricing model is a risky venture for a company and its service providers. Anything new and different involving investment in time, resources, and effort implies a certain degree of risk. Thought leaders agree, however, that the rewards of Vested Outsourcing can greatly outweigh the evaluated risk.

ARC Advisory Group's Adrian Gonzalez—a leading analyst who specializes in supply chain management and third-party logistics—offers this advice: "What differentiates Vested Outsourcing are not the risks, which are inherent in any outsourcing relationship, but the potential payoff for both service providers and customers. In other words, the benefits-to-risk ratio is much greater for Vested Outsourcing and the risk of remaining at the status quo—in terms of lower profits for service providers and continued diminishing returns for customers—trumps them all."[2]

What Gonzales articulates is the concept of relational economics and shared value that is so key to Vested Outsourcing. By working together, the companies can have a bigger payoff, but this is a payoff that must be shared. In chapter 1, we referred to the excellent work by Harvard Business School's Michael Porter and Mark Kramer on the concept of shared value.[3] Although their work mainly relates to how companies can work with society to create shared value, this concept is crucial to Vested Outsourcing. Your pricing model *must* share any value that is achieved by accomplishing the Desired Outcomes, and doing this requires a mind-set change.

Adopting a Vested pricing model requires resisting the urge and corporate pressures to demand the lowest possible prices from service providers. It also requires an open and transparent approach to pricing. In your Vested journey, the pricing model and incentives are where the rubber meets the road. At this point, organizations must go beyond merely saying and using the term *partnership* to creating a commercial pricing structure and associated budgets that equitably allocate risks and rewards with the purpose of realizing mutual gains for the duration of the agreement.

Step 1. Form the Team

Before you begin this part of your journey, we want to stress that creating a Vested pricing model can seem like a radical approach. It is a joint, fact-based effort; it is fair and not positional. *Both parties sit on the same side of the table and develop a mechanism*—the pricing model—that is the most effective and fair way to price the scope of work, given the dynamic nature of business and while also considering potential risks. The idea of jointly creating a pricing model may appear counterintuitive. It is common for the company with the most power in the relationship to establish the pricing model. In addition, parties often are taught to price high (or low, depending on their position) and then use tactics to negotiate concessions and move the other party from its stated position. There is much gamesmanship in price negotiations.

But consider: By creating the pricing model together, the companies have the opportunity to see the big picture and explore the hidden costs of the business venture. For example, companies rarely discuss the real costs associated with duplication of effort, multiple resourcing exercises, transition periods, post-contract management, or regulatory changes. Only through joint, candid conversations can the parties reach a pricing model that is fair to both companies for the duration of the agreement.

This is likely a new approach for many participants who are creating the pricing model. We caution you to go slow and make sure that the key stakeholders fully understand the purpose of a Vested pricing model and the steps you will be taking. We recommend three rules of thumb when putting together the pricing model team:

1. Use a peer-to-peer approach for selecting the people on the team, with peers from both parties participating. For example, do not just have a financial expert from the service provider; have one from both companies.
2. Always have at least one person from each party who has been involved with the Vested Outsourcing initiative from the start on the pricing team. If possible, everyone involved should have been on the team from the start, even if they were simply subject matter experts/participants.
3. On the team, always include a financial expert who has experience in developing pricing models.

Step 2. Establish Guardrails

Many teams start developing their pricing model only to find that, in the eleventh hour, corporate roadblocks prevent the parties from actually developing a formalized agreement to frame their Vested business relationship. For example, one team got to the pricing model stage only to find that the outsourcing company had a corporate policy that no business agreements could last more than one year. The service provider planned to invest millions of dollars in process efficiencies. A one-year contract term was a deal breaker because it was outside of the service provider's structured parameters. It took three months to get executive agreement from the outsourcing company that a longer-term contract was in the best interest of the parties.

These eleventh-hour roadblocks almost always emerge when the parties begin to discuss pricing and risk. Companies and services providers are very frustrated by these "surprises" and have started to rethink how they approach getting to an agreement. What has evolved is a progressive approach that involves establishing and openly communicating formal boundaries for conducting external business agreements at the start of the relationship. We refer to the agreement boundaries or structured parameters as *guardrails*.

Guardrails provide the company and service provider team that is drafting the agreement with the authority to develop a deal within clearly stated boundaries. Simply put, if the parties establish an agreement within the guardrails, no last-minute surprises will occur because, by design, the agreement is within the already established boundaries.

We introduced the concept of guardrails in chapter 1 when we recommended that the parties establish formal boundaries prior to beginning a Vested journey. If guardrails have not been set, now is the time to stop and establish them. Establishing clear boundaries also establishes the tone of "no surprises" and prevents eleventh-hour issues.

Figure 6.1 depicts a conventional approach to pricing an agreement and the concept guardrails.

On the figure, the dotted lines represent each party's guardrails. Any agreement outside the limits of the guardrails is the walk-away point for each party. The more risk a party is asked to bear, the closer that party will come to walking away from an agreement.

Let us examine the concept of guardrails with an example that looks at an information technology (IT) agreement between Company A and ITServiceCo. Company A had outsourced its IT department for two years. Company A had a corporate policy that no agreement could extend for more than two

Figure 6.1   Conventional Pricing Approach

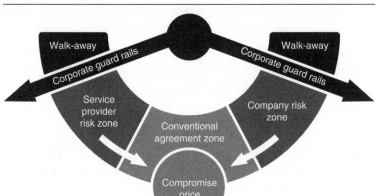

years. Under the agreement, Company A owned the IT infrastructure, such as the hardware and software. One year into the
agreement, ITServiceCo pointed out that the IT infrastructure
needed a very costly upgrade. Company A and ITServiceCo
agreed to reopen the contract and agree on new pricing that
would include ITServiceCo's investment in the IT infrastructure. The parties agreed to establish guardrails upfront, and
the two-year contract duration became a front-and-center issue.
ITServiceCo knew it could not justify such a large investment
with only one year left on the agreement. Company A knew it
would not like the prices that ITServiceCo said it needed to
charge to justify the upgrades and amortize the costs over the
remaining year of the contract.

By working together at the outset, the companies agreed
to establish guardrails that would help them set fair prices
to achieve the needed upgrade. The original guardrail for
ITServiceCo was a five-year extension; Company A's policy
stated that the agreement had one year left and there would be
no extensions without a rebid. Both parties worked with their
executive leadership and agreed that the guardrail would establish an extension of no less than three years and no more than

five years. Establishing formal guardrails up front empowered the team to create a pricing model that would work. The team could then agree on the optimal prices based on a fair return on investment for the service provider that ranged between three and five years.

Let us continue to review the illustration of a conventional pricing approach in Figure 6.1. Each party's risk zones are immediately within the guardrails. In a conventional approach to pricing, the parties negotiate back and forth and try to mitigate risk for their organization. The result is a tendency for the parties to settle on "fair" prices that are somewhere in the middle. We call this middle the agreement zone. We show the actual agreement price as the compromise price because both parties had to settle for something less than they had hoped for. In a conventional approach to pricing outsourced services, the agreement zone is relatively narrow as the parties try to mitigate risks and typically have to compromise—or trade off—when establishing prices. The ultimate agreed-upon price represents the size of the pie for both companies as depicted by the circle in the zone of agreement. For example, say the parties end up with an agreement that is expected to yield 12 percent profit margins for the company outsourcing and 10 percent profit margins for the service provider, with a book of business worth $100 million over three years.

An agreement that falls within the parties' risk zones is financially viable but risky. For instance, the service provider still may want to pursue an agreement in its risk zone if there are potential upsides for a reward in terms of profit margin or increased revenue. The result is that, with the right set of incentives, the service provider could be enticed to agree to a deal in its risk zone. We explore how to establish optimal pricing using a Vested pricing model in Step 8 of this chapter.

Use Figure 6.1 to physically plot each party's guardrails. Guardrails include clearly stating any assumptions that the parties feel are show-stoppers. In essence, the pricing model should yield an agreement that is mutually agreeable and avoids surprises. If the pricing model does not yield an agreement that fits within the guardrails, each party likely will walk away. Examples of key guardrails are:

- EBITDA (earnings before interest, taxes, depreciation, and amortization) targets and minimum acceptable EBITDA targets—meaning the company will walk away from a deal that does not generate a certain EBITDA target.
- An acceptable threshold deviation from EBITDA for given circumstances.
- Rights of use of inventions and innovative practices developed during the term of the agreement.
- An agreement duration that must be a minimum or maximum of a set number of years.
- Not accepting risks for natural or man-made disasters.
- Defined insurable risk assumptions.
- Nonnegotiable legal terms, conditions, or corporate policies.
- Transformation initiatives that generate a return on investment (ROI; internal hurdle rate) of X percent.
- Intentions regarding investment in other companies within the same market.

When corporate executives provide clearly defined boundaries, the integrated team can construct a pricing model that best stays within those established structural parameters. The guardrails become the conditions the parties must meet before the integrated team can agree to the pricing model.

It is important to note that guardrails also may come in the form of so-called corporate policies, legal policies, or standard terms and conditions. Your job is to balance established corporate and legal policies with your pricing model. For example, a company may have a corporate policy that all agreements have certain standardized terms and conditions. By design, Vested agreements discuss and optimize for risk and reward structures. For that reason, a Vested agreement almost never uses a standardized corporate contract template and almost always requires formal endorsement from corporate authorities. Getting executive endorsement for variances upfront will save you many headaches and prevent last-minute surprises.

As you work through your pricing model, set up formal checkpoints with internal stakeholders using a formal decision-making framework that ensures proper buy-in from authorities within each company (e.g., a steering committee). Until now we recommended using your gate review process, which provides for project structure and risk assessment to determine whether to move forward, after the completion of each element. The stakes get high as the parties allocate risks and discuss prices. For that reason, we now recommend that you move your gate reviews to *after* each pricing model step instead of after each element to ensure complete buy-in from company authorities.

Step 3. Document Input Assumptions

It is now time to document specific assumptions on the scope of the business. We like to think of input assumptions as the levers that will affect the parties' prices and bottom lines. When the lever is pulled (triggering increases or decreases), the profit potential of one or both of the companies is impacted. By documenting scope assumptions, the intention is to smooth out any profit peaks and troughs.

A Vested pricing model always includes input assumptions. The parties will use them to establish actual prices and to model estimated profits. The impact of variances in the assumptions can be modeled and also serve as a discussion point later to determine risk allocation when there is a variance from agreed-upon baseline assumptions.

Some common input assumptions include:

- Cost of raw materials and unit cost. The cost of raw materials often fluctuates, sometimes by large amounts.
- Market share assumptions. Strong market share encourages growth. A service provider will be motivated to innovate in order to increase market share.
- Variations in the conditions and rates in which products and services are used.
- Acceptable percentage levels for indirect costs, such as overhead.
- Currency assumptions and base exchange rates. Here revenue is accrued at a different real-time value than planned or in a different currency from the cost of raw materials or distribution costs. The parties must agree on the base assumptions and how to share the risk of deviations in currency values over time, either via joint hedging or joint risk sharing.
- Volume variability. For example, volumes rising above a certain level may prompt the service provider to add fixed costs, such as additional buildings, or add assets, such as more testing equipment, forklifts, or servers. Likewise, if volumes drop below a certain level, the service provider still will have fixed costs that are embedded in the price model.
- Inventory holding policy and costs.
- Workload mix. Workload mix is often the cause of frustration between companies and service providers when it comes to pricing. This is because service providers typically establish a price based on the units of workload.[4]
- Minimal order levels, lead times including expeditious lead times.
- Base-level assets. These are the assets specified to deliver Desired Outcomes. Base-level assets should be monitored and measured regularly as

fluctuations occur. They measure the impact on required assets or the use of existing assets if fluctuations occur.

- Payback period, the optimum return on capital employed (ROCE). ROCE is a ratio that indicates the efficiency and profitability of a company's capital investments. It is calculated by using a formula that divides EBIT by the result of Total Assets minus Current Liabilities.

Step 4. Identify Total Ownership Costs and Perform Best Value Assessment

We strongly encourage pricing decisions that are based on concepts known as total cost of ownership and best value. Best value concepts are closely associated with the concept of total cost of ownership and total landed costs that are espoused by supply chain professionals. While closely related, there are differences between these concepts, and their purposes are different.

Total Cost of Ownership

The calculation of total cost of ownership (TCO) first emerged in the 1950s with leading academics such as Don Bowersox challenging conventional approaches to understanding the costs associated with logistics.[5] He and a few colleagues believed that warehousing professionals needed to understand the *total* cost of a shipment—not just the warehouse and transportation costs. Bowersox and a group of thought leaders established the National Council of Physical Distribution Management, which is now known as the Council of Supply Chain Management Professionals, to advocate for what they called total landed costs.

The concept of total landed costs has evolved and expanded outside of the logistics profession. Today most industries refer to the concept as TCO. TCO analysis includes determining the direct and indirect cost of an acquisition and operating costs.

Its concepts are used now most notably to gauge the viability of capital investments.

For example, a TCO calculator is available free on the Internet to help people determine the costs of owning different types of cars; it includes such costs as depreciation, interest on the loan, taxes and fees, insurance premiums, fuel costs, maintenance, and repairs.[6] TCO concepts have been widely adopted in the aerospace and IT sectors, but they are not widely used when determining the costs of outsourced services.

By determining the TCO, information is available in order to make clear decisions regarding pricing. Considering only some of the costs will result in a poor decision. TCO is the foundation for any best value decisions that need to be made.

Transparency: The Foundation for Discovering TCO

As with buying a car, there are trade-offs in buying services. Unfortunately, it is much harder to uncover the real total costs when buying services. The only way to get to the real total costs is to understand all of the factors that influence a fair price associated with the business. If you have done a thorough job developing your baseline (as part of Step 2 of the Vested Outsourcing implementation plan), you should have at least a preliminary understanding of the total costs.

The only accurate approach is to document total costs from an end-to-end perspective—*capturing the costs from both the service provider and the company*. Doing this requires transparency. A transparent approach to sharing both company and service provider costs often is called an "open-book approach." We believe that an open-book approach is the best way to establish true end-to-end total cost, because it builds a fact-based discussion around "price." In fact, it is difficult to envision a Vested agreement that does not include an open-book approach. Unfortunately, many companies and service providers are fearful of such an approach. Criticisms about open-book pricing are real, and the parties should address any concerns early in their discussions. We find two primary concerns when it comes to transparently sharing costs when creating the pricing model.

First, service providers often feel "naked" when they share their costs. If a service provider exposes its true costs, it is easy for the other company to determine the service provider's profit—a sacred cow for many service providers. The biggest fear is that the company will use that information to attack the service provider's margins. Or the company could create competition by bidding out the work to other service providers to reduce spend.

If you are this far along in your discussions, it is highly unlikely that the company will switch service providers at this point. One way to mitigate this fear is to ensure that your Statement of Intent (developed in chapter 2) clearly states your margin targets. In addition, your guardrails should have expressed profit targets, market share, and other key assumptions. If you have done a proper job in setting margin targets early in discussions, you will find transparently sharing costs and margins more comfortable.

In our experience, most service providers are not making exorbitant profits; actually, they want and sometimes even need higher profits to be sustainable and invest in their business. If a service provider is unhappy with the status quo, why not put a stake in the ground for an agreement to make more profits— subject to performance and the service provider *earning* those profits for achieving the company's Desired Outcomes?

A second criticism about transparency concerns the company doing the outsourcing. Often when it comes time to share, the company defines transparency in terms of a one-way street—the service provider is supposed to share, but the company does not have to. This situation often occurs in real life. We offer two bits of advice:

1. To ensure that the spirit of transparency is addressed early, we encourage including the concept of transparency in the Statement of Intent.

2. Service providers should explain *why* they are asking
    for certain information. A good explanation of why
    certain information is needed helps allay company
    concerns. For example, in one case, a third-party
    logistics service provider asked its client about the
    three-year outlook—was it going to stay the same,
    grow, or decline? Once the company realized that
    the service provider needed this information to
    estimate the maximum size of the building it would
    need to secure for the duration of the contract, it
    felt more at ease.

Although we strongly favor transparency in establishing true
costs, we realize that it may not be feasible for some companies.
We accept this and encourage you to share as much information
as you can. Over time, companies get more trusting, and they
can revisit and refine the pricing model as they learn more.

Total Cost Buildup and Basic Business Case

We hope you have chosen a path of transparency, as it will enable
a much higher shared understanding of the baseline costs. The
baseline costs include the costs under the current scenario as
well as what you project them to be under the agreement based
on the assumptions that are set. Understanding and documenting current, as-is costs go beyond simply understanding the cost
of the planned outsource activities to the total operating costs
of the organization. The reason is that the outsource provider
is being chartered to drive total costs down. Often the biggest
improvement areas are in the "handoffs" between organizations. It is critical to identify the costs of poor cross-functional
performance and to target these costs for improvement.

Let us look at the cost of poor handoffs in a supply chain to
make this point. MarketOp was a marketing firm that designed
and manufactured marketing items such as cups, hats, pens,
and other promotional items. MarketOp worked with FulfillCo
to ship its products to more than 1,000 mid-tier retailers.

Calendars were one of the products in FulfillCo's warehouse. Unfortunately, some of the calendars were five years old! MarketOp did not have a strong operational background, and managing obsolete product was not a strong point. Each month FulfillCo charged MarketOp a fee to store pallets of its products. In this case, the cost of poor process in managing obsolete product ran into the millions. By working together the companies would have had end-to-end visibility of product on hand and the storage costs associated with old product.

Figure 6.2 illustrates the importance of understanding total costs. Understanding only acquisition costs is analogous to seeing only the tip of the iceberg. Often what is out of sight causes the greatest damage. This concept is referred to as the "priceberg" by practitioners.

Unfortunately, establishing real total costs is not entirely straightforward and often not easy. Companies establish a

Figure 6.2　Total Cost of Ownership

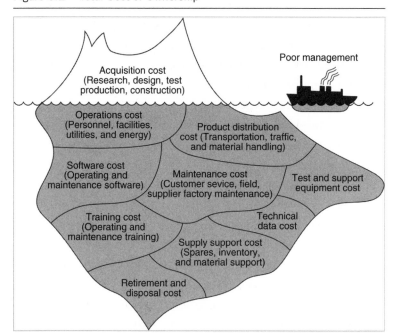

price, but there are almost always hidden costs, soft costs, and risks that are often overlooked when agreeing on a price. These costs need to be added into your pricing model equation.

When companies try to add as little profit as possible to the service provider's costs, service providers then hide the real costs, which results in a virtual shell game as service providers shift costs around in an effort to maintain their target margins. Often the buying companies will demand that service providers not include overhead and management costs in prices. But like it or not, these costs are real. Thinking service providers will magically absorb the costs is like burying your head in the sand. The preferred approach is *always* transparency, where the total costs to own a product or have a service over time are factored into the price. These total costs include:

- Hard costs such as labor and assets
- Soft costs such as overhead and any "corporate allocations"
- Governance costs (e.g., cost to manage the relationship)
- Software costs
- Supply chain support costs
- Retirement and disposal costs
- Opportunity costs
- Transaction costs
- Cost of switching suppliers
- Costs associated with a competitive bid and contracting process

Once you have captured a good baseline of the total cost—including the hidden and transaction costs—you should perform some basic analysis to determine the impact of the baseline on profitability for both companies.

There are two schools of thought when it comes to comparing business cases and basic financial analysis, and each is discussed next.

The first approach involves each company creating its own profit and loss (P&L) and balance sheets for the business in scope and then sharing these. This approach is fairly simple because typically each party already has created a business unit or a customer P&L based on a standard set of assumptions. Using this approach, the service provider's "revenue" in essence becomes one of the company's "cost" items. The goal is to identify as many of the costs as possible so both companies can understand the true cost of doing business and its impact on profit.

The second approach—and one that we recommend—is to create a pro forma or mock P&L. Such a P&L statement represents what the financials of the business would look like if the companies operated under an investment-based business model and shared one P&L and balance sheet. Using this approach helps the parties look at the scope of the service delivery through a new lens, one of a unified perspective that helps them focus on improving the bottom line of the business and not just each one's company. Creating a mock unified financial statement enables the parties to capture the overall financials in one place. To visualize how this works, think of an interlocking P&L statement. The company outsourcing has a "cost" that is paid to the service provider. This "cost" in turn is the service provider's "revenue." This portion of the joint mock P&L is then a snapshot of the service provider's P&L. By combining P&Ls in this way, the parties can see the entire scope of costs and can make value-based decisions about the cost of providing the service.

Regardless of your approach, we hope you take the time to understand the true costs to develop a baseline business case to establish the profit projections for the companies.

Best Value

The concept of best value is closely related to, but slightly different from, TCO. Best value bases pricing decisions *on the value associated with the benefits received, not on the actual prices or cost.*

Best value assessment goes one step further than TCO because
it compares alternative solutions based on value derived, not
just on cost. TCO looks at all costs; best value assessment adds
decision criteria to include intangibles, such as market risks,
social responsibility, responsiveness, and flexibility. According
to researchers Jaconelli and Sheffield, the intent of best value
is to enable a balance between cost and quality considerations
in service provision while ensuring ongoing value for money
and promoting continuous improvement to further value for
money.[7]

The easiest way to explain the concept of best value is
through an example. We will use picking a restaurant for
lunch. There are many reasons why someone might pick one
restaurant over another. Some criteria might include proxim-
ity for reduced travel time, service levels, taste of food, variety
of food, atmosphere, and price. You likely run through these
options every time you decide where you want to go to lunch.
Depending on your situation, you might pick different restaurants. What is a great choice for a business lunch with a client
might not be the same choice you would make for a quick bite
to eat so you can get back to the office to finish working on a
report. Determining best value for your workscope is no different—it is about picking the best option that fits your need. The
options go well beyond price.

Surprisingly, the government in the United Kingdom has
been the most notable advocate in the area of shifting procurement decisions to adopt best value thinking. In 1997, it
announced an initiative to abolish compulsive competitive
tendering (CCT) and to introduce a new concept for government termed *best value*. Between 1997 and 2003, adoption of
the best value concept was voluntary in the United Kingdom.
Scotland quickly emerged as a notable leader in applying best
value thinking.[8] Adam Smith, father of modern economics,
likely would be proud to know that his fellow countrymen
are progressive thinkers when it comes to the economics of
outsourcing.

Scotland has been a leader in applying the concept of best value because of a unique political situation whereby the Scottish Parliament was separated from that of Great Britain only in 1999. Under the devolution, the Scottish Parliament established 32 local authorities that suddenly gained significant power and budget in procuring public services ranging from education, to street cleaning, to housing, to leisure and cultural services, to welfare services. The local authorities were eager to improve the services received for their money.[9]

Because of Scotland's success using best value principles, its Parliament enshrined best value concepts into legislation under the Local Government in Scotland Act in 2003. The act sets out eight main criteria to define best value:[10]

1. Commitment and leadership
2. Competitiveness and trading
3. Responsiveness and consultation
4. Sustainable development
5. Sound governance and management of resources
6. Equalities
7. Review and option appraisal
8. Accountability

Note that the 2003 act does not even list a price component. Although the list is a good one, best value criteria are different for every workscope. Your integrated team should determine the criteria you will use to establish best value. We also suggest adding a cost element—especially one that focuses on quantifying the hidden transaction costs.

Last, we also recommend that best value be performed against major workscope components. It is rare that workscope will shift entirely to a service provider. Review the taxonomy you created in chapter 4 and go through a best value analysis for each major workscope. Doing so will help you develop deeper discussions regarding value instead of just price.

Companies buying services tend to make two common mistakes when it comes to determining best value.

1. Far too many companies still look solely at purchase
    price. Everyone has heard the idiom "penny-wise
    and pound foolish"; this thinking is no different for
    outsourcing deals.
2. Companies that have moved beyond purchase price
    to include other factors often fail to include hidden
    costs. For example, an original equipment manu-
    facturer chose to outsource contract manufactur-
    ing to China. The original estimates showed a price
    savings of almost 75 percent compared to work
    performed in region. What the company did not
    factor in were the increased costs to manage the
    relationship with the contract manufacturer. The
    company travel budget increased by 400 percent as
    engineers and quality teams flew business class to
    visit with the supplier for new product launches and
    quarterly reviews.

Let us explore another example that involves an intangible
around responsiveness when it comes to a life-or-death situation.
Valeant Pharmaceuticals International manufactures Virazole,
the only drug available for infants and children with respira-
tory syncytial virus (RSV). The University of Wisconsin Medical
Center in Madison had a rare instance in which two infants had
been hospitalized with severe cases of RSV. The infants needed
to complete their treatments by midnight Central Time, and
the hospital did not have any more dosages available.

Valeant's longtime logistics service provider, Kenco,
jumped into action to solve the problem. Normal shipment procedures for a rush order from Kenco's distribution center in
Chattanooga, Tennessee, would mean getting the medicine to
the hospital by 2 AM. However, this was too late—the medicine
had to be administered before midnight. James Levi, Kenco's

warehouse supervisor, took control of the situation and found a direct flight to Chicago arriving at 6:50 PM local time. He also organized a courier to meet the plane and rush the medicine to the hospital by 10:30 PM—an hour and a half before the last required treatment. As harrowing as the experience was, this was hardly an unprecedented situation for Valeant. For Valeant, having a service provider such as Kenco, with employees like James Levi who are empowered to use their judgment and expertise to solve problems, is a key part of the decision criteria when it determines the value of working with a service provider.[11]

In order to derive best value, the parties must move beyond the initial acquisition or purchase price and look at the price in terms of the best value when compared to end-to-end total costs—including the costs of market risks, transaction costs, and opportunity costs. You can make a good choice only after you understand the real total costs. Using best value thinking, the parties learn that there is much more to the price (and therefore procurement spend) than they first thought.

The concept of best value is underdeveloped in the outsourcing world. The good news is that organizations like the nonprofit Global Sourcing Council[12] are trying to raise awareness of the true costs and impact of social, economic, and political effects of global sourcing arrangements.

The homework section will challenge you to create a best value assessment for your workscope. Once you do this, you will be ready to move to Step 5, where you develop a risk assessment and allocate risks fairly.

Step 5. Perform Risk Assessment and Allocate Risks

Risk Allocation

Risk is an important factor when determining best value. Well-known outsourcing lawyer George Kimball[13] notes five types of risk in his research paper, "Risk-Allocation Liability Limits and Disputes in Outsourcing."[14] These are:

1. *Operational risks.* These risks relate to workscope
    and workload allocation. For example, poor service
    from the service provider or poor forecasting from
    the company creates operational risks.
2. *Financial risks.* These risks relate to overconsump-
    tion of services (poor assumptions) or inaccurate
    baselines impacting pricing and margins.
3. *Scope.* These risks result from the actual implementa-
    tion of the workscope, such as unmanageable work-
    load allocation and unforeseeable project overruns
    ("business happens").
4. *Compliance and security.* These risks impact highly
    regulated industries and pose significant legal liabil-
    ity issues for both companies. Your company's law-
    yers are especially eager to document these issues
    properly.
5. *Extraordinary risks.* These risks are your worst-case
    scenarios. Although they have little likelihood of
    occurring, when they do occur, they can result in
    financial ruin or worse, loss of life.

A mistake many companies make is blindly shifting risk to the
other party. This is especially common when one party has
more power than the other. Companies often feel a sense of
self-gratification when they have "won" by shifting performance
or investment risk to the service provider. Or worse, they do
not understand the magnitude of the operative impact or the
cost associated with the risk they have shifted. Some companies' legal and contracting groups develop "standard contract
templates" that include onerous terms and conditions designed
to protect one party. These standard contract templates often
are presented with a policy of "take it or leave it." Heavy-handed
approaches usually are met with the shell game, where the service provider calculates the risks into the final price while hid-
ing actual costs. Thus, because risks are deeply buried, they are
not managed. When an event occurs, the parties' legal teams

wave limitation of liability and indemnification clauses at each other.

Legal departments are duty-bound to protect their company from all perceived risks and to attempt to limit liability for those risks. Likewise, many procurement professionals have personal incentives to reduce cost and are dependent on certain service providers. The best approach is to allocate risks to the party that is able to eliminate the risk. When that is not possible, the next best approach is to allocate the risk to the party that is best able to manage and mitigate it in the most cost-effective manner.

We strongly caution against using contractual terms and conditions in order to shift risk; this is a financially shortsighted tactic. Indeed, Oliver Williamson states: "Using a muscular approach is myopic and inefficient. Companies not only use their service providers—they use up their service providers."[15] Williamson suggests that shifting risk will only add to the hidden transaction costs. Companies will not save money; rather, they will likely increase their total costs from an end-to-end perspective. Instead of shifting risk, companies should develop pricing models that are based on smart risk allocation. Risk exists. Do not bury your head in the sand.

It is entirely possible that while one party is accountable for delivering a solution, the other is better able to mitigate and control risk. In this case, a party that knowingly and willingly bears a risk must be compensated for it, as it will cost the business money to manage the risk within specific tolerance levels. The compensation for bearing a risk is a *risk premium*. In a Vested deal, risk premiums are discussed openly and mutually agreed upon by the parties. The parties must come to the relationship prepared to account for known risks. Both companies must examine the past to identify risks that have a high likelihood of occurrence or a high impact to safety, margin, operability, or reputation and tie a price or premium to the estimated cost of intervening, should one or the other company have to take action. An awareness of events that can create new risks is advantageous.

Both parties should strive to create a risk-aware culture as an integral part of the Vested agreement governance structure (see chapter 7). A risk-aware culture anticipates trigger moments when a risk moves from a stable, controllable form into a new, potentially uncertain or uncontrollable form. Vested teams map out the intersection point at which joint intervention is useless and build into the pricing model the costs of a joint business continuity plan to address trigger moments before they occur. This team approach makes risk more transparent and can avoid serious future event failures and save total cost. As changes occur in the marketplace, use the processes established in the governance structure to inform critical business decisions and trigger a review of the pricing model. We view this approach as a long-term investment in business continuity.

A five-step process is recommended to establish risk premiums that should be included in the pricing model.

1. Identify the risks. There is a tool for this in your homework section.
2. Understand the potential costs associated with the risks (if possible).
3. Agree and assign an actual risk premium used in pricing model calculations.
4. Determine which company is better suited to manage and mitigate the risks. Risks should be allocated to the party best equipped to deliver consistent performance and mitigate risk before an event occurs.
5. Establish a risk premium that will be paid to the service provider for taking on risk.

Step 6. Agree on the Compensation Model

Most companies rely on one of two compensation methods for their business arrangements: fixed price or cost reimbursement. In each case, a company is expected to pay the service provider for its costs and an acceptable profit increase.

Each of the compensation methods has significant drawbacks. A fixed-price agreement may encourage the service provider to cut costs and take undeclared risks, delivering services at minimally acceptable technical specification levels or worse, with limited safety or reduced operative reliability. Where products and services are used in high-risk environments, this can trigger a sequence of events that fails to achieve the Desired Outcome. A cost-reimbursement agreement may encourage the service provider to overspend, increase the scope and scale of work, and deliver more services than really are needed in an attempt to maximize revenue and associated profits. Each approach results in potential perverse incentives that harbor hidden risks and costs that are not always apparent until it is too late to reverse the impact.

Cost-Reimbursement Agreements

Under a cost-reimbursement approach, a company pays its service provider the actual costs to perform a service. By definition, cost reimbursement is a variable-price agreement, with fees dependent on the amount of service provided over a given time period. A cost-reimbursement approach is appropriate when it is too difficult to estimate a fixed price with sufficient accuracy and when the service provider will not agree to assume the risks associated with unknowns. Cost-reimbursement agreements often are used to develop a new product or service because it is difficult to specify the work clearly.

A primary disadvantage of a cost-reimbursement method is the lack of incentives for service providers to control costs, especially if the profit is based on the actual cost of service. Figure 6.3 shows a cost-reimbursement approach with fixed percentage fee tied to costs.

In such approaches, service providers are not motivated to bring cost-reduction solutions to their clients. If they do so, their revenue and profits decline. To address this issue, it is important to tie cost-based incentives to the pricing model. Incentives

Figure 6.3   Cost Reimbursement plus Fixed Fee

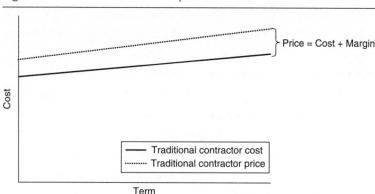

could include preserving the earned margin for given volumes of work.

Fixed-Price Agreements

In a fixed-price approach, the service provider's price is agreed to in advance and typically is not subject to adjustment. Because the total fee for the products and services is fixed, the service provider, rather than the company, absorbs the peaks and valleys. The service provider's ability to manage costs directly impacts its ability to make a profit. Thus, a fixed-price agreement provides incentives for service providers to control costs by implementing efficiencies that drive costs down. Fixed-price agreements also are the easiest contract type for companies to administer because there is no need to keep track of actual costs to determine payment.

From the outsourcing company's perspective, the real advantage to a fixed-price approach is predictability. Budgets are more easily created and approved. If, however, the actual cost of providing the services is more or less than expected, winners and losers are created by accident.

Service providers rarely "lose" because they do one of two things: they buffer their prices or they cut costs. If they have not added in a large enough buffer, they likely will want to renegotiate pricing once they realize that their costs are higher than expected. This is especially true when demand exceeds supply and the service provider has more power in the relationship. In this scenario, if the parties cannot reach a new pricing agreement, the service provider may choose to subsidize the company's operations in order to retain the business. Alternatively, the service provider could cut costs to maintain its target profit in ways not easily detected by the company. Even if the cost of providing the services is as expected, a service provider focused only on short-term gains may reduce service levels to increase its profits.

The second choice is to exit either by choice or by default if the service provider is forced into bankruptcy. Figure 6.4 compares agreement types.

Research from the Wharton School[16] suggests that risk-averse companies are more likely to choose agreements that combine fixed payment, a cost-sharing incentive, and performance incentives. Risk-neutral companies may prefer performance-based approaches. In cases where the company is more risk-averse than the service provider, the performance incentive increases while the cost-sharing incentive decreases with time. Conversely, if the company is less risk-averse than the service provider, the performance incentive decreases while the cost-sharing incentive increases with time.

Flexible Pricing Agreements

There is no right answer when it comes to selecting the compensation method for your pricing model. Purchasing goods is relatively simple. However, risks increase as the transaction becomes more complex, particularly when it involves the delivery of goods and services or pure services over time.

The bottom line in setting the correct structure requires an intimate understanding of the operational risk involved in doing the work. Each party should understand and appreciate the degree to which the other party is prepared to share or bear

Figure 6.4   Comparison of Pricing Agreement Types

	Fixed Price	Cost Reimbursement
Base Cost	The actual hours and/or cost of the service are NOT disclosed to the company by the service provider.	The actual hours and cost of the service are disclosed to the company by the service provider, and billed without mark-up. In cases involving a third-party provider, the company may pay that provider directly.
Profit	A management fee (profit) is added to the cost of the service. This is built into the "price" the company pays.	A management fee (profit) is added to the base cost of the service. This can be a fixed fee, a variable fee (such as a percentage markup based on costs), or a variable fee based on achieving specific incentives. It is possible to have a cost-reimbursement agreement with a zero profit margin where profit is solely based on the service provider's ability to perform against desired incentive targets.
Total Cost of Process	Price is agreed upon in advance and includes the service provider's costs and their profit. Typically the service provider does not reveal the actual profit margin.	Price is unknown and varies based on the actual costs.
Risk Transfer	Service provider bears majority risk as it delivers the requirements within a fixed reward.	Company bears majority risk as it controls the costs.

those risks. This understanding includes identifying the cost associated with assuming any risks.

Companies have succeeded using either solution. Your choice depends on what is best for your situation and market. Many of the agreements we have seen use a combination of compensation methods whereby different workscope elements use the method that best fits the nature of the work that is performed.

It is also possible to change the method used as the business relationship matures. For example, a new program without accurate performance or cost data is probably most suited for a cost-plus agreement in the early stages of the relationship. As the program matures, volumes may become stable and predictable, and the compensation method will tend to favor more of a fixed-price approach. Set clear definitions for the stable and predictable risk stage so that you know when you are moving from a stable state into a more variable environment that requires a review of the compensation method. We provide two examples that show the logic behind using a hybrid-based pricing model.

The first example is a flexible compensation structure from a company that teamed with a global business process outsourcing firm to standardize back-office administrative practices, reduce costs by 35 percent, and increase internal employee satisfaction by 90 percent. The complex scope of work included multiple services at dozens of worldwide locations.

The pricing model provided basic building blocks for the service delivery and transformation elements and used a hybrid approach including fixed price, cost reimbursement, and incentives. A key feature of the model was its scalability. The company wanted the flexibility to scale up volumes with the quarterly seasonal volume fluctuations. In the agreement, the company established fixed fees for each volume band and thresholds that would enable automatic pricing changes in response to volume movements. In addition, the service provider agreed to a firmly structured, or baked-in, "productivity index" whereby the service provider would commit to a 6 percent productivity improvement each year over the life of the contract.

These building blocks allowed the organizations the flexibility to best match the pricing model to the type of work. Figure 6.5 illustrates the agreement.

Base Services

In the example, the base services were fairly stable in terms of volume. The company guaranteed to pay the service provider the fixed fee for the minimum volume threshold regardless of whether volume commitments were met. As mentioned, key features of the model were scalability and the "productivity index."

Other Services

The pricing model allowed the company the flexibility to adapt to future business conditions. Both parties knew they did not have to plan for every conceivable contingency. They addressed this with a rate card that established a cost-reimbursement approach for the various resource types so that the company could purchase unanticipated services when required.

Figure 6.5   Flexible Compensation Structure

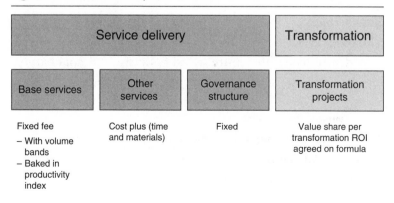

Governance

The parties agreed that to manage an outsourcing agreement as large and complex as their deal, they should set aside costs to cover governance. This included paying for individuals who performed contract compliance roles and for out-of-pocket costs for attending key business reviews and morale-building events.

Transformation Initiatives

The parties agreed to value share using a simple yet repeatable process and payment scheme. The payment scheme was agreed upfront based on a fair share of the ROI from each transformation initiative. The organizations viewed transformational incentives with the philosophy that together, both sides were creating a bigger pie: unlocking financial value that was not being realized by either party previously. Incentives therefore would be paid for successful implementation of transformation projects when value—or ROI—was realized. Increasing the size of the pie was fundamental to enhancing the spirit of partnership. Carving the existing pie differently would lead only to conflict between the two sides.

The second example is a hybrid pricing model used for facilities management. The overall pricing model was a cost-plus, fixed-management, fee-at-risk hybrid with incentives. Each component of the pricing model is discussed next.

Base Services

The base services were cost-pass-through. Although the service provider managed the entire spend budget, it did not charge a fee or markup on materials or second-tier suppliers.

Management Fee at Risk

The service provider was compensated for a predetermined management fee based on volume bands. The management fee represented the service provider's profit for managing the business. The volume bands allowed the outsourcing company to continue to increase its business through acquisition while establishing a fair fee up front. Pricing was pegged to volume against the baseline for volume bands. A unique feature was the at-risk portion of the management fee, where the service provider agreed that a portion of the management fee would be paid based on its ability to deliver success in three areas:

- The service provider's ability to achieve 12 critical performance indicators.
- The service provider's ability to beat market-based cost targets using a formal third-party benchmarking group.
- The service provider's ability to achieve a "relationship satisfaction" score. This was based on a mandatory quarterly survey of 40 key people, and the goal was to help the parties "get in synch."

Governance Fee

The parties wanted to ensure that the service provider would not feel pressure to reduce its level of effort on governance or to try to cut costs on governance efforts. They agreed to set aside a budget in order to manage agreement governance. They also agreed to have two dedicated transformation management process owners as part of the governance structure.

Transformation Incentive

The parties agreed to a gainshare incentive for the service provider based on their ability to deliver sustainable cost savings against core cost drivers. For example, the service provider received an incentive payout for improving energy efficiency that was measured in terms of kilowatts of energy used per hour.

Step 7. Determine Target Contract Duration

An essential component of the pricing model is the duration of the agreement, commonly referred to as the term of the contract. Longer-term agreements often are needed to achieve the Desired Outcomes. Also, achieving step-level improvements in process efficiencies takes time and a significant investment on the part of the service provider. In many cases, investments in process improvements, such as new equipment or IT infrastructure, can run into the millions of dollars. Service providers should have the ability to estimate their future revenue stream and other strategic investment choices before determining whether the ROI will be reasonable. Service providers likely are unwilling to invest in process efficiencies without the assurance of a longer-term agreement. In situations of increasing complexity, more assets are needed to ramp-up the service provider; therefore, costs are best amortized over a longer term.

Almost all Vested agreements are longer term in nature than conventional agreements; the added contract length gives the service provider confidence to invest in business process efficiencies that will yield year-over-year savings. Some highly integrated Vested agreements share investment risk in return for rewards over the term of the agreement. The general rule of thumb is that agreement duration is commensurate with the service provider's optimum time to make an ROI, therefore keeping prices reliably stable. We rarely see a Vested agreement with less than a five-year term, and we have seen several agreements with ten-year terms. The longest contract duration we have seen was for 20 years.

Long-term agreements have another significant advantage in the outsourcing arena. A longer-term agreement gives the parties business security and allows them to amortize switching costs over the life of the agreement. As discussed in chapter 3, outsourced services are typically more multifaceted than procuring simple goods or raw materials, such as steel or widgets. That complexity drives higher transaction costs.

One transaction cost associated with complex agreements is the cost of switching service providers, which can be very high in a services-oriented outsourcing agreement. Think of the costs Wells Fargo Bank would incur to change the real estate management provider that maintains and upkeeps all of its bank branches. Or what about the cost for Apple to switch its call center service providers and retrain new customer service representatives? Switching costs can run into the millions of dollars for larger deals, not to mention the fact that the service providers can invest 5 to 15 percent of the agreement cost in business development and "capture" costs while trying to win the business. The smart approach is to understand these costs and weigh them against the pros and cons of long-term agreements.

Let us look at three examples of companies that considered the impact of contract duration as they developed their pricing model.

1. Company A was able to receive a discount on the management fees from its service provider by locking into a longer-term agreement.

2. Company B, a pharmaceutical firm, required its contract manufacturer to make substantial investments on Company B's behalf during the launch of a new, innovative product that required heavy investment in new contract manufacturing assets. The long-term agreement allowed the service provider to amortize these high costs over a longer agreement span. This reduced the impact of the cost in the early years of the agreement as the product was launched.

3. Company C was able to balance the risk of investment in new assets, tools, and methods and create lean production capability. The surety of a minimum level of business over the term enabled the company to get lower interest rates on borrowing and to spread the investment cost over the life of

the term to avoid peak increases in prices. The service provider was then able to utilize its new spare
capacity to make higher margins on spot sales for
other non-Vested customers.

A final benefit of a long-term contract is that companies investing quality time and effort selecting the right service provider
and structuring the pricing model will need to write fewer
agreements in the future. The annualized costs associated with
writing and developing one ten-year agreement are substantially lower than creating two five-year agreements and much
less costly than creating five two-year agreements. One company had a corporate policy to bid and transition the logistics
work from service providers every two years. Their rationale was
that doing so helped it drive competitive market prices. But the
average cost of each transition was $700,000. When the parties
performed their total cost buildup, the company learned that
the service provider had $500,000 in business development costs
embedded in the price of the agreement. The result? Moving
to a six-year agreement reduced transition and hidden business
development costs by more than $2 million—or 12 percent of
the contract cost.

Given the scarce resources within many organizations and
continued downsizing of corporate functions, agreements
should continue for as long as possible, as long as they are fair
to both parties.

Step 8. Complete the Pricing Model and Establish Prices

After you complete Steps 1 through 7, you are ready to move to
Step 8 and develop the actual pricing model—the mechanism
you will use to trigger payments to the service provider. A Vested
pricing model goes beyond providing a means to transact business. It should reward service providers for helping the company achieve the Desired Outcomes and encourage providers

to innovate by making investments in processes, services, or associated products that benefit both companies.

The goal is to build a pricing model that allows the parties to leverage a wider range of value-generating elements instead of bargaining on sticker price to reduce spending. Vested Outsourcing does *not* automatically guarantee service providers higher profits. It is perfectly OK for company margins to fluctuate as business assumptions fluctuate. We address how to ensure that the economics do not get out of sync in the next step. At this point, you should work on developing a model that best captures how the parties can develop a mechanism for triggering payments that they are comfortable with.

The pricing model should then include details about the selected compensation method. Remember, it is perfectly reasonable to have a pricing model that has some fixed-price components and some cost-plus components. A hybrid approach works well.

Your pricing model now also has links to the TCO and assumptions relative to the work. These assumptions form the baseline service levels and targets in your pricing model. A great pricing model takes into account potential variables and includes sensible assumptions, thus refining the model and making it sensitive to specific deviations from normal business conditions. Any variation to the assumptions triggers a change to the agreement. Depending on the impact, the change could affect price, performance, and any service standards offered. This change process is outlined in the governance structure you develop later (in chapter 7) in your journey. In a Vested agreement, the parties acknowledge that economic and market forces will adversely impact the relationship, and both parties establish a process early on for addressing change.

Companies can use different tactics to create a Vested pricing model; what is important is that the pricing model balances risk and reward fairly. One approach we have seen deployed quite successfully is often referred to as a fee-at-risk approach. Under this approach, a service provider guarantees performance targets, given established price/cost parameters. Therefore, the service provider must leverage its unique skills, capacity, and capabilities to make processes more efficient, to the point that it can generate increased profit without necessarily increasing prices.

Another technique Vested pricing models often deploy is to create a provision for general market escalation, such as local labor costs, plus energy and raw materials expenses that can fluctuate greatly over time and are out of the service provider's control.

At the point of establishing actual pricing and incentives, the parties should keep in mind that the total financial arrangement must fall within previously established parameters agreed to in Step 2, Establish Guardrails.

Although the focus will be on establishing an agreement within the guardrails, we encourage you not to forget what's-in-it-for-we (WIIFWe) thinking when it comes to pricing. The conventional pricing approach makes it easy for the company outsourcing to succumb to Ailment 1, "pennywise and pound foolish" (see Appendix A) as it works through the pricing model to shift risk and get the lowest possible price. The problem is compounded if the company outsourcing has more power and leverage than the service provider, because the natural tendency is to use a heavy hand in establishing the pricing model and prices. Because outsourcing agreements are often multidimensional, outsourcing companies must discard the notion of power-based pricing and instead shift to facilitating a deeper economic discussion that will expand the pie for both parties.

Let us review Figure 6.1, presented earlier, and our previous example of a fair agreement to make this point. We outlined a sample deal with a zone of agreement that resulted in the service provider getting a 10 percent margin and the company getting a 12 percent reduction in total costs in a deal valued at $100 million over three years. In the example, we explained that the deal would be considered fair because the pricing lands between the guardrails in the zone of agreement and also avoids risk. If the companies agree on the pricing model, they have established a base price. The parties have likely negotiated trade-offs and settled on a compromise price. This base price was shown as a circle that represented the size of the pie for both companies.

Applying Vested thinking when establishing your prices helps to greatly expand the zone of agreement and the size of the pie for both parties. Figure 6.6 illustrates how a Vested pricing approach can produce better outcomes for both parties.

Figure 6.6 also shows the importance of WIIFWe thinking when it comes to pricing. The Vested agreement zone represents the opportunity for much greater gains through transformative innovation, in essence expanding the pie for both parties. But you will notice that with the larger pie comes more risk for the parties. In other words, for the companies to win big, both companies must bear some risk. You might be thinking "This is no different from going to the casino and betting more money—you win some and you lose some. And the larger the bet, the more you will either win or lose."

What makes this approach a good bet for both companies is the effort that is put into establishing the agreement, including transparently identifying all total costs and ensuring that

Figure 6.6   Vested Pricing Approach

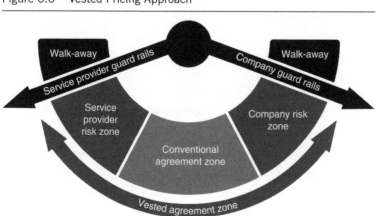

all work is allocated through best value practices with the party
most suited to do the work actually doing it. In addition, the
parties have jointly identified risk and created a risk mitigation
plan. By doing their homework, the parties can feel more confi-
dent about taking on additional risks and therefore expanding
their zone of agreement, which in turn expands the size of the
pie for both parties. In addition, a Vested pricing model uses
incentives as a key reward structure. Both parties become highly
motivated to work together to achieve Desired Outcomes. The
more closely the parties work together to achieve success, the
more likely they are to succeed. The more they succeed, the
more they are rewarded with incentives. One or more of the
parties takes on more risk with the clear understanding that
this risk is being balanced with incentives that will yield higher
rewards for both parties.

Using a WIIFWe approach helps prevent the natural tendency to hunker down and get positional when it comes to
establishing prices. Both parties can clearly identify—and
value—the potential upside of their various choices. By working together, they can allocate workscope smartly and develop
incentives that encourage each party to unlock untapped value
that neither party had before. Creating a Vested pricing model
drives proper behaviors because the parties see the reward of
working together efficiently and effectively. Partnership no
longer is something that is merely spoken. It is something con-
tracted and paid for.

Step 9. Test the Model and Agree on the Baseline

If your business has a high degree of complexity with multiple
dependencies, it may be sensible to invest in risk simulation
software using the Monte Carlo method[17] to help boost awareness of the various risk probabilities and their impact. Monte
Carlo simulation methods were originally used for space explo-
ration but are used routinely by many businesses. Businesses
that have used these simulations report higher degrees of event

awareness and are better situated to put in place proper risk mitigation efforts. Once companies understand risk probabilities, they can create pricing model approaches that help offset the risk in the smartest manner. Offset approaches could include insurance, training, and detailed protocols. With Monte Carlo simulations, extra checks likely are needed if the risk is in a highly complex environment, such as rotating airline equipment, nuclear facilities, IT, and banking services or complex construction in remote areas or underwater.

The best approach for testing the pricing model is to create realistic scenarios. The parties should test the pricing model to determine the impact of various assumptions and risk factors. When testing the pricing model, each party should rank the probabilities of specific outcomes. The next step is to choose a factor that allows adjustments for events that could affect target margins. This analysis will educate everyone involved and will help facilitate sound business decisions.

Step 10. Define Margin Matching Triggers and Techniques

The maxim that the only thing that is certain is change is all too true when applied to business. All businesspeople know that business is dynamic. We like to say "business happens." For this reason, your pricing model should include a mechanism for fairly adjusting prices as business happens.

Margin matching addresses market events and fluctuations by creating a mechanism to fairly adjust prices based on movements in the defined underlying pricing model assumptions. The pricing adjustment is based on trigger points that, when activated, reset prices as fluctuations occur. The goal of using margin matching is to maintain economic alignment in the relationship as the business environment changes, ensuring fairness for both parties.

Companies should proactively create a process that allows for margin adjustments so that both parties involved in the agreement win and lose in accordance with equitable ratios. The analogy is a rising tide, as in the saying "A rising tide floats all boats." Margin matching works in much the same manner. If business happens to effect positive change, when situations change positively, a margin windfall is created not for one company but for both. Likewise, when situations change negatively, margin and spend pressures are created for both companies.

Margin matching works by comparing and harmonizing various disclosed elements of the underlying assumptions that make up the business case, response to risk, and price. When unexpected events occur or when operating assumptions change, adjustments are made to the price and incentive framework to keep pace with the parties' intentions and expectations. Margin matching ensures that no one party gains a windfall or bears an undue loss at the expense of the other party simply because economic changes occur midway in the agreement.

To illustrate, let us consider the impact of rising energy costs on a facilities management agreement. A facilities management service provider (call it AssetWiseCo) charges the company (Estates R UsCo) a price of $2.00 per square foot to manage Estates R Us properties. In the agreement, AssetWise is responsible for all costs, including energy costs. When energy prices increase, AssetWise loses profit margin due to costs beyond its control. When energy prices decrease, AssetWise gains profit margin for the same reason. However, the price Estates R Us pays per square foot remains constant. Therefore, when "business happens" and energy costs rise and fall with market conditions, one company is a winner and the other company is a loser.

A margin matching approach achieves a different result in this example. Estates R Us and AssetWise set the base price assuming that energy costs will remain within a certain range, securing profit margin expectations to a specific price model assumption. If the energy price rise varies from the baseline assumption, the net price is adjusted accordingly. Estates R Us would change the base price up or down depending on whether energy costs went up or down; in this way, the service provider's margins would remain intact. No credits or charges come as a surprise to the company.

In the case of AssetWise and Estates R Us, the parties agree to share the impact of the change up to the point where the service provider's margins fall below a certain percent or rise above a certain point. In the event of a wild swing, Estates R Us would bear the risks and windfalls. In a margin-matching scenario, the parties are fully aware that they will bear some of the risk associated with the cost of energy at some point in time.

The margin matching approach is used for all the potentially variable items in the pricing model where the parties agree to share economic alignment risk. As discussed, the risk discussion must determine which company is better suited to assume and mitigate risks.

Margin matching is a far more transparent pricing strategy for mitigating and sharing risk than the shell game most companies play when shifting risk to another company. One thing remains clear, however: It is necessary to discuss and account for all assumptions and costs in the final pricing model. There are many benefits to the margin-matching approach.

Margin matching:

- Is designed to maintain economic alignment at the most fundamental level as business happens.
- Is flexible, efficient, and easy to administer because all factors are transparent and assumptions are clearly stated.
- Is linked to known inputs, so the parties potentially can automate the invoicing and tracking system.
- Is positively focused on business continuity, stability, and much-needed certainty.

- Is friendly to end users or internal stakeholders because service providers avoid cutting corners on service delivery due to pricing pressure.
- Avoids the need for midterm renegotiation by triggering proactive change through the governance process.
- Is focused on a culture of understanding risk and maintaining business continuity.

Margin matching techniques work best when they are integrated into the governance section of your Vested agreement. Meetings should occur when predefined thresholds are likely to cause either a positive or negative variance to the stated targets. Ideally, the parties periodically should examine the pricing model as well as the actual prices.

A margin matching approach levels the playing field over the long term and mandates reciprocity. Because the starting point is a mutual objective, the parties help each other achieve optimal margins and derive the best value from their relationship. Margin matching also helps the parties both identify and mitigate risks that are prevalent yet rarely accounted for in non-collaborative relationships.

Margin matching is designed to watch out for the bottom lines of the parties in an agreement in a fair, collaborative manner. That is why we highly recommend its use.

Step 11. Agree on Incentives

Primer on Incentives

As discussed in chapter 3, firms using a transaction-based pricing model while wanting innovation or transformation at the same time are at odds with the business and pricing models in their outsourcing agreements. We also showed that using firm fixed-price or cost-reimbursement approaches is inherently flawed because both methods can generate perverse incentives.

Companies always should incorporate incentives that are mutually beneficial to the parties in order to offset the flaws of using conventional approaches. The challenge becomes establishing the right incentive to motivate the parties to make decisions that ultimately will meet the Desired Outcomes.

Many companies are familiar with incentives; their inclusion in business agreements is not new. In chapter 5, we shared the story of how the United States Army wrote performance metrics into the Wright brothers' contract.[18] Let us review this again as it relates to the pricing model and incentives:

- Target price: $25,000
- Minimum speed requirement: 36 mph
- Target speed: 40 mph
- Incentive: For every mph over the 40 mph target, the Wright brothers would receive an additional $2,500; for every mph under the target, the Wright brothers would lose $2,500.

The final delivered speed was 42 mph, and the Wright brothers earned a $5,000 incentive bonus.

The compensation type was a fixed-price approach, and the price was $25,000. Under this agreement, the Wright brothers were accountable for meeting the Army's requirements to deliver a plane that flew at a price to the Army of $25,000. If the Wright brothers' costs went over $25,000, they would make less profit. In addition to the fixed fee, the Army had an incentive based on the performance standard of 40 mph whereby the Wright brothers would be penalized or rewarded based on how fast the plane flew. The result? A pricing model where the Wright brothers had a vested interest in meeting (and beating) the Army's target. The downside to this pricing model was that there were likely many unknowns for the Wright brothers.

We have no idea what the business case looked like—the brothers' first flights occurred in 1903—but we have to assume that they either understood the risk before signing on the dotted line or simply were prepared to take the risk because of the potential reward. They could claim they built the first powered, human-controlled, heavier-than-air flying machine for the Army.

Although coupling incentives to business agreements is not new, it is not common, and it is easier said than done. The wrong incentive structure can result in perverse incentives with undesirable outcomes.

Gainsharing versus Valuesharing

We have said throughout the manual that gainsharing (called shared savings in some agreements) and valuesharing are not the same thing. Many companies include a mechanism in their agreement to share the savings that come from reducing the cost of products or services. In these cases, the companies look at the difference in the original cost of the product or service and the new cost. Then this difference or saving is split in some fashion. But gainsharing does not capture all the value that comes from change. In valuesharing, the parties look beyond cost savings to include the change in the total *value* the solution brings to the company. Let us use a simple example to illustrate how the two models differ.

A third-party logistics (3PL) service provider provides ware-housing and distribution services to a consumer products company that designs and manufactures printers. As part of the service, the 3PL takes printers shipped from China in bulk and repacks them in retail packaging. Each retailer has a unique model, but the printer itself is the same for all retailers. The printers are packaged when the consumer products company receives an order from a retailer. The 3PL sees that the box could be redesigned to be smaller and less expensive while still meeting the company's specifications. If this agreement includes gainsharing, the two companies would calculate the difference in cost of the old box and the new box and then split the savings based on an agreed ratio.

However, in a valuesharing agreement, the companies would look beyond the cost savings of changing the box to how this change would benefit both parties and impact costs in the supply chain. For example, a smaller box would allow the placement of more printers on a pallet for shipping to the retailer, lowering the retailer's cost of freight and storage. The smaller box also may allow a retailer to place more printers on the store shelf. These savings are considered in valuesharing when allocating a share of the total savings (value) between the parties.

But what if the cost of the box actually went up by $1 per unit but the total transportation was reduced by $1.50 per unit? In a gainsharing agreement, the 3PL would not have an incentive to make the change because it would not *directly* contribute to savings. Why bring a cost increase to the company, even though it would be better off from the net transportation savings? Gainsharing in this case does not offer the service provider any incentives to share value. The power in valuesharing is that it encourages service provider innovation to increase overall value. In this case, the company would reward the service provider for implementing new ideas.

The key to designing the right mix of incentives is aligning interests and developing a pricing model that rewards proper behaviors and results. Microsoft's senior director of the OneFinance program, Henric Häggquist, after the joint Microsoft-Accenture team won the Shared Services Outsource Network's "Best Mature Outsourced Services Delivery" award, said:

> So why do we get these awards?
> I say it is because of TOGETHER.
> We face all things TOGETHER.
> We win TOGETHER.
> We face difficulties TOGETHER.
> We never go YOU against US.
> We have all seen what that leads to.[19]

Häggquist's statement reflects a key point: Why fight over whose idea is it when you are sharing something you never had in the first place?

Our second favorite piece of advice concerns the common criticism that companies find it hard to quantify the value of some Desired Outcomes—for instance, what is the value of a customer loyalty point? We recommend that instead of getting stuck, try to think of nonmonetary incentives, such as an agreement term extension or providing good press for the service provider, such as issuing a press release, co-presenting at a conference, or committing to a set number of referrals for new business.

Types of Incentives

Some of the most common incentives that can and should be added to a standard agreement in order to help drive performance and cost improvements include cost, performance, non-monetary, award fee, and award term incentives.

Cost Incentives

A cost incentive is a margin adjustment and is intended to motivate the service provider to manage costs effectively. Cost incentive clauses in contracts should include a target cost, a target profit or fee, and a profit adjustment formula. Typically when a service provider meets the stated target cost objectives, it receives the stated profit target objectives. Actual costs that exceed the target typically result in a downward adjustment to the service provider's profit; actual costs that fall below the target typically result in an upward adjustment of the profit. Cost incentives have variable or firm targets.

Performance Incentives

Performance incentives typically are tied to specific performance requirements. The desired performance generally is stated in terms of a quantitative service target (e.g., percentage on-time completion) and/or qualitative targets (e.g., customer satisfaction). A performance incentive ideally is designed to relate the service provider's profit to achievement of specific targets. The incentive fee is fixed or variable but always corresponds to specific, agreed target ranges of service. Fees typically are paid quarterly. Performance incentives are a great way to ensure performance because a service provider *must* deliver in order to get paid.

Nonmonetary Incentives
Incentives such as public recognition, case studies, willingness to provide references, sharing processes and techniques, sharing knowledge, and other goodwill gestures and endorsements are powerful intangible incentives that increase visibility and market worth.

Award Fees
Award fees are paid at the conclusion of a fixed-duration agreement for achieving a desired goal. Award fee incentives typically are used when the service provider's performance is not objectively measureable or when the nature of the work makes it difficult to devise predetermined objective incentive targets applicable to cost or performance. Usually the fixed-duration agreement specifies an award fee if the service concludes with a desired result. The incentive fee can be variable but usually is fixed.

Award Term
The best agreement incentive is more business, and a service provider always should strive to increase market share. An award term is an automatic renewal incentive. If the performance meets the agreed targets, the agreement is extended— usually for one year. In some cases, this can occur annually, with or without an agreed final end date.

As you create your incentives package, it is important to create incentives that are not too cumbersome to track and monitor. The simpler the incentives are, the better. Administrative costs should not, under any circumstances, exceed the expected benefits, and the incentives must be easily measurable. We recommend creating an incentives framework, which is a mechanism that the parties use to measure performance and trigger incentive awards or payments. Typically the value of the incentive is calculated using a mathematical formula.

Agreements also should provide for evaluation at stated intervals so that the parties are regularly informed of performance quality and the areas in which improvement is expected. Partial payment fees generally should correspond to the evaluation periods. This partial payment approach will induce the service provider to improve poor performance or to continue with good performance.

Linking Incentives to the Requirements Roadmap

Link incentives to your Desired Outcomes developed under Rule 2. The Requirements Roadmap can be used to identify incentives that support the Desired Outcomes in the agreement.

Learning by Example
Incentives—Foodservice

At this point we can complete the Requirements Roadmap for the foodservice example. In chapter 4 we defined the Desired Outcomes and statement of objectives. In chapter 5 we developed a performance standard that included standards and tolerances for each objective. We also developed a quality assurance plan that defines who is responsible for the data, the source, how the metric is calculated and how often it will be collected. All we need to complete the requirements roadmap for this example is to document the incentives that are tied to each performance objective, as illustrated in Figure 6.7.

Not all performance objectives will require incentives, as shown by the objectives *eliminate company subsidy immediately and pricing to employees should remain at or below established benchmark,* these objectives have no incentive tied to them. The objective *increase employee utilization rate of the cafeteria at lunch time* is tied to an incentive. This objective had variable target performance

Figure 6.7 Example—Incentives

Desired Outcome	Performance			Annual Incentive	Inspection			
	Statement of Objective	Standard	Tolerance/AQL		Who	Data Source	Calculation	How Often Collected
Foodservice that eliminates subsidized costs to the company, and	Eliminate company subsidy immediately	For standard cafeteria (6AM–2PM)	None	None	Corp acct'g dept	Invoicing system	No subsidy to be charged on monthly invoice	Monthly
		For catering services	None	None	Corp acct'g dept	Invoicing system	No subsidy to be charged on monthly invoice	Monthly
increases utilization by employees	Increase employee utilization rate of the cafeteria at lunchtime	Target levels: • Yr 1—57% • Yr 2—62% • Yr 3—64% • Yr 4—66%	Target level must be achieved to earn incentive. Targets do not change even if exceeded in prior year	$50,000 for each 1% above specified target level	Corp HR & Supplier	Cash register transactions for time period 11AM–2PM; HR records	Average weekly transactions (by supplier) divided by average weekly full time employees (by HR)	Collected weekly, posted quarterly, evaluated annually
	Pricing to employees should remain at or below established benchmark	Benchmarks (values to be established) • Hot entrée • Sandwich • Salad bar • Pizza	Benchmark value can be adjusted semi-annually for changes to consumer price index	None	Corp program manager	Posted menu in cafeteria	Compare current pricing against benchmarks and record variance	Collected monthly, reviewed in QBR (quarterly business review)

for utilization of the cafeteria at lunchtime established for each year of the agreement. The target levels are:

- Year 1—57 percent
- Year 2—62 percent
- Year 3—64 percent
- Year 4—66 percent

The incentive is based on exceeding the target level: the service provider is paid $50,000 for each 1 percent above the specified target level for that year. We know from the quality plan that it is evaluated and paid annually. The incentive is directly tied to the Desired Outcome, *foodservice that eliminates subsidized costs to the company, and increases employee utilization.*

The requirements roadmap is now complete. It forms the backbone of the SOO in the agreement and clearly communicates the Desired Outcomes, defines success and any incentives.

Step 12. Document Deployment Processes

As mentioned, a great pricing model takes into account potential variables and includes sensible assumptions. Because the model is based on the underlying assumptions, you must revisit the assumptions as business happens and events transpire. A key pricing model component is to document the deployment process to monitor for changes and trigger events.

In a Vested agreement, the parties acknowledge that economic and market forces will impact the agreement, and they establish a process for addressing change early. Thus, when setting up your governance structure, we recommend including a component that monitors the pricing model and assumptions. Any variation to the margin-matching assumptions will trigger a change to the economics of the agreement. Depending on the impact, the change also could affect service standards offered. This change process should be outlined in the governance structure you create later in chapter 7.

H O M E W O R K

Element 6

Pricing Model and Incentives

Before you start working on the pricing model, pause for a quick sense-check in your journey and make sure each organization can address the next questions.

1. Are the Desired Outcomes and joint intentions outlined in enough specificity to create a Vested pricing model?

2. Is senior leadership on board to get beyond traditional pricing approaches and guardrails?

3. Have you completed the workload allocation homework from chapter 2? Do you understand the scope and scale of the work required and who is accountable for the workload allocation?

If either party answers no to any of the questions, we recommend going back to review the work completed in Steps 1 to 3 of the Vested Outsourcing implementation framework. (These can be found in chapter 6 of *Vested Outsourcing: Five Rules That Will Transform Outsourcing.*) Often companies find that they have skipped one or more of the suggested steps and deliverables (e.g., such as skipping the baseline) in their haste to get to an agreement. We have found that companies that skip steps often have to go back and complete them in order for executives to feel comfortable in moving to a Vested pricing model.

Overall Guidance

First, remember that there are no magic potions or easy answers when it comes to creating a Vested pricing model. We have seen many models from many companies covering various types of workscopes, and they are all different. Although we cannot offer a generic template or a spreadsheet to help you, we can offer sound advice in the form of the 12 steps you should take and the questions you should ask as you develop your pricing model and incentives. The checklists provided will make sure you have thought through the key factors to help you make a good decision about your pricing model. For some of the steps, we also provide generic tools and simple examples that can aid you in your discussions.

As we stated at the beginning of this chapter, the Vested pricing model is designed to reward both the company outsourcing and the service provider for achieving the Desired Outcomes. A properly structured pricing model should generate returns in excess of target margins for both parties when the parties achieve the Desired Outcomes.

A good pricing model includes these components:

- The total cost build-up and best value assessment
- Underlying financial and operational assumptions
- Risk factors and allocations
- The desired compensation method (e.g., fixed price, cost plus, hybrid)
- Margin matching triggers and techniques
- Contract duration
- Incentives

Figure 6.8 illustrates the 12 steps you will need to take as you develop your Vested pricing model.

The homework for this chapter addresses each of the 12 steps. We include a checklist for each step and, where possible, tools and templates to help you complete your homework. Significant effort and commitment are required to complete this homework, but doing so will bring you closer to an equitable Vested Outsourcing agreement and pricing model designed to reward the company and the service provider for achieving the Desired Outcomes.

Figure 6.8   12 Steps to a Vested Pricing Model

12 steps	Vested pricing model
Step 1	Form the team
Step 2	Establish guardrails
Step 3	Document input assumptions
Step 4	Identify total cost ownership and perform best value assessment
Step 5	Perform risk assessment and allocate risks
Step 6	Agree on compensation
Step 7	Determine target agreement duration
Step 8	Complete pricing model and establish prices
Step 9	Test the model and agree on baseline
Step 10	Define margin matching triggers and techiques
Step 11	Agree on incentives
Step 12	Document deployment processes

Step 1. Form the Team

Getting Started

Make sure that the team developing the Vested pricing model is an integrated cross-functional stakeholder group including legal, contracting, finance, and other technical experts. This is a cooperative effort.

1. Use a peer-to-peer approach for selecting the people on the team, with peers from both parties participating. For example, do not just have a financial expert from the service provider; have one from both companies.

2. Always have at least one person from each party who has been involved with the Vested Outsourcing initiative from the start on the team. If possible, everyone involved should have been on the team from the start, even if they were simply subject matter experts/participants.

3. On the team, always include a financial expert who has experience in developing pricing models.

4. Make sure that team members understand the purpose of a Vested pricing model and the steps that will be taken to develop it.

5. Ensure that the (people, IT, budgets, etc.) assigned to the team have the support of their managers to participate in the pricing process.

> ***Tools of the Trade***
> Stakeholder mapping,[20] developed in Step 2 of the Vested Outsourcing implementation plan, will help you identify stakeholders in both organizations that have a stake in the pricing aspects of your Vested agreement. Figure 6.9 charts this identification process. Choose your pricing team members from these stakeholders.

✓ ***Check Your Work***
Are all stakeholders on board and signed up to review the pricing model as an integral part of a cross-functional and joint governance structure?

Figure 6.9   Stakeholder Importance

High Importance	Higher importance Lower Influence: SECONDARY (score: 2) Communication Director Procurement Director Marketing Director Individual Employees	Higher importance Higher influence: PRIMARY (score: 4) Chief Executive Chief Operating Officer Chief Financial Officer HR/Diversity Director
Low	Lower importance Lower influence: OTHER (score: 1) Clerical Staff External Suppliers	Lower importance Higher influence: SECONDARY (score: 2) IT Director Line Managers
	Low Influence **High**	

Step 2. Establish Guardrails

Getting Started

The parties should clearly understand any formal boundaries for conducting external business agreements. Clear guardrails support the steps listed below to follow as you establish your pricing model and will prevent eleventh-hour issues.

1. The parties should clearly understand any formal boundaries or guardrails for conducting external business agreements.
2. Establishing clear guardrails also establishes a tone of "no surprises" that likely will be a relief to both corporate authorities and the team creating the pricing model.
3. Develop your detailed assumptions by clearly stating what each party feels are show-stoppers for moving forward.
4. Clearly define target outputs for each company; if the pricing model does not provide the outputs, each party likely will pursue other options.
5. Openly express concerns and get clarification of limits from the parties.

6. Share the base assumptions and risk/reward toler-
    ances with regard to potential incentives.

> **Tools of the Trade**
> Have your financial experts create a pricing model with the
> base case assumptions around sales, costs of sales, escala-
> tion factors, targets, and challenges. The model should have
> scenario planning capability so that the parties can test the
> basic assumptions against potential future situations. The
> parties should then agree on the major base case assump-
> tions and the resulting target margin.

✓ Check Your Work

1. Have your basic assumptions been endorsed by
    all senior officers of the company and the service
    provider?
2. Have you agreed on all base case assumptions that
    will deliver the desired outcomes for the company
    and the target EBITDA for the service provider?

Step 3. Document Input Assumptions

Getting Started

Agree on the input assumptions you will use. The input assumptions document specific suppositions relative to the scope of
the business and affect the price and bottom line of each party.
These assumptions will support the workscope and the desired
outcomes. Some tips:

1. Define assumptions, intensity, and volume with the
    team that actually delivers the service. That team
    should know everything about how the company
    uses the service.

2. Where possible, use the service provider team to design what-if scenarios to test assumptions.

3. Work with the financial team to translate their knowledge into a service utilization formula with clear work example spanning two or more years.

4. Define what happens if the company is unable to use the service for a limited or extended time. The parties may need to establish a pricing floor to cover the service provider's fixed costs plus a proportional cost for it to work with the company through crises.

5. Benchmark the current situation carefully against assumption parameters. This is especially important when converting from an existing agreement. The benchmarking process will create a bridge to the new Vested model.

6. Establish clear usage guidelines. The company and the service provider may choose to provide price reduction incentives for good purchasing behavior. Ideally, the parties want to reduce wasteful duplication.

Tools of the Trade
Review the list of common input assumptions presented earlier in this chapter. You will use these input assumptions when modeling the impact of variances in them and as discussion points to determine risk allocation when there is a variance from agreed baseline assumptions.

✓ *Check Your Work*

1. Have you documented your assumptions?

2. Have the parties agreed to the input assumptions that will be used to establish the actual prices and model-estimated profits?

Step 4. Develop Total Ownership Costs and Perform Best Value Assessment

Getting Started

In this step, you will make pricing decisions based on total cost of ownership and best value, or the value associated with the benefits received, not the actual prices. Document total costs from an end-to-end perspective, capturing the costs from the service provider and the company. Doing this will require transparency to establish the real total cost; remember that there are almost always hidden costs, soft costs and risks that are often overlooked when agreeing on a price. Add these costs to your pricing model equation. There are two approaches to getting started with a transparent approach.

Approach 1. Each company creates and shares its own P&L and balance sheets for the workscope and shares these side by side. This approach leverages the P&L that each party already has created based on a standard set of assumptions. The service provider's "revenue" in essence becomes one of the company's "cost" items. The goal is to identify as many of the costs as possible so each company can understand clearly the true cost of doing business and its impact on profit.

Approach 2. Create a mock P&L, or pro forma statement. The P&L is a representation of what the financials of the business would look like if the companies were operating under an investment-based business model and shared one P&L and balance sheet. This approach helps the parties examine the scope of the service delivery in a unified way that helps them focus on improving the bottom line of the business—not just one or the other's company.

Ensure that the financial experts of both parties mutually agree on the P&L model, its calculations, currency assumptions, and detailed rates and hurdles. Create at least one example spanning a two- or three-year period to ensure that the parties understand the exact calculation methods used in the P&L. Put this example in the agreement as an appendix to the compensation section. It will serve as a reminder of the core intention of the pricing assumptions, account for personnel changes and avoid the risk of misinterpretation of detailed financial calculations in the future.

Once you have established the base business case, determine best value criteria and try to quantify values. Update your pricing model to include best value elements.

> ### Tools of the Trade
> Use your pricing models and standard P&Ls to capture and test your pricing assumptions. Remember to work up the total cost structure by grouping costs into logical key components over the service lifecycle. Also, understand the capabilities of the parties and whether they are planning any major investments in future capability.
>
> Do you understand the total value that a partner can add to the supply chain and your competitive position?
>
> It is helpful to create an Excel spreadsheet to define and rank best value decision criteria.

✓ Check Your Work

1. Did you take the time to understand the true costs of developing a baseline business case that establishes the companies' profit projections?
2. Have you documented the total end-to-end costs?
3. Are your assumptions clear?
4. Have you developed a parallel or mock joint P&L?
5. Have you determined the best value criteria and ranking?
6. Have you revised the taxonomy to finalize workload allocation based on best value?

Step 5. Perform Risk Assessment and Allocate Risks

Getting Started

Through this process you will identify and prioritize the risks associated with your agreement. You will apply costs to selected risks that have a high probability of occurring or that could pose a significant impact.

1. Identify the various risks related to the service delivery that might impact the business assumptions and pricing model. The simple risk template in Figure 6.10 can help you document the risks associated with your agreement.

2. For each risk, understand risk patterns, have event awareness, and assign a probability of occurrence and impact on the agreement. Assign a priority to each risk.

3. Tie a price or premium to selected high-probability, high-impact risks, estimating the cost of intervening if one or both companies have to take action. Understand the potential costs associated with the risks.

4. Establish a firm cost associated with each risk in terms of added cost to the service or product.

5. Determine which company is better suited to manage (and mitigate) the risks. Allocate risks to the party that is best equipped to mitigate them, and pay a risk premium to the company for taking on risk.

Tools of the Trade
See Figure 6.10 on the next page.

Figure 6.10   Risk Template

ID Date	Risk Description/ Reason	Probability of Occurence	Impact on Project	Category—Red, Yellow, Green	Mitigation	Responsible Party	Target Date to Resolve	Status

✓ *Check Your Work*

1. Have you completed your risk assessment?
2. Have you identified risks with a high probability or impact?
3. Have you assigned costs to selected risks? Are these risk premiums factored into the pricing model?
4. Have you included in the review process the legal and the contract management group along with other stakeholders?

Step 6. Agree on the Compensation Model

Getting Started

Use Figures 6.4 and 6.11 to help you select the compensation method for your pricing model. Think through the best method—fixed price, cost reimbursement, or a hybrid—for your agreement. Remember that you can use different pricing structures within the agreement. Also document your pricing model framework. Even a simple graphic will give clarity to the framework and assist in building stakeholder agreement.

> *Tools of the Trade*
> See Figure 6.11 on the next page.

✓ *Check Your Work*

1. Have you worked through the key components of your pricing agreement?
2. Have you determined the best compensation method?

Figure 6.11   Pricing Model Selection Criteria Guidance

Criteria	Favors Firm Fixed-Price When…	Favors Cost-Reimbursement When…
Level of understanding of the work to be performed	Work is clearly defined	Flexibility to adjust the work tasks is required
Ability to influence service provider behavior	Low level of need to influence service provider behavior	High level of need to influence service provider behavior
Flexibility to adjust work tasks	Regulations or policies will not allow flexibility in tasks	Opportunity to adjust the tasks to gain efficiencies
Level of inefficiency in the operations being outsourced	Current processes are well defined and efficient	High degree of inefficiency in current processes
Budget predictability	Need for predictable budget	Ability to tolerate budget fluctuations to achieve performance goals
Level of understanding of price/high level of competition	Strong competition/high certainty of price	Weak competition/low certainty of price
Need for visibility of cost data	Visibility of cost data is not required	Visibility of cost data is required
Level of confidence in cost data	High level of confidence in cost data and cost history	Low level of confidence in available data and/or cost history
Administrative burden	Low tolerance for administrative burden	Ability to handle administrative burden
Tolerance for Risk	High service provider risk Low company risk	High company risk Low service provider risk

Step 7. Determine Target Contract Duration

Getting Started

Almost all Vested agreements have longer terms than conventional agreements; the additional length gives service providers confidence to invest in business process efficiencies that will yield year-over-year savings. Some highly integrated Vested agreements share investment risk in return for rewards over the term of the agreement. The general rule of thumb is to align the agreement duration with the service provider's optimum time to make a return on investment.

> ### *Tools of the Trade*
> There is no right or wrong answer regarding contract duration. Almost all Vested agreements have a duration of three to five years or more. The best way to establish a duration term is to assess the total costs associated with the goods or services over the lifecycle of use. Companies that prefer more flexibility than a long-term commitment can build benchmarking targets into the agreement at various checkpoints and reward service providers with continuation of term.

✓ *Check Your Work*

1. Does your pricing model allow you to conduct a risk assessment?
2. Does your pricing model include a financial sensitivity analysis on the term of agreement?
3. Have you done a Monte Carlo–type risk analysis?
4. Can you model investments over time to see the impact on prices or required increases in volume or reduction in costs?
5. Have you established an optimum timeframe for your Vested agreement to avoid duplicated

management, administration, resourcing, and transition costs?

Step 8. Complete the Pricing Model and Establish Prices

Getting Started

The goal is to build a pricing model that allows the parties to leverage a wider range of value-generating elements instead of bargaining only on the initial sticker price to reduce spend. With a range of economic assumptions and parameters already in the pricing model, you can begin to model various scenarios of volume, duration, unit price, and risk to create the desired target margin. Depending on the focus of the parties, their approach to risk, and the duration of the agreement, the price may be different from initial assumptions.

Tools of the Trade

Use the pricing model as the starting point to establish the fixed-price components, cost plus components, and any hybrid prices. Then link the TCO and assumptions relative to the work. These assumptions will form the baseline service levels and targets in your pricing model and set the threshold for variability and deviations from normal business conditions. Agree on any performance or service standards that are affected. Enter the volume of work desired and the total cost. The first initial price should reflect the elements in the pricing model in order to deliver the target return. Then compare the initial price with competitive price offerings as a benchmark.

✓ Check Your Work

1. Have you included all the input and output assumptions in the pricing model?

2. Have you calculated the TCO of goods and services over time?

3. Have you calculated any investments required to meet the Desired Outcomes and the optimum period of amortization of costs against a market price?

4. Have you factored in the risk premium?

5. Is the price the market will bear fixed or variable?

Step 9. Test the Model and Agree on the Baseline

Getting Started

The best approach for testing the pricing model is to create realistic scenarios and query the pricing model for its sensitivity to each one, noting the impact that various assumptions and risk factors may have on the target price. Rank the probabilities of specific outcomes, and choose a factor that allows adjustments to the price for risks and events that affect target margins. Each party should consider a range of upside and downside scenarios to test the balance of fairness in risk allocation and any subsequent price adjustments. If one party controls revenue through flexible pricing and one party controls only cost, how is the revenue allocated fairly over the cost base?

1. Revisit your assumptions based on the risk assessment.

2. What is your approach to spare capacity and the ratio of resources required to service the total capacity?

3. Do you have accurate demand forecasting? What are the levels of predictability in volumes over time?

4. What risk factors have been applied to the volume assumptions? Who bears this risk?

5. Is there a cost and price differential for differing levels of service or standards of service?

6. Are there pricing choices to be made based on a base service level or higher quality standards?

7. Are there seasonal fluctuations, peaks and troughs in demand that can be smoothed over time?

8. Are there any functional constraints? (These might include local pricing considerations at different locations where the impact of losses in a highly competitive market is balanced against gains in less competitive markets.)

9. Have you considered the impact of substitutions, new innovations, and cost improvement techniques over time relative to increases in firm orders?

10. Is there an optimum point to review the price to ensure that multiple dynamic events affecting price do not detract from meeting the Desired Outcomes?

11. Now test your assumptions and adjust the pricing model accordingly to set the baseline.

Voila! You now have a target *price* for a given set of assumptions and time span.

> ### Tools of the Trade
> Off-the-shelf scenario modeling methods are available to assist companies in establishing dynamic business cases and flexible scenario-driven pricing models. The real tool of the trade in a Vested pricing model is that assumptions are built with transparency and that the parties all understand the drivers and levers underneath the price that can be adjusted in the event of deviations from the core assumptions.

✓ Check Your Work

1. Have you tested your pricing model?

2. Will your pricing model allow the parties to leverage value-generating elements while not focusing on bargaining on the sticker price to reduce spend?

3. Have you tested your pricing model with a range of economic assumptions and parameters including various scenarios of volume, duration, unit price, and risk?

4. Have you made required adjustments to your assumptions based on your testing?

Step 10. Define Margin Matching Triggers and Techniques

Getting Started

Develop a margin matching plan and prepare for the unknown. The parties must agree that there are causes outside their control (because business happens and events, incidents, and accidents occur) and that these causes impact the pricing model. Maintain the variables in balance or readjust them according to a simple formula so that the underpinning assumptions for margin (EBITDA) in the pricing model do not deviate too widely from the projected returns. In doing so, it is important to be clear and precise regarding the underlying assumptions that drive margin. Other points to consider:

- This analysis will give the parties a reference point and provide further clarity about the accounting method used to execute the margin matching terms.

- List all factors that may cause large swings in profit gains/losses.

- Mutually agree on the accounting treatment in the event of positive or negative variances. The cost to provide the service may not track at the same pace as service utilization.

- Avoid complex adjustment formulas. They look nice but are costly to administer and are impossible to understand in a crisis.

> *Tools of the Trade*
> Every Vested deal is unique in its suite of outcomes and there-
> fore in its construction. There are no magic potions or silver
> bullets. The margin matching method must be carried out
> on a case-by-case basis and in consultation with all relevant
> experts using a transparent pricing model as the baseline.

✓ Check Your Work

1. Did you clearly state your margin matching objectives?
2. Do the parties agree to the margin matching plan?
3. Are you prepared to continually align the pricing model based on changes to your assumptions and input parameters?

Step 11. Agree on Incentives

Getting Started

A Vested Outsourcing partnership must have a properly structured pricing model that incorporates incentives to encourage
optimization for the best cost and service trade-off decisions
and, if possible, to encourage the service provider to achieve a
trade-up to higher service and lower costs.

The essence of Vested Outsourcing is the service provider's strategic bet that it will meet service levels at the set price.
Inherent in the business model is a reward for the service
provider to make investments in process, service, or associated product that will generate returns in excess of agreement
requirements. However, the company that is doing the outsourcing needs to understand the risks it is allocating to the service
provider and to ensure that it sets a value on the cost of those
risks when it develops a fair price for outsourcing.

Revisit the earlier Step 11 discussion for the list of the common incentive types used in Vested agreements.

Use the next questions to determine if there should be a performance incentive for each of the objective statements. For each objective, answer these questions.

1. Review each objective and its standard. Can you develop an incentive that will support the Desired Outcome?
2. Would an incentive be meaningful? Why or why not?
3. What type of incentive would best induce the service provider to reach the objective?
4. Does the incentive fit your overall pricing model?
5. Are incentives clearly linked to Desired Outcomes?
6. Will the incentive motivate the service provider to develop and establish innovative, cost-effective methods for performing work, such as driving down total cost, improving service, increasing market share, or making customers happier?
7. Will the incentive help offset risk by providing proper reward?

Incentives work best when applied to performance objectives where the service provider has process control. If the service provider is not able to make improvements to the process or is highly dependent on the company or outside providers for success, the incentive will not drive the positive behaviors required to support the Desired Outcome.

> ***Tools of the Trade***
> Use the requirements roadmap in Figure 6.12 to document the incentives and to tie them to a performance objective. The form can be found in Appendix C. An Excel version of the template can be downloaded from the Vested Outsourcing website: www.vestedoutsourcing.com /resources/tools.

Figure 6.12   Requirements Roadmap Template

Desired Outcome	Performance			Annual Incentive	Inspection			
	Statement of Objective	Standard	Tolerance/ AQL		Who	Data Source	Calculation	How Often Collected

✓ *Check Your Work*

1. Do the incentives reward the service provider for making investments in process, service, or associated product that generate returns in excess of agreement requirements?
2. Are the risks allocated to the service provider reflected in the incentives or in a fair price for the service?
3. Are incentives supportive of the Desired Outcomes and tied to performance objectives?
4. Do incentives promote innovation and improvement?
5. Are incentives consistent with the overall pricing model?

Step 12. Document Deployment Processes

Getting Started

Because your prices are based on underlying assumptions and have an element of variability, it is vital that you revisit the assumptions as business happens. Document the deployment process to monitor for these changes and trigger events, and incorporate it into the agreement governance structure.

Tools of the Trade
Deployment Checklist

1. Set a specific time horizon to manage fluctuations on an aggregated basis. Do not manage every fluctuation. Keep the approach simple and automated where possible, and bundled into a quarterly or biannual review dependent on the level of variability in the product or service structure.
2. Agree on the decision governance framework and the people from each company who will participate in reviewing deviations from pricing model assumptions. Ensure that resources to monitor the pricing model are available for the life of the agreement.
3. Set approval boundaries, and ensure that all statutory financial instructions and regulatory procedures are followed.
4. Record movement in prices, incentives, and performance to create trends that will inform future pricing strategies.

✓ ***Check Your Work***

1. Have the parties agreed on the pricing model?
2. Have you documented how to manage the pricing model for the life of the agreement?
3. Have you developed a deployment plan for inclusion in your governance statement?
4. Have the parties assigned resources that will monitor the pricing model for the life of the agreement?

The tips in Figure 6.13 are offered as an aide-mémoire when completing the pricing model.

Figure 6.13 Tips of the Trade: Element 6: Pricing Model

Tips of the Trade – ELEMENT 6 – Pricing Model	
Tip 1	Remember WIIFWe! Develop the pricing model jointly. Developing the pricing model that aligns the organizations involved is perhaps one of the hardest parts of a Vested Outsourcing initiative. Organizations implementing Vested Outsourcing must not revert to a win-lose mind-set when it comes time to develop the agreement and stay in tune with the shared vision and Statement of Intent.
Tip 2	Follow the 12 Steps to build your pricing model first – then negotiate. Ensure the pricing model is based on solid principles supporting continuous economic alignment and not a revenue generating price alone. This helps to bring an element of "fairness."
Tip 3	We recommend that the team hold off and "negotiate" the actual pricing and incentive payouts until after the economics of the agreement and the broad terms have been developed and documented.
Tip 4	Your Vested pricing model does not have to be a One Size Fits All. Pricing models often can have cost-plus and fixed-price components. The goal is to ensure the right agreement type aligns with the nature and risk profile associated with the work.
Tip 5	A pricing model can change over time as the teams learn more. For example, an early stage Vested Outsourcing performance is probably suited for a cost-plus agreement. As the outsourcing program matures, the pricing model can be migrated to more of a fixed or hybrid price structure with an innovative incentive framework.

CHAPTER 7

RULE #5: A GOVERNANCE STRUCTURE THAT PROVIDES INSIGHT, NOT MERELY OVERSIGHT

Governance is the last Vested Outsourcing rule, but it is perhaps the most important. A sound governance structure provides consistent management along with cohesive policies, processes, and decision rights that enable parties to work together effectively and collaboratively. A governance framework enables the parties to manage performance and achieve transformational results throughout the life of the agreement.

Following the first four rules helps you get to a good agreement—but you have to manage it. For this reason, we are embedding the concept of agreement governance into the Vested agreement. Simply put, agreement governance is the governance—or management—of your agreement and relationship. This chapter will help you understand what agreement governance is and enable you to create the proper agreement governance structure for your relationship.

Although companies recognize that there are benefits to reaching deep collaborative relationships with select service providers, many lack clear direction on how to build and govern effective partnerships.

To help you establish your governance structure, we have divided this chapter into two parts. The first part provides fundamental concepts for developing an agreement governance structure. All parties involved in both design and ongoing management of your Vested agreement should understand the basic nature and purpose of governance structures. This will help the parties understand why putting the effort into a governance structure is crucial. First we share the leading academic and applied research thinking regarding governance structures and the key themes and principles needed to develop a sound governance structure.

This chapter also addresses how to create a Vested governance structure. We delve into the how by discussing each of the four elements that must go into a successful governance structure: your relationship management structure; a transformation management process; an exit management plan; and other special considerations and external requirements, such as local regulations, and how the parties will manage strategic prerequisites, such as security, technology, and intellectual property.

FUNDAMENTAL CONCEPTS OF GOVERNANCE STRUCTURES

Guidance regarding the fundamental concepts of governance structure is necessary before you can implement the four elements of your agreement governance structure. We have teamed with the Corporate Executive Board (CEB) and the International Association for Contract and Commercial

Management (IACCM) to capture the latest thinking regarding governance structures.

Although it may be tempting to skip over the first part of this chapter and begin working on the elements, we encourage you to think of this part not as a detour in your journey but rather a pit stop. Think of this part of the chapter on the fundamentals as fuel for your journey. Take the time to soak up as much as you can to help you not only cross the finish line but sustain momentum through proper governance. We (and you) should not assume that everyone involved in developing—and eventually managing—your relationship has a comprehensive background in the fundamentals of governance. By studying this material, you will have that background.

Governance Structures in Theory and Research

Four constants recur in the study of agreement governance and structure:

1. Agreements are incomplete or inadequate.
2. Agreements should have a flexible framework.
3. There is no clear, standard definition of *governance*.
4. Agreement governance is not widely adopted

These constraints lead us to the troubling assertion[1] that today's governance structures are broken (or nonexistent) and are causing performance failures. Successful agreement governance structures address all four constraints, each of which is addressed next.

Agreements Are Incomplete or Inadequate
By their very nature, agreements are incomplete works in progress, and most still are rooted in the classic approach to contract or agreement law, designed to address transactions and legal protections, such as pricing and price changes, service

levels, limitation of liability, indemnification, and liquidated damages. According to legal scholar Ian Macneil: "Somewhere along the line of increasing duration and complexity [the agreement] escapes the traditional legal model."[2] Macneil's work points to a key reason why traditional legal theory is not adequate in today's business environment: "Classical law views cooperation as being 'of little interest' and external to the agreement. This argues for an agreement framework that encourages cooperation and dialogue." He taught that agreements can be "governed efficiently only if the parties adopt a consciously cooperative attitude."[3]

Oliver E. Williamson, the Nobel laureate economist, also contributed to this theme, writing that "all complex agreements will be incomplete—there will be gaps, errors, omissions and the like."[4]

Agreements Should Have a Flexible Framework

If a contract or agreement is incomplete due to the dynamic nature of business, what can the business and legal communities do? According to Williamson, an agreement should be a flexible framework and a process for understanding the parties' relationship. Structuring agreements with flexibility prevents what Williamson called "maladaptations." A maladaptation is an aspect of the agreement that was designed into it but that has become more harmful than helpful.

An example of a maladaptation is a consumer packaged goods company (CPGCo) that outsourced its distribution and transportation to LogisticsCo. LogisticsCo invested in an expanded fleet of trucks to handle the volume and shipped CPGCo's products to the major retailers, including Wal-Mart. When Wal-Mart—the largest retailer in the world—changed its corporate policy to state that it would take over all inbound transportation,[5] a maladaptation arose for LogisticsCo, because the original agreement called for it to handle a large amount of transportation. With Wal-Mart's volume taken out of the mix, the pricing assumptions were no longer accurate.

A flexible agreement can address the dynamic nature of business head-on by crafting mechanisms that can cope with unanticipated disturbances as they arise. The authors believe that a good governance structure should include mechanisms to enable the parties in a relationship to adapt and to adopt business changes—in effect, helping to keep the parties aligned and continually working toward the Desired Outcomes. The Desired Outcomes in essence are the beacon, the governance structure a mechanism for the parties to stop and redirect their efforts when detours occur.

There Is No Clear, Standard Definition of Governance

Research by the European academics Florian Moslein, Humboldt University of Berlin, and Karl Riesenhuber, Ruhr University in Bochum, Germany, suggests that the time companies spend on corporate and agreement governance is a critical component in managing a firm toward achieving its goals.[6] This is especially true when service providers play vital roles as key extensions of a firm's capabilities. Moslein and Risenhuber's work points to a weakness in agreement governance: the lack of a generally accepted definition of the term *governance.* To make matters worse, Moslein and Riesenhuber note that governance structures typically are customized to the scale and scope of the work. How can you define what a governance structure is when there is a moving target on what you are governing?

Agreement Governance Is Not Widely Adopted

The final concept raised by academics is that companies are not widely using agreement governance to help them manage both the relationship and the agreement itself. In a 2002 paper,[7] Williamson observed that while a contract is an exercise in organization or structure, economists "have been skeptical that organization matters and that it is susceptible to analysis." He continued: "The surprise is that a concept as important as governance should have been so long neglected."

It is clear that business professionals generally are remiss in adopting sound agreement governance. Of course, who can blame practitioners for not adopting something when there is not even a clear definition of what they are supposed to do?

Governance Structures in Practice

In the early days of outsourcing, many companies made the mistake of simply tossing the work over the fence to the outsource provider. Companies then compounded this mistake with inadequate or no performance monitoring or agreements. We call this the "driving blind disease" (see Appendix A). Fortunately, our experience has shown that most companies realize abdication is a bad practice. Unfortunately, most have gone overboard in the other direction to the point of micromanaging service providers against dozens or hundreds of discrete task-level metrics, which we call the "measurement minutiae" ailment (also described in Appendix A).

The CEB found that in a typical outsourced relationship, the outsourcing company can erode up to 90 percent of the anticipated value by poor governance of the relationship.[8] This is often called "value erosion" or "savings leakage" and presents a pressing problem for companies.

Other leading organizations studying outsourcing agree that governance structures are typically nonexistent or broken. While studies on outsourcing show various results, they have a common theme: Governance structures definitely matter. Poor governance often is cited as the major reason for agreement failure. Some of the more reliable sources that have studied governance are described next.

- The Outsourcing Center reported that poor governance plays a role in outsourcing failures as much as 62 percent of the time.[9] The center also identified unclear expectations on objectives from the beginning and misalignment of parties' interests over time

as the business environment changes as two major
factors for outsourcing failures.

- The London consultancy Hudson & Yorke states that
  governance "is one of the main reasons why managed service or outsource agreements succeed or
  suffer."[10]

- ARC Advisory Group found that changing the way
  people work and interact with each other in a performance-based or Vested relationship—both internally and between companies—necessarily requires
  the proper metrics to create alignments that drive
  desired behaviors along with high degree of trust,
  but "no true change will occur" without the support
  of the chief executives or other top-level executives.[11]
  In addition, there must be a culture and relationship
  structure that embraces continuous improvement.

- PricewaterhouseCoopers' Global Pharmaceuticals
  and Life Sciences Industry Group concluded that
  most companies found it difficult to monitor partner compliance because as companies "assess controls, they find it challenging to ensure that these
  arrangements work effectively" due to confidential-
  ity constraints and "lack of critical information from
  alliance partners."[12] PwC added that 90 percent of
  its agreement examinations "identify misreporting
  that leads to increased revenue or decreased expenses. As a result, most companies that do not have
  an effective contract compliance program do not
  receive the maximum financial benefit from their
  alliances."

Fortunately, companies and industry organizations are starting
to become aware of the problem and to understand the need to
include agreement governance as a critical component of outsourcing relationships. The next section provides a definition
of agreement governance as a starting point.

Defining Governance

Thought leaders at the IACCM, the CEB, and the University of Tennessee believe there is a need to define *agreement governance* in a new, more relevant way—one that not only embraces good management practices but also deeper collaboration with service providers. They recommend establishing a governance structure that has a vested interest in managing what are often highly multidimensional contractual arrangements in a more collaborative, aligned, and credible way. One distinct, standard definition of *agreement governance* is hard to pin down; indeed, it may not exist.

A good place to begin to define *good governance* starts with Vested Outsourcing's Rule #5: Insight versus oversight governance structure (see chapter 2). First, using the Macmillan Dictionary, let us look at the definitions of *governance* and *insight* to help gain clarity around a governance structure based on insight.

> Governance: The process of governing a country or organization.
> Insight: (1) A chance to understand something or learn more about it. (2) The ability to notice and understand a lot about people or situations.

Thus, we define *governance insight* as the process of governing an organization, enterprise, or agreement through learning and understanding. A good governance structure creates an environment for understanding the business better and to make proactive changes that can help the company control its actions, with the goal of reaching Desired Outcomes.

We submit this working definition for *Vested governance*:

> A framework that uses a relationship management structure and joint processes as controlling mechanisms to encourage organizations to make proactive changes for the mutual benefit of all parties.

As a general rule, effective agreement governance will maximize the potential for successful agreement implementation. It also will provide a framework for decision making, renegotiation, and modification as circumstances change.

HOW TO CREATE A VESTED GOVERNANCE FRAMEWORK

Now we turn our attention to the elements needed to craft a Vested governance structure that will provide insight, not just oversight. As Moslein and Riesenhuber noted, governance structures typically are customized to the scale and scope of the work. We have chosen to craft a framework that can be used for all types of outsourcing arrangements, from the simplest to the most complex. By doing so, organizations can tailor the framework rather than guess what else to add.

The Vested framework incorporates these elements:

Element 7: Relationship management. The relationship management structure formulates and supports joint policies that emphasize the importance of building collaborative working relationships, attitudes, and behaviors. The structure is flexible and provides top-to-bottom insights about what is happening with the Desired Outcomes and the relationship between the parties.

Element 8: Transformation management. Vested agreements are transformative because change in the Vested environment is both desirable and expected. Change will surely happen. Transformation management supports the transition from the old to the new as well as improvement of end-to-end business processes. The focus is on mutual accountability for attaining Desired Outcomes and the creation of an ecosystem that rewards innovation and a culture of continuous improvement.

Element 9: Exit management. The future is unknown. Even the best plans fail or events will change the business environment. An exit management strategy provides a template to handle these unknowns. In keeping with the Vested culture, the plan is fair and seeks to keep all parties whole in the event of separation.

Element 10: Special concerns and external requirements. The final element recognizes that all agreements are different and that many companies and service providers must understand and adhere to special requirements and regulatory protocols. Thus, the governance framework may need to include additional provisions. These additional provisions must recognize external influences and support rather than hinder the Vested agreement.

Figure 7.1 summarizes these four elements of a Vested governance structure. Then we explore each element and explain the key differences between a Vested governance structure with insight versus a governance structure based on an oversight mentality.

There is no magic elixir for creating a Vested governance structure; no one-size-fits-all approach exists. For this reason, we have teamed with the CEB to share examples of how companies are employing various best practices in agreement governance.

The remaining sections of this chapter provide specific insights and examples to help you address each of the four elements that you will need to include in your governance structure. We take some of the best-of-the-best thinking and provide real-world examples of how companies are applying each element. We suggest you review and discuss the various examples as you create your own Vested governance structure.

Figure 7.1   Four Elements of a Vested Governance Structure

Element	Vested (insight) Mentality	Oversight Mentality
Relationship Management	Relationship Management Focus – Reverse Bow Tie structure, Layers – Joint policies that emphasize the importance of building collaborative working relationships, attitudes and behaviors.	Service provider Management Focus – Bow Tie structure – Agreements viewed as risk avoidance mechanisms that monitor transactions/functions
Transformation	Agreement components viewed as a flexible framework. – Regular contact/review systems for service, performance, IP, and IT management updates; joint review boards for potential agreement changes and service issues. Focus on performance and transformation. – Emphasis on end-to end business metrics as well as service provider SLAs; mutually accountable for top level desired outcomes; focus on root cause analysis. – An ecosystem that encourages and rewards innovation. Ideas directed to the right people.	Agreement components viewed as fixed. – Infrequent communication or only when emergencies arise. – Little or no provisions for regular reviews beyond monthly revenue/cost accounting reports. Focus on service provider metrics and scorecards – Narrow SLA focus on the service provider SLA targets; focus on reporting. – No clear systems or attitudes that set joint processes for innovation as a continuing culture beyond 'feel-good' PR.
Exit Management, People /Change Management	Addresses how to handle future unknowns – Based on fairness – Seeks to keep parties whole in the event of a separation when separation is not a result of poor performance	Focus on T's and C's that are risk averse – Entity with the most power typically uses that power to negotiate in their favor without regard to fairness
Special Concerns and External Requirements	Support Vested ideals – Remain flexible enough to support applicable local laws, cultural norms and smooth processes – Focus on supporting the Desired Outcomes	Prescriptive provisions that are inflexible – Based on rigid or standard templates and existing processes

Element 7: Relationship Management

Effective relationship management involves not only establishing the mechanisms for how the relationship and business
will be managed but how the parties will addresses changes in
the key components of the agreement itself. For this reason,
Element 7 is divided into two primary sections that should be
included in your Vested agreement: organizational alignment
and change management.

Organizational Alignment

Organizational alignment is the process the parties use to
place the people and systems to manage the outsourcing agreement. We recommend six techniques to use when aligning your
organizations:

1. Create a tiered management structure.
2. Establish separate service delivery, transformation,
    and commercial management roles.
3. Establish peer-to-peer communications protocols.
4. Develop a communications cadence, tempo, or
    rhythm.
5. Develop a process to maintain continuity of
    resources.
6. Establish a performance management program.

Each is discussed in this chapter. Before we go into detail
regarding each technique, we provide some general advice and
guidance.

Manage the Business and the Relationship, Not the Service Provider

Many companies that outsource believe that they have a best
practice because they have deployed supplier relationship management (SRM) techniques. SRM is the practice of creating
mechanisms to increase the efficiency and effectiveness of how

a company works with its service providers. The goal of SRM is to create effective processes for a company and its service providers to work together, which in turn yields lower costs of doing business. Some SRM efforts are designed to build deeper relationships that foster improved collaboration and innovation. A benefit of SRM is that it establishes a common frame of reference for companies and their service providers to use, creating unified business practices and terminology for how the organizations work together.

We are advocates of many of the SRM concepts and highlight some of the best practice approaches in this section. You should leverage many of these best practice elements. However, for true organizational alignment, we suggest that you deploy the SRM practices with a unique spin—by putting on your what's-in-it-for-we (WIIFWe) hat when you develop processes for jointly managing the business to meet the Desired Outcomes.

The biggest difference between *managing a service provider* and strategically *managing a relationship* starts with a philosophy of how the parties work together. While SRM is most definitely not a whose-throat-to-choke exercise, experience shows that companies applying SRM typically have a what's-in-it-for-me (WIIFMe) attitude in managing their service providers. The wider view of the Vested approach is that the processes should encourage a shared accountability for achieving the Desired Outcomes. Companies should manage their Vested relationships with the same level of intensity as customer and employee relationships. After all, your strategic service providers really are an extension of your own firm. A Vested governance structure applies the best practice thinking behind SRM *but in a unique manner*. A Vested structure deeply embeds WIIFWe thinking into each of the SRM best practices. Figure 7.2 shows how Vested Outsourcing shifts thinking from conventional service provider management approaches of WIIFMe to the WIIFWe thinking that is critical to a Vested relationship.[13]

Figure 7.2   Transitioning from WIIFMe Service Provider Management to WIIFWe Relationship Management

WIIFMe thinking		WIIFWe thinking
Getting the service provider to meet our needs	BECOMES	Finding a way to meet both our needs
"It's in the agreement, now it's the service provider's problem"	BECOMES	Work together to achieve the performance and compensation goals
Blame and punish the service provider	BECOMES	Communicate the issues, jointly find solutions
Unpleasant surprises	BECOMES	Integrated planning and communications

The second biggest difference between traditional SRM philosophies and a Vested approach concerns the number of resources that remain within the company to "manage" the service providers. As you develop your transition agreement, think carefully about the post transition resources that will manage the ongoing business. Companies typically follow one of two schools of thought with regard to the resources they should maintain after the work is transitioned.

One school of thought believes that the company outsourcing should keep a staff of "experts" to provide technical guidance and to manage the service provider. We oppose this approach for two reasons.

1. If you have chosen a good service provider and put in an effective agreement and governance structure that includes resources that "manage" that provider, you add overhead.

2. Keeping staff members who know the business at the managerial level often leads to the "junkyard dog ailment." In this ailment, employees sometimes go to great lengths to hunker down and stake territorial claims to certain processes that

simply must stay in-house. One corporate executive said, "Our only mistake was keeping too many
people on our own staff. However, we wanted to
keep 'key' people and were nervous to reallo-
cate too many individuals. After six months we
knew we had made a mistake because we found
many of our staff having too much time on their
hands and trying to butt in and micromanage the
suppliers."[14]

The second school of thought lays off or transfers employees to the service provider. The rationale is that since the function has been outsourced, it is no longer necessary to keep
any technically skilled workers or managers on staff. This is
extremely dangerous, as it effectively results in an abdication
as opposed to service provider management. We recommend
a small number of experienced people remain within the firm
based on the size and scale of the workscope. If in doubt, we
find the fewer the better. We also want to remind you that it is
possible to avoid layoffs when outsourcing. Procter and Gamble
chose to transfer employees to Jones Lang Lasalle upon outsourcing its corporate real estate management services to the
latter company.[15]

There is a fine line between delegating responsibility to a
service provider while remaining accountable for the results
and managing the service provider so tightly that the process
might as well not have been outsourced at all. The company
still needs high-powered talent to gain the most benefit from
Vested Outsourcing. As mentioned, in the best approach, the
company retains a limited number of senior employees who
are knowledgeable about the technical aspects and are highly
skilled in overall management. This combined expertise allows
the company outsourcing to understand what the service provider is doing while resisting the urge to micromanage. The
handful of employees who remain must resist the urge to
tell the service provider how to do its jobs or to nitpick small

problems. Individuals must shift their thinking to managing the business *with* the service provider instead of managing the service provider or, worse, managing the service provider's people.

Earlier we outlined six specific techniques that you can use when aligning your organizations. We address each technique in more detail in the following pages, sharing examples from the CEB's applied work with members where possible.

Create a Tiered Management Structure

Once an initial agreement is signed, the focus changes to day-to-day operations and getting the work done. Too often the parties put the "strategy" on the shelf in a vinyl binder and never refer to it until a new executive comes in and wants to create his or her own plan. This is often referred to as strategic drift. To avoid strategic drift, your governance structure should start by establishing an organizational structure that ensures vertical alignment between the executives and the employees in the organizations that are charted to get the work done. A tiered structure with peer-to-peer alignment helps ensure not only that day-to-day priorities are executed efficiently but also that neither party loses sight of strategic goals.

A tiered management structure uses a layered approach, with each tier having specific responsibilities for managing different aspects of the business. This structure creates vertical alignment among the upper management, middle management, and day-to-day workforce. Each layer is accountable for examining the relationship and business success from its own point of view and is accountable for ensuring that the relationship is focused on the strategic and transformational components as well as the tactical elements. Using a tiered structure also greatly enables the resolution of problems in a timely manner. Regardless of how often people communicate, not all issues can be resolved at the lowest levels in the relationship. Some matters will need to be escalated.

We recommend creating a tiered organizational framework. The common usage consists of these three levels:

1. *Board of advisors.* The board provides overall sponsorship, strategic direction, and feedback regarding progress against Desired Outcomes and overall performance. This group also makes decisions related to escalated issues and approves of large transformation projects. The board should meet at least quarterly for the first two years of the agreement and after that semiannually. It should be composed of senior executives from both parties.

2. *Joint operations committee.* This committee provides direction regarding service delivery and monitors progress of the outsourcing relationship and scope of work. It is responsible for service quality across all locations. The group also sets continuous innovation and implementation priorities. The committee should meet monthly for the first year of the project and quarterly thereafter, pending mutual agreement.

3. *Management groups.* These groups oversee day-to-day operations in each location. There may be several working management groups. For example, there might be regional service delivery management groups and project-based transformation groups.

Figure 7.3 illustrates a three-layered structure to work with service providers.

A three-layered governance structure can work well for almost any type of Vested relationship. A layered approach ensures that each different level in the organization provides guidance across three key areas—functional working levels, operational levels, and executive levels—in a timely and consistent manner.

Figure 7.3   Three-layer Governance Structure

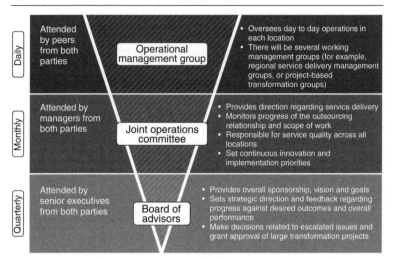

Establish Separate Service Delivery, Transformation, and Commercial Management Roles

A Vested agreement by design is meant to drive transformation. Thus, your governance structure should promote and drive your transformational efforts. Your governance organization should be aligned to support three primary governance roles: service delivery management, transformation management, and agreement compliance management. For larger outsourcing deals, we recommend creating three functional groups or roles for each of these areas. Smaller deals can work with at least one person dedicated to transformation management and agreement compliance. Next we outline each governance role.

Service Delivery Management
This function is responsible for the efficient and effective delivery of service, for responsive customer service, and for ensuring that service delivery complies with regulatory and internal policy requirements. The size of this group will vary according to the size of the deal. We suggest that only a very limited number

of people in the company participate in this role to manage the work scope the service provider is taking on.

Transformation Management
This function has responsibility for driving ideas, innovations, and process changes across both parties. The goal of this function is to identify and deploy transformation projects. The size of this group also will vary according to the deal size. All deals—regardless of size—should have at least two transformation management resources staffed full time on the agreement, one from the company and one from the service provider. For larger deals, we recommend that the company have a "process champion"—a dedicated person for large processes. For example, in a finance and administration business process outsourcing project, a Fortune 100 company had three process champion roles: one for accounts payable, one for accounting transations, and one for procurement.

Agreement Compliance Management
This function is responsible for managing the commercial and contractual aspects of the outsourcing relationship and the overall relationship across the various stakeholders in the two organizations. It is responsible for ensuring that the parties follow the Statement of Intent and manage performance. This group also manages scope/pricing changes and ensures that the actual agreement stays up to date as the business needs and pricing assumptions change.

The functional structure is layered across each of the tier levels shown in Figure 7.3. This ensures that all of the key governance roles work together at each of the hierarchical levels, as illustrated in Figure 7.4.

These functional governance roles should be embedded in each layer of the governance organization. The larger the deal,

Figure 7.4   Governance Organization: Core Functional Roles

Service Delivery Management	Transformation Management / Process Champions	Commercial, Relationship, and Contractual Management
– Efficient and effective service delivery – Customer engagement and management (users of service) – Ensuring statutory, regulatory, and internal policy compliance	– Overall process stewardship (must approve any process changes) – Leading transformation efforts – Thought leadership, market intelligence, and benchmarking – Ensuring statutory, regulatory, and internal policy compliance	– Managing the overall relationship with the service provider and governance process, including escalations – Driving service excellence and transformation through appropriate contractual and commercial arrangements – Managing the commercial and contractual aspects of the agreement (physical agreement change management)

the more people in each of the roles. For example, a Fortune 500 company outsourcing a large global outsourcing deal had seven full-time people as part of its governance team. The team included:

- Three regional service delivery directors
- Three regional tranformation management directors (one for three different core processes)
- One commercial relationship and agreement management program manager

Often the first reaction we get is "My gosh, we can't put that kind of overhead on our project!" Governance is not free; you must devote the right resources not only to achieve service excellence but also to help drive the desired transformation. Without proper governance, companies can experience up to a 90 percent value erosion and savings leakage.

Establish Peer-to-Peer Communications Protocols

Once you have determined your tiered structure and have established the various functional roles within it, the parties should
focus on horizontal integration. One way to do this is to map
the various individuals into the structure using a peer-to-peer
alignment approach commonly known as reverse bow tie. Many
companies insist on using traditional hierarchical structures,
where everything flows through the outsourcing company's
program manager and the service provider's account manager.
This approach, depicted in Figure 7.5, is known as a traditional
bowtie model, as shown on the left.

We recommend that you change to direct functional
communication through the appropriate contacts in the
respective organizations, as shown in the "TO" section of the
diagram in Figure 7.5. Using this reverse bow tie approach,
managers of individual components are responsible for keeping the company's program manager and the service provider's account manager aligned and informed about program
management.

Let us use the earlier example of the large outsourced deal
that dedicated seven people to governance. With peer-to-peer
alignment, the joint governance structure team likely would
include 14 people.

A peer-to-peer communication model improves the flow
of information and helps empower the company and service
provider teams. Information flow is specified and guiding
communication principles are established between the parties. As you implement this model, note that it is essential

Figure 7.5   Creating Horizontal Alignment

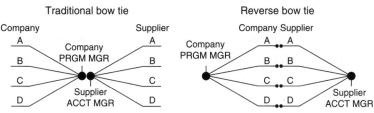

that managers hear about problems from their teams first. Failure to communicate about problems early on will doom this model.

Peer-to-peer mapping must be performed for each level established for the governance structure. Often companies establish peer-to-peer communications protocols only at operational levels, focusing on performance management and resolving day-to-day tactical issues. Although the majority of the communications will occur at the operational level, the real benefit of using the reverse bow tie approach is that it streamlines communications across *all* layers. At the lower levels, the conversations tend to be about day-to-day tasks, while the higher levels channel discussions around providing executive direction. The executive level is critical to helping establish the Shared Vision and Desired Outcomes, but executives still should continue to engage in performance management discussions and be integral parts of supporting and approving collaborative transformation projects.

Establish a Communications Cadence

Establishing a regular communications cadence process is an important aspect of the governance structure. We like to think of the communications cadence as the rhythm of the business because it helps the parties establish a formal mechanism for managing the business. We believe the frequency should be shortened during the first year of the outsourcing relationship. Frequency should change only once the parties establish a solid footing and the business is working smoothly. We recommend that the executive layer meet quarterly, the operating committee meet monthly, and the sourcing/functional teams meet weekly and even daily if needed.

Figure 7.6 presents an example of providing the purpose of each type of review mechanism and the general meeting cadence between Merck and their third-party logistics (3PL) service providers.

The Merck example shows the need to formalize the timing and nature of communications with key partners in order to make these interactions both regular and effective. Continuous interaction between Merck and its service providers makes it much easier for the company to identify collaboration opportunities and generate operational efficiencies. As an added benefit, Merck's close relationships across the 3PL base puts it in a position to foster cross-3PL collaboration that enables providers to find joint opportunities to reduce waste and inefficiencies in the Merck supply chain.

As with any team, regularly scheduled conference calls, team meetings, and face-to-face formal reviews are the grease for the wheels. Governance involves free-flowing communication between operational groups, their managers, and the executives of the companies. The most successful teams have formal mechanisms (and informal protocols) for talking daily, weekly, monthly, quarterly, and annually. Figure 7.7 provides a communications frequency framework. Use this framework as a template for creating your own communications cadence.

Develop a Process to Maintain Continuity of Resources

One of the most common responses from organizations wanting to adopt Vested Outsourcing is "I love the concept, but what if we sign up for risks under the agreement and the players change and throw out the rules? We have had trusting relationships and when a player changes, the pendulum swings and any progress we have made is lost."

This is a real fear and needs to be addressed. Consider this real-world example from the real estate sector. A large company we will call TelCo outsourced its entire corporate real estate services to a large real estate service provider we will call RealCo. TelCo had gone through two other service providers and was unhappy with them. TelCo's new chief procurement officer wanted a change. He loved the value proposition that

Figure 7.6 Global Relationship Value Management

Executive Steering Committee				

MRK Contact
CEO/CFO/CIO
Sr. VP GP[1]
Director Stakeholder[2]
Director GP
Relationship Manager[3]
	Supplier Contact
	CEO/Owner
	VP Sales &
	Marketing
		Purpose
		• Executive sponsorship
		• Establish partnership vision and goals
		• Generate collaboration options
		• Address collaboration obstacles
		  – Resolve organizational issues
		  – Provide resources
		• Approval of collaboration programs
		• Address major performance issues
			• Meeting notes
			• Partnership goals
			• Action plans
			• Opportunity lists
				Twice a year

Operation Committee				

MRK Contact
Director Stakeholder[1]
Director GP
Relationship Mgr[2]
Sourcing Mgr[3]
	Supplier Contact
	VP Sales &
	Marketing
	Account Managers
		Purpose
		• Set direction and priorities; drive compliance
		  – Identify/assess collaboration opportunities
		  – Develop collaboration programs
			• Meeting notes
			• Opportunity assessments
			• Collaboration plans
			• Justifications
			• Action plan
				Quarterly

Sourcing/Functional Teams		Purpose		Monthly or as often as needed

MRK Contact	Supplier Contact	• Execute collaboration programs
		  – Assign/deploy resources
		  – Conduct performance reviews
		• Conduct performance reviews; address issues
		• Drive development of annual plan
			• STPs
			• Performance reviews	

Relationship Mgr[1,2]	Account Managers	• Prepare performance reviews
		  – Address performance reviews
		  – Lead collaboration programs
		  – Manage win/win relationship
			• Meeting notes
			• Scoreboard and agenda
			• Performance development plan
			• Action plans	

Sourcing Mgr	Technical Managers			
Key Stakeholders[3]	Technical experts			
Technical experts				

Notes:
[1] Driver
[2] Facilitator
[3] Secretary

Source: "3PL Collaboration Scoring Model." Arlington, VA: The Corporate Executive Board, 2010, p.10

Figure 7.7   Communications Frequency

Frequency	Purpose	Attendees
Daily	• Address issues as they arise • Short "stand-up" meeting first thing in the morning and/or last thing before going home • Phone calls as needed	Functional team leads
Weekly	• Progress check/weekly performance • Reaffirm the Vision and Intent • What the metrics are showing • Issues, if any • Discuss upcoming events, and/or issues that are coming up at other companies	Program manager, account manager, functional team leads
Monthly	• Reaffirm the Vision and Intent • Review end to end business metrics against Desired Outcomes • Address performance issues • Assess relationship metrics • Review continuous innovation opportunities	Departmental managers, program manager, account manager, functional team leads
Quarterly	• Reaffirm the Vision and Intent • Full Quarterly Business Review • Formal agenda including performance against desired outcomes, incentives and trends • Review and set strategy • Review continuous innovation opportunities	Corporate managers, departmental managers, program manager, account manager, functional team leads

RealCo brought, including some innovative ideas that would reduce TelCo's corporate real estate budget by 30 percent. This was music to TelCo's ears. TelCo and RealCo signed a three-year agreement with a classic gainshare agreement to split the costs savings that RealCo achieved. (As discussed chapter 6 gainshare is a monetary incentive where the service providers share in costs savings. The focus is on driving out costs that are of limited value and sharing the costs savings.) The deal, although it had a gainshare provision, was not a Vested agreement. TelCo also suffered from these outsourcing ailments (see Appendix A):

- Aliment 2: *"Outsourcing paradox"*. Although the procurement department was the "buyer" for the deal, TelCo Corporate Real Estate would manage the deal. The parties wrote a 600-page contract, detailing exactly how the service provider should aerate the grounds.
- Ailment 4: *"Junkyard dog"*. The Corporate Real Estate group did not trust RealCo. It had churned through two previous service providers, and many employees who remained in the group were still upset that TelCo had outsourced at all.
- Ailment 9: *"Measurement minutiae"*. Because of the lack of trust, TelCo created a vendor scorecard that had more than 300 key performance indicators (KPIs). Many of the KPI metrics were subjective and not measurable.

To make matters worse, the Procurement Group and the Corporate Real Estate Group were revolving doors when it came to the people managing RealCo. In the first two years of the agreement, RealCo had three "strategic directions" that shifted from "You are the expert—just go do it," to "I need a 20 percent fee reduction," to "We need you to invest in our business to deliver win-win innovations." Needless to say, RealCo was hesitant about making investments. In addition, TelCo had churned through two vendor account managers.

On the flip side, service providers also have issues when it comes to continuity of resources. One of the main complaints we see is that service providers sell the A team but then quickly switch to the C team. We recommend that your governance framework contain a process for ensuring continuity of resources. Here are five best practices for maintaining continuity of resources:

1. *Mutually identify a limited number of personnel who are designated as key personnel for both parties.*
2. *Establish a provision that prevents either party from unilaterally removing, replacing, or reassigning key personnel for a specific timeframe.* Two to three years is a reasonable duration that enables promotions.
3. *Develop a process for communicating key personnel changes.* For example, establish communications protocols when key personnel become unavailable (e.g., sickness, jury duty, resignation, etc.).
4. *Establish a provision for replacement of key personnel.* This might include having the service provider propose a replacement resource three months prior to the replacement or enabling the company to interview a limited number of potential replacements and approve the new person.
5. *Use a formal escalation process for personnel mismatch concerns.* For example, we have seen employees of one party (typically the company outsourcing) denigrate or verbally abuse the service provider's personnel. This is intolerable. The agreement should have provisions that address escalating improper behavior between the parties or between employees.

At the end of the day, an agreement is managed by people. The governance framework should include a people management component.

Establish a Performance Management Program
Vested Outsourcing is not just about driving innovations. The day-to-day business and the relationship also must be governed.

We recommend creating a performance management program that:

1. Measures end-to-end performance against KPIs and Desired Outcomes, not just service-level agreements (SLAs).
2. Provides a mechanism to measure the overall health of the relationship and effectiveness of transformation efforts.
3. Enables the parties to score performance to capture perception gaps.
4. Includes a neutral third party to help facilitate decisions on final performance scores and other aspects of governance.
5. Includes a proactive problem-solving and dispute resolution process.

Each attribute is discussed next.

Measure End-to-End Performance
For many companies, the most efficient way to oversee normal operations is through a well-designed scorecard. Scorecards play a key role in tracking performance against the agreed-upon metrics you outlined in chapter 3. A common mistake when developing a scorecard is using a service provider scorecard that focuses on the detailed SLAs rather than the end-to-end Desired Outcomes and business needs. It is critical to have a business-focused scorecard because the parties will need to work together to achieve the business goals. An integrated, business-focused scorecard can help the parties emphasize performance against the Desired Outcomes and business needs, not just performance against the service provider's tasks. Far too many service provider scorecards are all green yet the business is not performing against its Desired Outcomes. We fondly refer to this as a "watermelon effect" because the relationship is green on the surface but red when you dig in. When developing

the scorecard, remember that it is the business that needs improving, not just the service provider's role.

Mechanisms to Measure the Overall Relationship

Performance management also should include understanding the overall health of the relationships. For example, look at how Whirlpool applies this concept with its strategic 3PL service providers. Whirlpool's Kevin O'Meara, director of supply chain operations, has embedded five key principles to ensure the overall health of the relationship. Figure 7.8 illustrates the Whirlpool approach. (Note that the figure uses *company* for what we term *service provider.*)

Although the figure specifically refers to how Whirlpool works with a 3PL, the model is relevant to *any* Vested Outsourcing relationship. What is attractive about this model is its emphasis on transparency of communication, collaborative problem solving, trust, and finally service provider profit opportunity. The tenets of Whirlpool's framework map very closely to those

Figure 7.8   Whirlpool Approach to Understand Overall Relationship Health

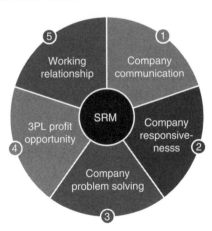

1. Company communication
   - Open and honest communications
   - Adequate and timely information transfer
2. Company help (responsiveness)
   - Joint efforts to achieve cost/ quality objectives
   - Collective responsibility; joint problem solving
3. Company problem solving (proactiveness)
   - Elimination of barriers; ease of doing business
   - Alignment of key processes (product development, S&OP, ect.)
4. 3PL profit opportunity
   - Opportunity to make advantaged returns
   - Rewards for strong performance/ joint process improvement
5. Working relationship
   - Mutual trust/alignment of objectives
   - Senior management ownership

"Five critical components to managing logistics providers." Arlington, Va.: The Corporate Executive Board, 2009, p. 5.

laid out in the Vested Outsourcing approach in Figure 7.1. The Whirlpool management framework graphically illustrates how each of the principles meshes to enable the parties to work effectively together to guide the governance of their key relationships. It also illustrates how the parties evaluate overall relationship health, enabling them to look at more than the actual performance against KPIs and SLA. One very successful relationship we studied allocated a full 20 percent of the service provider's profits to "relationship health."

Joint Scoring of Performance to Measure Perception Gaps
A well-designed scorecard also allows both parties to rate each other's performance and their own. This joint approach for scoring performance will highlight gaps in perceived performance and prompt better conversations about why this gap exists and potential resolutions. Figure 7.9 is an example of a scorecard using a joint measurement approach.

When Microsoft outsourced its facilities management services to Grubb & Ellis, it used a similar joint measurement approach where both parties provided a score for the key metrics. The results? Initially, there was a significant gap in

Figure 7.9   Performance Scorecard

Service Provider Scoreboard						
KPI	Possible score— 100	Scores				Comments/ examples
		Client			Self score	
		Individual Score		Client score		
Category weighting—25%	KPI weight					
1 KPI example 1	20%					
2 KPI example 2	40%					
3 KPI example 3	20%					
4 KPI example 4	20%					

expectations and performance as measured by Microsoft versus Grubb & Ellis. Over the first two years, the gap decreased by 91.5 percent, resulting in tight alignment between the two companies. In addition, the final performance score improved by 47.6 percent over the same period.[16]

To illustrate why this approach is so important, we share a real story of a disconnect between parties. One of the authors facilitated a contentious meeting between a firm we will call Company A and PayEx, a payroll service provider. Under that agreement, Company A had responsibility to provide accurate and timely employee wage and benefits information to PayEx.

Company A accused PayEx of serious performance failures and was threatening to terminate the agreement. Company A called PayEx to its headquarters for a thorough tongue-lashing. During the course of that meeting, PayEx executives showed Company A's upper management a string of email correspondence to Company A employees. Those email messages warned Company A that its own information was inaccurate and untimely. PayEx further warned that Company A was compounding the failure by randomly fixing inaccuracies rather than highlighting and fixing all inaccuracies.

Because there was no formal governance structure for escalation, Company A's managers had not seen any of the warnings. They were completely unaware of the problem its own employees were creating. To make matters worse, Company A's employees consistently blamed PayEx for the service failures in an effort to protect their department from scrutiny.

Clearly, no company wants to throw its service provider under the bus, and vice versa. Without a two-way scorecard—in the case just mentioned including a score for accuracy and for timeliness of information and time to fix known inaccuracies—the parties can and likely will be completely unaware of the performance problem.

Include Neutral Third-Party Facilitation

This story illustrates the need for a joint measurement approach and points to the fact that the problem escalated to the point where a third-party mediator was needed. There is a trend to use neutral third-party facilitators in overall agreement governance and in particular for the performance management aspects. We support this concept and have seen it work well; however, we advocate including the neutral third party as part of the overall governance team from program inception. Microsoft and Grubb & Ellis have used a third-party firm since the first days of the agreement to help them create "truth" on their scorecard and incentive payouts.[17]

Including a neutral third party offers many benefits. Even great relationships have moments when parties misunderstand each other or disagree about how to resolve a situation. Vested Outsourcing is no different. The collaborative approach to developing a Vested agreement will not eliminate the need to resolve differences of opinions. In fact, the opposite might be true. As a natural result of the collaborative process, parties are more open to discuss underlying issues and willing to get to the root causes.

Jim Groton, veteran attorney, mediator, and Standing Neutral[18] in the construction industry, has been an advocate on the use of neutral third-party resources for many years. The parties select a trusted neutral expert as the "Standing Neutral" to assist in the prompt resolution of any disputes throughout the life of their relationship.

A Standing Neutral is slightly different from a mediator. Mediators are typically brought in by the attorneys once the dispute is a full-blown controversy, whereas a Standing Neutral is brought in by the business unit as part of the governance structure. Groton's pioneering work in the construction industry has shown that including a neutral third party almost always helps prevent formal disputes. Neutral third-party experts allow the parties to work through conflicts in a fair manner and significantly reduce discontent and lawsuits.[19]

We would like to draw a distinction when we refer to a Standing Neutral, and that is with the word *neutral*. It is becoming popular for outsourced advisory service firms to provide governance services to their client organization. We perceive these relationships as very "neutral." Here is an example of why we see a potential conflict of interest. DrugX was a drug store retailer that hired AAAdvisors to help them with their RFP, contract development and supplier governance. The potential conflict was that AAAdvisors felt compelled to act in its client's best interest. Every day they set out to prove their value by nitpicking the service provider, micromanaging, and finding errors. We encourage companies to avoid finger-pointing at all costs, and in this case AAAdvisors was getting paid to finger point.

Include a Proactive Problem-solving and Dispute Resolution Process
At this point in your journey, likely you feel positive about the future. This is precisely the time to talk about how to raise and address issues and concerns. After all, the parties have proven that they are capable of working together to develop a multifaceted, long-term agreement. Why would the same people not be equally capable of solving problems together?

By *proactive problem solving*, we mean establishing a process for channeling problems in a constructive and meaningful way. Embedding a formal problem-solving process into the agreement creates a sense of accountability to solve problems in a timely manner using an agreed-upon escalation and decision process. This proactive approach prevents parties from ignoring problems until they get to the point of needing intervention, such as arbitration or litigation. Because the parties have established the process in the beginning, they often are successful in following it. More important, a problem-solving process prevents people from falling into bad habits and WIIFMe thinking.

Some issues can, and ought to, be handled at the day-to-day level of implementation. As business happens, problems may arise that require internal escalation. Decide now how to identify those issues, who should address those problems, and what type of third-party intervention the parties may choose if the problem cannot be resolved.

Proactive problem solving has three equally important components, which include identifying the situation, determining the degree of urgency, and resolving the situation. Take some time to define terms from least problematic to most problematic. You will want to consider what types of actions and inactions will trigger a potential problem. Figure 7.10 illustrates this point by suggesting definitions and corresponding problem-solving procedures.

For example, you may be concerned that the service provider's performance is not trending in the right direction in a specific area. Concerns should be placed on quarterly business review (QBR) agendas. Problems, however, are more urgent and require middle management's attention. Conflicts likely are unresolved problems demanding senior-level attention.

Talk about these terms at this stage of formulating the governance framework process now, because one party's issue is another party's problem. Who gets to decide if something is

Figure 7.10   Problem-Solving Procedure

Situation	Degree	Resolution
Issue:	Medium impact; low urgency	Resolved in routine conversations
Concern:	Medium impact; medium urgency	Resolved in QBR meetings
Problem:	High impact; high urgency	Escalate and call special meeting
Conflict:	Unresolved problem	Escalate to senior management or neutral third party
Breach of Contract:	Unresolved conflict	Third party intervention, such as arbitration

labeled an issue or a problem? In our experience, this is an easy exercise to undertake at this point. Look back at your homework for Elements 4 and 5. Decide the variance or tolerance level for performance indicators. From that discussion, you can decide at what point a variance triggers a problem-solving approach. By documenting this thought process now, you can save countless hours exchanging emails as you try to understand how much attention to pay to a situation.

You also may want to define the term *conflict*. The words *dispute* and *conflict* are often loaded with negative connotations. We suggest that you reserve the term *conflict* for all unresolved problems. No party should tell the other party that they are having a conflict unless there is an intention to involve senior management. In our opinion, a conflict is any circumstance that cannot be resolved by middle management. Conflicts, by their very nature, threaten the relationship and the agreement; for that reason, they require senior-level attention.

Once you have defined terms to use when differentiating issues that have little impact or little urgency from those that do, it is time to design a process for addressing issues, concerns, and problems. For example, routine daily conversations should resolve almost all issues. Issues usually are identified and addressed as a matter of course. A high percentage of all issues will get resolved. A concern has more urgency. Therefore, concerns ought to be addressed at the QBRs. Place concerns on the agenda and set aside time to discuss them.

Problems are high impact and urgent. Parties must act immediately to solve problems using a predefined process. For example, you may decide that a problem requires three measures:

1. A middle manager at one company will notify the corresponding middle manager at the other company in writing about a problem.
2. The parties agree to convene a meeting within five business days.

3. The parties agree that each company will send someone with decision-making authority to that meeting.

If such a clear process is set forth in the agreement, implementing it, even in a time of high emotion, will be easy.

Map out the process for solving a conflict. If middle management cannot resolve the problem for any reason, senior management must engage. A good governance process often prevents a problem from rising to a conflict demanding senior-level attention. Putting that escalation process in writing actually forces middle management to stay in a conversation until the problem is resolved. We doubt that any manager wants to throw a conflict on a superior's desk. But without defining the implications of taking the conflict to a superior, it just might happen.

A word of caution: Some companies encourage their employees to escalate issues directly to the service provider's senior management if they do not get a timely response. This behavior is unacceptable and must be avoided. It is inappropriate for a company to escalate anything other than a full-blown conflict to the service provider's senior management. Do not cry wolf. The problem-solving process will work if you follow it.

The parties must address the worst-case scenario: a breach of contract and contract termination. It is important for the business units to outline the contract termination procedures, which become the exit management plan. The parties' respective legal teams will help you outline the process for holding the other party legally accountable for a breach of contract.

HOMEWORK

Element 7

Relationship Management Framework

Getting Started

As you can see by the examples in this chapter, your Vested governance framework must be customized to fit your relationship and the workscope of the agreement. Use a flexible and anticipatory governance framework to guide your agreement. Use the checklist in the Tools of the Trade section to ensure that your Vested relationship management framework includes all the important attributes to support your agreement.

Also, later in the homework sections for each element there are Tips of the Trade tables that provide important summary points and takeaways for each element.

Tools of the Trade
Relationship Management Framework Checklist

- Develop an organization chart showing the relationship between members of both parties.
- Identify senior-level managers from both parties to sit on the governance committee.
- Empower the governance committee to manage the relationship and all aspects of the agreement.
- Focus communications on:
  - Vision and strategy.
  - Collaborative problem solving.
  - Collaborative innovation.
  - Partnership goals.

- Working relationship health (trust/align-
  ment/ownership/responsiveness).
- Service provider opportunity, risk, and
  reward.
- Tactical performance.
- Establish multilevel communications with functional communication through appropriate contacts in each organization so that management is
  fully informed.
- Set in place strategic communications with the
  governance committee to guide the relationship
  and manage progress toward meeting Desired
  Outcomes.
- Establish formal timing and nature of communications including QBRs conducted between
  the company, the service provider, and key stakeholders as well as more frequent operational
  meetings and reviews.
- Define a communications plan with messages
  tailored to different key constituencies.
- Set in place leadership that fosters improved
  relationships.
- Set in place processes to track your relationship
  health.
- Include a communications plan to support
  change.
- Include definitions for various levels of conflict:
  issue, concern, problem, and conflict.
- Include a plan for resolving levels of conflict within the existing governance structure.
  Make sure to determine when and how senior
  management should be engaged for conflict
  resolution.

✓ *Check Your Work*

1. Does your relationship management framework promote open and transparent communications?
2. Have you documented and mapped relationships between the parties?
3. Are expectations between parties clear?
4. Do you have an issue resolution plan?

Figure 7.11   Tips of the Trade: Element 7: Relationships Management Framework

Tips of the Trade – Element 7: Relationship Management Framework	
Tip 1	Formal communications include what, how and when information will be communicated.
Tip 2	Map organizational relationships between parties.
Tip 3	Strategy is shared between parties.
Tip 4	Relationship health is tracked and there is a formal effort to improve collaboration and trust.

Element 8: Transformation Management

There is an obvious overlap in getting from the initial agreement, to transitioning the workscope, to maintaining the business in an ongoing and dynamic environment. These transitions require a sound process for making changes to the actual agreement. As we have done previously, we start by getting grounded with regard to what transformation management is by referring to the Macmillan Dictionary.

Transformation—a change into someone or something different, or the process by which the change happens.
Management—the control and operation of a business or organization.

When the words are combined, we can define transformation
management as the operation of helping an organization to
become different with regard to both people (someone) and
processes (something).

To be successful, your agreement should include transformation management processes to help your organization
stay aligned in a dynamic business environment. This is crucial, given that the one thing that is certain is that change is
the only constant. It is also why scholars such as Ian Macneil
and Oliver Williamson advocate that businesses engage in
cooperative behavior under a flexible agreement. Change
puts pressures on even the steadiest of relationships. A Vested
agreement should create mechanisms for dealing with those
changes to ensure that the organizations stay aligned and
continue to work effectively together toward their Desired
Outcomes.

Transformation management processes should allow the
agreement to evolve in a controlled manner. They should
support—not hinder—continuous improvement and innovation. When a change impacts key elements of the agreement,
such as the price or related service costs, service delivery, or
the obligations of either party, follow a documented process
that includes an assessment of the impact of the proposed
change.

The transformation management element of your agreement should contain four key components, each targeted for
different types of transformation.

1. *It should document a common understanding on how
    the initial transition of workscope is managed.* This
    will ensure that the relationship gets off to a good
    start by establishing a clear understanding of the
    transition.
2. *It should include philosophies for driving overall trans-
    formation initiatives—what we call a continuous*

innovation management process. This part of the agreement is designed to establish the protocols and processes for how the company will manage ideas that the parties need to agree upon and invest in order to help them achieve their Desired Outcomes.

3. *The agreement should contain a process for managing day-to-day continuous improvement efforts or business problems that arise.*

4. *It should include a process for updating and managing any changes to the actual agreement.* This is also referred to as contractual document management.

Only by establishing clear protocols and processes for transformation management can the parties achieve maximum effectiveness.

Initial Transition Management

For some teams, the overall agreement may represent a transition from a company-operated function to a new service provider or from an old service provider to a new one. For others, it simply may entail a scope change and a new way of doing things between the same parties. If there is considerable workscope shift between the parties, the Vested agreement should include a formal process that covers how the parties will manage the initial transition. A checklist of the typical items for a transition agreement is included in the Homework section.

Regardless of what you include in your transition agreement, the transition process consists of three key aspects:

1. Maintain team continuity from the initial sourcing process, through transition to day-to-day operations.

2. Include an effective communication and training
    campaign around the transition.
3. Include the high-level target plan.

Maintain Continuity: Keep the Team(s) Together
Service providers typically are very knowledgeable regarding
transitions. Many larger companies have formal transition or
ramp-up teams solely focused on successful ramp-ups. In fact,
one item you might consider specifying in your transition agreement is the actual roles or job description of the people on the
transition team. Having at least some dedicated resources to
transition any work is smart because the skills needed to develop
an agreement, to project manage the startup, and to manage
the day-to-day business after implementation are often very different. For example, it is fairly common for larger outsource
programs to have a full-time project manager assigned to the
project who likely transitions off the project once the transition
is complete.

There is one caveat to having a dedicated transition team.
It is critically important that at least one person on the original
team designated to get the work under the agreement is part
of the transition and the ongoing business teams. In short, the
transition team is a bridge from the initial sourcing team to a
performance team.

Up until now your team has likely comprised an integrated
multifunctional solutions team comprised of various participants. Likely it has included representatives from the technical,
supply, business/operations groups, procurement communities
and possibly the customers they serve. As the team designs the
transition, there is a natural need to expand it to include more
members from the parties responsible for the actual transition
and day-to-day business. To be successful, *at least a core of the integrated solutions team must remain on the project.* This group has the
most knowledge of why and how things are structured and of
what has to happen next. Their roles will change and adjust to

new post-agreement award roles, and their responsibilities will be remapped as required. Learning the business is very different from keeping the business. For this reason, it is important that the agreement includes a clear understanding of the roles, responsibilities, and major timeframes for transitioning the work.

Include an Effective Communication and Training Campaign
As you develop your transition plan, you will need a formal resource plan. The transition should include the deliverable of creating a formal blueprint of the work once it is transitioned to ensure that key workscope elements are transferred and personnel are properly established. The taxonomy and workload allocation is an excellent source for crafting this blueprint. As you work through the workload allocation, the parties should agree on a formal process for the service provider to assume day-to-day management, staffing, and operational responsibilities. The transition management plan should clearly spell out workscope transfers, staff transfers, and the roles of third parties involved in the transition or setting up interfaces.

The plan also should include training procedures for such processes as work-shadowing, knowledge capture, and knowledge transfer. This training plan also should include creating training material and process documentation, especially if there are any local statutory requirements or processes. If the service provider did not create a performance work statement, one should be completed once the work is transitioned.

Avoid underestimating the need to conduct required training and education. It is important to educate not only customers but also any new agreement administration personnel. All training plans must incorporate a validation process to ensure that the training is delivered as intended and that personnel can provide the operational requirements.

Include a High-Level Target Plan
The last part of the transition management plan is documenting the actual high-level plan itself. The finite details will change, but the agreement itself should outline the agreed-to transition plan. It should include documenting:

- Assumptions
- Target transition schedule, including:
  - Key activities, milestones, and decision points
  - Key dependencies
  - Performance criteria to be measured and achieved at each stage of roll-out
  - Go-live criteria
- Quality control and delivery management procedures
- What each party company has to provide or other special requirements (such as not transitioning during peak months)
- Testing methodology and criteria
- Transition project management protocols, such as:
  - Progress reviews
  - Issues resolution

The team also should outline potential risks to the transition. A risk assessment exercise at the inception of the relationship enables the parties to look at potential relationship landmines before they occur and jointly design methods to overcome issues as they arise. The team can use the same risk assessment template that was used when discussing the pricing model (see chapter 6), but this time it will be looking through the lens of implementation risks.

Finally, make sure you start your transition by implementing the organizational aspects first—putting in place the resources for each of key positions you outlined in your relationship management structure. Keep in mind this is a partnership, a new phase in outsourcing. It is a team working together and learning from each other.

Start positive and stay positive.

Continuous Innovation Management

A Vested relationship and agreement is designed for change. For this reason, we recommend your Vested agreement include a formal process for managing ideas, opportunities, and innovations that can help the parties achieve their Desired Outcomes.

A Vested agreement is designed to reward service providers for innovative ideas and investments that deliver results against the Desired Outcomes. It is important to understand that innovation is the key driver of economic growth for businesses. In fact, Robert Solow won a Nobel Prize for his work linking innovations in business products and processes to the key reason for business growth. He found that a staggering 87 percent of all economic growth for businesses comes from these innovations.[20] Establishing a joint continuous innovation management process is thus a fundamental part of your Vested agreement. The agreement should spell out exactly how the parties will communicate and make investment decisions with regard to potential innovations that can help them achieve the Desired Outcomes.

Before you develop a continuous innovation management process, we must address two primary misconceptions associated with innovation. The first is the confusion between invention and innovation. The second is that innovation only applies to research and development (R&D) as it relates to new products or services.

Regarding the first misconception—confusing invention with innovation—for our purposes, invention has at its heart the idea that something—an idea, a concept, a physical element—is created or constructed that did not exist before. The telephone is an example of an invention. Innovation, however, is modifying what already exists. It is continuous and incremental in nature. Cynthia Barton Rabe, author of *The Innovation Killer*, defines innovation as "the application of an idea that results in a valuable improvement."[21] For example, telephone innovations led to cordless devices and the development of cell phones.

Significant revenue streams can come through continual improvements of a product or service. Innovations can be risky, but doing nothing is riskier. As the economist Joseph Schumpeter put it, companies that resist change are "standing on ground that is crumbling beneath their feet."[22]

The second misconception is that innovation applies to R&D only in terms of developing new products and services. The American Productivity and Quality Center is debunking this myth. Its studies have shown that innovation applies in virtually all parts of a company and its underlying processes. One area where innovation has been mostly untapped is in business operations. Your Vested agreement should focus on making the business more effective through process innovations. In short, innovations help make the pie bigger for the parties when they are focused on delivering results against the Desired Outcomes.

Business leaders agree that innovation can yield great benefits; almost all also point out that investing in innovation involves costs and risks that could have a negative effect if the efforts do not result in successful end products or services. For this reason, it is crucial that your agreement include a continuous innovation management process where the parties can review potential ideas and jointly agree whether an idea is worth pursuing and, if needed, investing in.

Continuous innovation management relies not only on the parties' abilities to collaborate and generate ideas but also on their abilities to implement ideas that can deliver value. A problem can arise not from a dearth of ideas but their execution. The framework from Merck outlined in Figure 7.12

Figure 7.12 Collaborative Scoring Model for New Projects

Value and growth project evaluation and monitoring process illustrative

Collaborative project scoring model for new projects

Business impact (revenue): What potential revenue impact will this opportunity have for Merck and the 3PL? (1 = Very low impact, 10 = Very high impact)	8
Resource required: How resource intensive is this opportunity? (1 = Very resource intensive, 10 = Not very resource intensive)	6
Resource available: What ability does Merck and the 3PL have to allocate the resouces necessary to take advantage of this opportunity? (1 = Not readily available, 10 = Readily available)	8
Timeliness: How well does this opportunity support Merck's and the 3PL's overall business strategy? (1 = Not timely, 10 = Very timely)	8
Total project score	30 pts

Next steps for high potential projects

• Assign resources
• Establish project success metrics
• Build business case

Meeting details

Owner: Global logistics with input from global procurement

Time requirement: 1.5 hours per month per supplier

Attendees: Global procurement, regional logistics staff, relationship manager, and 3PL regional account manager

Agenda items:
• Collaboration project launches and updates
• Removing roadblocks and project obstacles
• Performance updates
• Move completed or discontinued projects out of value and growth monitoring portfolio

Project examples:
• Cold chain packaging
• Supply chain risk mitigation
• Greenhouse emissions

"3PL Collaboration scoring model," Arlington, Va.: The Corporate Executive Board, 2010, p. 6.

demonstrates an effective way to identify good continuous innovations by scoring the projects for value. Merck's framework helps the parties prioritize their ideas through a formal scoring process.

Using the collaborative scoring model helps both parties understand the nature of the projects they want to run. Companies should differentiate between long-term collaborative projects and shorter-term quick wins. Both are equally important but require a different level of effort as the ideas go through the continuous innovation management process.

Service providers often tell us that they propose ideas only to have them rejected. They often complain that clients are "junkyard dogs" (see Appendix A, Ailment 4) and are not receptive to change. For this reason, we highly recommend that the parties develop a formalized process and guidelines for managing and picking ideas and innovations to implement. We recommend the governance board of advisors play a key role in vetting and approving ideas and transformation initiatives. We also recommend creating a portfolio of ideas and, as they are implemented, measuring their success.

Consider these approaches as you create your innovation management process.

- Keep ideas in an innovation pipeline. Just because an idea was rejected once does not mean that it cannot be brought forward again.
- Measure how many ideas are generated relative to how many get implemented. The best companies implement a large number of ideas—as much as 90 percent.
- Develop a graph, for example a Pareto chart that shows the most frequently occurring problems or sources of problems in descending order. This will show why ideas do not get implemented.
- Clearly document desired hurdle rates for projects and create a formalized process that teams can use to help them capture and quantify their ideas.
- Develop a decision framework and process for selecting ideas to implement.

Continuous Improvement Program

The third component of transformation management is putting in place a continuous improvement program for managing day-to-day operations. Continuous improvement programs are different from the continuous innovation management process because continuous innovation management tends to focus on larger-scale transformation initiatives that often need investments or resources. Transformation initiatives are often cross-organizational in nature and are tied to the Desired Outcomes. Improvement initiatives come in all shapes and sizes. Six Sigma and Lean programs are two of the most popular approaches.

Regardless of the continuous improvement approach you adopt, it should have the following five attributes.

Joint, Not Separate, Approach
In many cases, one or both of the parties have their own continuous improvement program. This is great for improving efficiencies separately within the four walls of each company. It does not help much when many of the improvements planned or made are cross-company. The parties should decide on a single approach for managing joint continuous improvement efforts across the scope of work.

Transparent, Fact-Based Decisions
Building trust starts with a transparent relationship based on facts and the ability to see critical components of the business in a timely manner. We highly recommend developing a formalized root cause analysis process to determine service failures. The process should highlight—rather than hide—the data and how the process is not yielding the performance against the Desired Outcomes. The parties' ability to engage fully in this process is entirely dependent on a "no blame approach" to fact finding. Individuals at the companies are accountable for sharing the facts that led to the service failure, but are not required to be liable for the service failure.

End-to-End Focus on Accountability
Regardless of who performs the analysis for failures, it is understood that the root cause may reside with either party. Most continuous improvement processes are one-sided and focus on the service provider. We believe that the parties should look at the end-to-end process, measure failures at the highest level, and then drill down into root cause analysis.

Customer Satisfaction Survey
It is important that the parties measure not just their internal performance but also external performance. This may

include end users (such as the case with call center outsourcing) or internal customers (such as the case with
back-office outsourcing). Getting direct feedback from
customers helps keep the parties aligned on how the users
define success.

Formal Benchmarking Reports
When possible, the parties should adopt a formal benchmarking process. The purpose of benchmarking exercises is to monitor progress toward goals, identify successes and problems,
measure scorecard performance, track customer satisfaction,
identify new opportunity areas for improvement, and quantify
business value delivered. A good example of using external
benchmarks is Jaguar and Unipart. They use the J. D. Power
ranking as a key indicator for their success at ensuring they
have outsourcing customer loyalty.

Change Control Procedures
Your Vested agreement should contain change control procedures that the parties use to request, assess, process, and approve
or reject modifications to the agreement. The parties develop
a formal written change request process that either party can
use to initiate a formal change to the agreement. A change
request is required for modifications that affect the price or
related costs of the services, impact the delivery of the service,
or impact the obligations of either party under the agreement.
Typical events that trigger change requests include, but are not
limited to:

- Changes in applicable law that have a material
  impact on the services
- Changes in relevant policies and procedures by
  either company
- Introduction of new or updated technology tools
- Changes in volumes not included in the agreed
  upon pricing

- Changes in workscope not included in the agreed-upon pricing that will require additional staffing or costs
- Changes to service-level targets
- Changes in key personnel
- Requests for additional work for one-time projects that will require additional staffing
- Material increase in any reporting requirements
- Changes in assumptions outlined in the pricing model

Change control procedures should include:

- A formal change form
- A formal process outlining steps and suggested time-frames for approvals
- An approval process, such as signatures needed
- An escalation procedure
- Formal documentation procedures for updating the agreement itself

A change management process is most crucial during the transition phase. In the early phases of the relationship as workscope transitions, key stakeholders in the old and new models may be unreceptive to the change, may not understand why the change is necessary, or may be new to the entire process. In all cases, the team responsible for implementing Vested Outsourcing principles will likely find it has varying degrees of supporters and detractors. You will use a good change management process throughout the life of your relationship to manage any jointly agreed transformation initiatives, not just during the initial transition.

There is a natural tendency for the focus on documenting changes to wane after the initial transition phase is completed. Prevent this by establishing a commercial management role within your governance framework (as discussed earlier under Element 7, Relationship Management). The commercial manager should document trigger events that drive an update of the agreement. Figure 7.13 lists the Ten Elements of a Vested agreement and shows some of the most common reasons for changes. We also recommend that the parties' commercial managers formally review each of the Ten Elements at regular intervals.

Figure 7.13   Frequency of Change

10 elements	Reason for change	Frequency
Business model	• When there is a significnt change in the operating environment	At contract renewal (5+ years)
Shared vision/statement of intent	• When there is a significnt change in the operating environment	At contract renewal (5+ years)
Exit management plan	• May be revised with new SOO	New SOO (5+ years)
Statement of work, workload allocation	• When there is a significnt change in the operating environment	Under continuous governance (yearly)
Relationship management framework	• When there is a change in the governance structure	Under continuous governance (yearly)
Transformation management	• With improvements	Under continuous governance (yearly)
Top level desired outcomes	• Change in the outcomes	Under continuous governance (yearly)
Pricing model	• Improvement plans • Change in incentives • Revised assumptions • Margin matching	Under continuous governance (yearly)
Special concerns and external requirements	• With major contract revisions	Dependent on other changes, likely yearly
Performance reporting quality plan processes	• Change to the business rules • Change in processes • Change to operational measures	As required (weekly, monthly, yearly)

Increasing level of details

Increasing frequency of change

HOMEWORK

Element 8

Transformation Management

Getting Started

Transformation management is about improvement opportunities and governing performance to ensure that the relationship delivers expected outcomes. Your transformation management plan will manage the transition, improvements, and innovations. Vested agreements are designed to drive change. The Vested governance structure must support change as follows:

1. *Develop your transition plan.* Maintain the team from the initial sourcing process, and develop an effective communication campaign for the coming transition. Expand the team to include the service providers who will provide the products and services.

2. *Manage improvement and performance.* Continuous improvement is the result of a series of small changes, or adjustments, so establish a culture of continuous improvement. The process should be simple, clear, and constructive because improvement efforts benefit both parties. Assign roles and responsibilities to team members for managing the process. Define the process for submitting and evaluating ideas, and communicate it to everyone who touches the process: company, customer, user, service provider, and so on. Ideas for improvement should come from everyone but be organized to facilitate evaluation and action on the high-potential ones.

3. *Provide for shared control and management.* This is especially important in the Vested framework. Develop your scorecard by allowing the service provider to

rate the company and the company to rate itself. Insight requires a back-and-forth conversation about the reality of the performance; a one-sided scorecard gives the impression of providing only oversight and micromanagement.

4. *Manage innovation.* Innovation relies on an ability to collaborate with the partner and implement ideas that can deliver value to the parties. The problem is not a dearth of ideas but their execution. Your governance process should include a methodology to review innovations. The governance committee must have the ability to approve ideas and to watch over their implementation and track results.

Tools of the Trade
Use Figure 7.14 as your checklist to establishing your transformation management plan.

Figure 7.14   Key Attributes of a Vested Transformation Management Plan

Parameter	Attributes
Transition:	• Start positive and stay positive • Maintain team continuity, remap responsibilities as required • Expand the team to include the service provider • Establish an effective communication campaign • Build checkpoints or milestones to confirm the transition is on track • Conduct training and education • Perform transition risk assessment at the start of the transition
Improvement:	• Define the process for submitting and evaluating ideas • Communicate it to all stakeholders • Commitment to collaboration • Assign roles and responsibilities • Collect feedback from the stakeholders and review it to evaluate the continuous improvement strategy

Continued

Figure 7.14   Continued

Parameter	Attributes

Innovation:	• Define the process for submitting and evaluating ideas
	• Assess the appropriate level of investment and the Desired Outcomes of each initiative idea, including:
	  • estimated gain or benefit
	  • estimated percentage of benefit
	  • split between parties
	  • scoring process creates a prioritized list of opportunities
	• Steering Committee evaluates and approves the business case for each transformational opportunity
	• Clear method to share the winnings from collaboration
	• Measurement and reporting to track the success of each initiative

Measurement:	• Track metrics critical to meeting Desired Outcomes • Continuous tracking of performance • Scorecards that focus on overall performance delivery • Two way scorecards • Allow the service provider to provide its own scores • Score relationship health • Regular reviews

✓ *Check Your Work*

1. Did you retain part of the integrated solutions team on the project?
2. Did you keep technically skilled managers on staff?
3. Did you implement an effective communication campaign in support of the coming transition?
4. Does your governance process include a methodology to review innovations and approve projects?
5. Is the improvement process simple, clear, and constructive?

6. Will your transformation management plan support change, including performance improvement
opportunities, and ensure that the relationship delivers expected outcomes?

Figure 7.15 Tips of the Trade: Element 8: Transformation Management

Tips of the Trade – ELEMENT 8: Transformation Management	
Tip 1	Plan it, leverage it and celebrate it.
Tip 2	Transformation Management includes managing the transition, improvements and innovations.
Tip 3	Vested Governance Frameworks provide for shared control and management based on insight. Insight requires a back-and-forth conversation about the reality of the performance implementation and a two-sided scorecard to track performance.
Tip 4	Vested Agreements transform processes; your Vested governance structure must support transformation.

Element 9: Exit Management Plan

What happens at the end of the agreement? On one hand, if the
agreement is properly structured and is achieving the Desired
Outcomes while continually improving performance, the
agreement likely will be renewed. Most companies would like
to envision a long-term productive relationship that spans
decades—such as the Coca-Cola and McDonald's relationship that is in its fifty-fifth year.[23] Since we have been studying
Vested Outsourcing relationships, we have not seen any parties
separate after they made the paradigm shift to become Vested
with each other.

Unfortunately, relationships can fail, no matter how prom-
ising the start, how well written the statement of intentions is,
or how well structured the governance framework is. Business
and market conditions can change suddenly; people move on;
projections fail to transpire; and companies get acquired. An

important facet of the governance framework therefore is a credible exit management plan.

One of the potential dangers of outsourcing is that the company can become so entwined with and dependent on the service provider that the potential benefits of changing to a new provider cannot match the pain of extraction. This occurs most often when a company's management of the service provider becomes a service provider abdication. By maintaining proper insight and a balanced relationship between company and service provider, two very good things happen:

1. The likelihood of the partnership degrading is minimized.
2. The ability to dissolve the partnership as required by new circumstances remains in play.

It is in the best interests of the company and the service provider to work toward an ongoing balanced partnership.

Outsourcing agreements often address what happens at the end of the agreement purely from a liability point of view, through termination clauses either for convenience or for cause. These clauses may address the notice period or financial obligations under the agreement but do little to set forth how to unwind the business relationship. In fact, these clauses may provide incentives for the service provider just to dump and run, stripping resources from the program long before the transition is complete. In such cases, services may be seriously disrupted and customers impacted.

An exit management plan will facilitate a smooth, effective transition of services delivery, minimum disruption of ongoing delivery, and efficient completion of all agreement obligations. The plan is invoked with the issuance of a formal termination notice under the agreement, which specifies:

•   The portion of services included in the scope of termination

- The estimated exit transition period and vendor delivery centers affected
- The period of time following a termination notice that the parties will have to agree on the specific scope of transition services provided by the vendor

One company we studied provides an excellent example of planning ahead. The company was creating a 12-year agreement and included a nine-page exit management plan "just in case." The plan was very specific about the roles, duties, and expectations of both the company and the service provider should the parties decide to terminate. It is far easier to work through an exit management plan at the beginning of a relationship than when the parties are in heated debate and separation is imminent. Your plan may not need to be as detailed as in the example, but it should detail how essential elements are managed when the agreement ends (in part or in full). The components of an effective exit management plan include:

1. Termination notice
2. Exit transition period
3. Exit transition plan
4. Exit governance and reporting

Termination Notice
The exit management plan enters force when a formal termination notice is delivered by either party or when services are transitioned once the agreement or workscope expires. The termination notice must be specific about the services included (including processes and geographies) and also should include an estimated exit transition period, service provider delivery centers affected by the transition, location of replacement delivery centers, and vendor transition assistance charges. Each party should establish exit management teams within one week of the termination notice issuance, and the

detailed exit plan should be developed and submitted in less than a month.

Exit Transition Period

Just as there is a transition period when an outsourcing agreement is first implemented, there is a transition period in the event of agreement termination. The transition period generally encompasses the time from the date of the termination notice until the date upon which any transition services are completed.

Exit Transition Plan

The object of developing an exit transition plan is a smooth, effective, and uninterrupted transition of service delivery with a minimum of disruption and efficient completion of an agreement obligation. This can happen only if there is a plan to make it happen and if the transition is managed. The exit process is managed through an exit management governance process that is set up specifically within the overall governance structure of the agreement. The transition is run by an exit manager who supervises the exit management team, which is made up of representatives from the company and the service provider. The team oversees the entire transition process. If the work being transitioned is spread over a large geographic area, team members from each location may need to be included. The exit transition team will be responsible for:

- Program management
- Due diligence
- Services transition and continuity (including knowledge transfer, documentation, and enabling systems transfer)
- Facilities transfer
- Human resources transfer

- Fully answering all reasonable questions about the services or transfer
- Coordination with the respective company and service provider organization members to sustain continued service delivery as per statement of objectives requirements in the agreement

Although the plans will vary by the workscope and complexity of the agreement, all exit transition plans will include:

- Timelines for the various activities required to exit the business
- List of the personnel responsible for planning, managing, and implementing the services transfer
- List of the information required for continued performance of services in an orderly manner that minimizes disruption in the operations during the transition period
- Preparations for a transfer of knowledge regarding the transferred services
- Support for the transfer of resources used in the delivery of services
- Communication plans for external customers and all impacted stakeholders
- Identification of all security and disaster recovery tasks
- Inventories of all licenses, permits, and other agreements that require notification, assignment, or transfer of rights
- Personnel and resource transition/transfer procedures
- Lists of confidential information, equipment, materials, and intellectual property so that it can be returned or destroyed

Governance and Reporting

The exit management process and resolution of any issues arising from exit transition should be managed within the overall governance structure developed as part of the agreement.

Despite the parties' best intentions and efforts, some relationships may end because of an alleged breach of contract. Exit management discussions ought to include a process for handling legal disputes. In effect, you are choosing now what forum the parties will enter to resolve a lawsuit.

There are several options, and they are not necessarily mutually exclusive.

The parties may choose mediation. Mediation is often the most cost-effective method for resolving disputes because mediation does not mandate discovery or hearings. Depending on the issues raised, the parties may choose arbitration, which can be binding or nonbinding, depending on the parties' choice. Arbitration differs from mediation, because arbitrators make rulings based on evidence presented to them in the form of documents and testimony. This option is a wise choice when the parties may encounter issues requiring legally technical expertise. The parties may also choose to initiate a lawsuit. The question then becomes in what court and in what country will the parties sue each other?

Although it is not easy to discuss the catastrophic failure of the relationship resulting in legal action, it is wise. Outline these legal procedures while the parties are on good terms, not when the relationship has disintegrated. The exit transition plan should specify the reporting requirements. Reports to the governance committee must be issued frequently. If the exit transition period is short (under 60 days), daily or weekly reporting is advisable. Reports to the governance committee will:

- Provide status on progress against the exit transition plan
- Identify key issues impacting the delivery against the plan

- Identify potential risks to the plan
- Detail key actions that need to be taken by the various stakeholders to facilitate a smooth transition

The detailed exit management plan will provide a sort of reverse snapshot of the entire governance framework, making it vital to get the structure right at both ends of the relationship.

HOMEWORK

Element 9

Exit Management Plan

Getting Started

A Vested agreement is flexible, and part of that flexibility comes from preparing for the relationship to end. Your exit management plan will facilitate a smooth, effective transition of services, should the need arise. The primary goal of the plan is the minimum disruption of ongoing delivery and the fair and efficient completion of all the agreement's obligations.

Using the exit management plan checklist in the Tools of the Trade section, develop the exit management framework for your agreement.

> *Tools of the Trade*
> *Exit Management Plan Checklist*
>
>   • Include a governance statement in your exit management plan.
>   • Document what constitutes notice of termination. The notice should include:
>   • A specific statement of the services included in the scope of the termination.
>   • The estimated exit transition period (based on the predefined exit plan).
>   • The period of time following notice that a specific transition plan will be provided by the service provider and agreed to by the company.
>   • Document the structure of the exit transition team: the personnel responsible for planning,

managing, and implementing the services transfer.

- Document the timelines for the activities related to exiting the agreement, including notice periods, transition periods, and final payment periods.
- Document the reporting requirements, including the report frequency and essential information that will be reported.
- Document communication plans for external customers and stakeholders.
- Identify all security and disaster recovery tasks.
- Create a financial plan to finalize invoices, open credit/debit memos, and document how specific sections of the pricing agreement are managed (such as undispersed incentives, capital reimbursements, etc.).
- Document who will develop inventories of all licenses, permits, and other agreements that require assignment or transfer of rights, when the list is due, and what information is to be included on the list.
- Develop personnel and resource transition/transfer procedures.
- Plan for the return or destruction of confidential information, equipment, materials, and intellectual property.

✓ *Check Your Work*

1. Is your exit management plan fair and well documented?
2. Does the plan address all essential criteria?
3. Is the plan clear and executable?

Figure 7.16   Tips of the Trade: Element 9: Exit Management Plan

Tips of the Trade – ELEMENT 9: Exit Management Plan	
Tip 1	Including an exit management plan in your Vested Agreement is good business, it is vital to get the governance structure right at both ends of the relationship
Tip 2	Agreement includes adequate exit criteria, and equitable on- and off- ramps for both parties

Element 10: Special Concerns and External Requirements

By now you have completed the lion's share of your agreement. You have created a Shared Vision and Statement of Intent. You have established the statement of objectives, allocated workscope, and developed a Vested pricing model and metrics that will help drive end-to-end performance improvement and expand the proverbial pie for the parties. You have set up your transition plan and established your governance structure.

What is left? That is precisely the point. No agreement is perfect, and you will forget things. That is the purpose of Element 10: it serves as a placeholder for all those little (and big) things you did not think about or that will come up. In fact, this element is for those things that warrant special attention but not necessarily a full section of the agreement.

Element 10's basic message is to pay attention to all the things that are unique to your Vested deal to help make it work more smoothly over its term. Spend the time now to document and bundle these elements into one group, and address the special considerations and external regulations that are unique to your agreement. Where special aspects require more detailed governance, such as technical specifications, operating manuals, and procedures, pull them out into their own individual element.

Your particular Vested agreement may consist of more than Ten Elements, depending on the special considerations that arise. The concept is akin to fine-tuning an engine and putting in just the right amount of gas for the journey.

Next we present a list of some of the more common things we see included in Element 10.

- *Security.* How will the parties manage specific security concerns (e.g., in remote or developing locations for a contract manufacturing agreement or services delivered at international border control points)?
- *Hazardous materials.* How will the parties manage chemical and hazardous materials with special handling, packaging, security, and transportation challenges and when specific local government regulations could become an integral part of the governance framework?
- *Intellectual property.* This is particularly important in a transformational relationship. It concerns how the parties will handle background, emerging, and current intellectual property, ownership, and rights of use.
- *Special tax issues.* International and cross-continental deals may have special tax provisions and laws that require expert guidance.
- *Import and export and transportation.* How do the parties deal with transfer of goods and services across national and international boundaries? Who takes care of insurance for goods in transit? What standard transport is used—road, rail, ship, or air—and who pays for the freight and the charges?
- *Information management.* Be aware of any special data management considerations, security of data, location of servers, and other matters pertinent to information security.
- *Law and jurisdiction.* How will the parties make an informed decision about the legal framework that underpins the agreement? Agreements across international boundaries with parties in different

countries require careful consideration as law and jurisdiction may vary.

- *Care of documents.* Do you have all the relevant safety records and validated insurance certificates, training records, and other such documents that validate the capability of the parties to deliver the work safely? *Always* keep these with the agreement and propose an annual review so that in the future anyone picking up the agreement file has everything. It is a special consideration to colleagues who may come after you. Keeping a clean and tidy file is such a little thing it hardly bears mentioning—but it is worth its weight in gold to many a contract manager waiting for the auditor to visit!

- *Local labor law.* Accommodate special ratios and laws pertaining to the hiring of local people at the asset or work level. Is a diversity balance required in the governance structure? Are there rules about hiring via local agencies and are there any regulations around transferring of undertakings and personnel from an existing partner to a new partner, and are the terms and conditions of employment different? Determine if these considerations need to be included in the pricing model.

- *Ethics and compliance issues.* Do the parties support Fair Trade or other similar causes related to sustainable operations, clean working conditions, and environmental safety and compliance? How do the parties ensure joint social and corporate responsibility? How do the parties deal with ethics in trading practices and are there joint rules and processes?

- *Publicity and marketing.* Even though the parties are separate entities, the public and the media will likely be interested in the new relationship between the parties. Coordinate public relations activities and promotional marketing messages around the Vested agreement.

- *External regulatory issues.* Do special local laws and regulations exist in the work location? Decide if international or local convention applies, for example, in health and safety matters.
- *Special safety issues.* Most important of all, how will the parties ensure continuous safe and reliable service, comply with specific regulations and any special local practices pertaining to the particular location or operative environment? How will the parties coordinate and manage any rectification action in the event of a safety incident or event requiring major action to resolve? Do the parties have a mutually agreed business continuity plan pertaining to the loss of function or service such as major loss of power, mission-critical capability, or loss of confidential data? How will the parties work together to resume normal working conditions?

These special concerns and external requriements should be clearly vetted and understood by the company and service provider at the outset. The parties should include special conditions at the master services agreement and Vested agreement levels. We could go on and on about the myriad special requirements we have seen. The point is that you need to think of them and determine the best way to document them in the agreement.

We would like to bring up one last recommendation when it comes to all of the special requirements you might feel compelled to add to your agreement: The simpler the better. One technique that works effectively concerns dealing with regulatory compliance issues. There is a trend for agreements to point to the regulation rather than try to list each and every regulation and try to keep the agreement updated with every change.

Consider OSHA (Occupational Safety and Health Act) regulations as an example. One way to ensure that OSHA requirements are followed is to include in the service agreement a simple statement saying: "The service provider will abide by all OSHA regulations. The service provider is responsible for monitoring changes and updates in OSHA regulations." This is a much more effective way to manage the issue than baking the details into the agreement itself and trying to keep track of any changes.

One common response we get to this approach is: "How can I trust the service provider will keep up with the regulations? I have to keep the service provider updated." Our response is to have the service provider write *how* it will do this in its performance work statement. Remember: The company that is outsourcing should define the *what* and the service provider should determine the *how*.

HOMEWORK

Element 10

Special Concerns and External Requirements

Getting Started

Governance frameworks are not one-size-fits-all. It is probable that you will need to document special conditions or requirements in your agreement. Review these attachments through the Vested filter. If the attachment conflicts with Vested principles or hinders the parties in attaining the Desired Outcomes, decide if these requirements or conditions truly must be part of the agreement. Change the requirements or conditions to bring them in line with and to support Vested philosophies.

Tools of the Trade
Special Concerns and Requirements Checklist

- Identify specific requirements or conditions for inclusion in the agreement that are not already part of other elements.
- Review company requirements that support the workscope of the agreement, including:
  - IT data specifications, interface requirements, data format, coding rules, and so on
  - Licenses, permits, lease agreements, and so on
  - Safety standards or requirements
  - Customer contract requirements
  - Facility-related requirements
  - Intellectual property
- Review the impact of the requirement to the pricing model.

> • Review the impact of the requirement to the Desired Outcomes and the SOW.
>
> Each agreement will be unique in the additional requirements that must be incorporated.

✓ *Check Your Work*

1. Have you reviewed the need for any additional requirements or conditions?
2. Have you assessed if these requirements impact Vested principals or if they will impact the ability to achieve the Desired Outcomes? Will the requirement or condition impact the service provider's control over the SOWs?
3. Do the requirements impact the pricing model or the workscope in the agreement?

Figure 7.17   Tips of the Trade: Element 10: Special Concerns and External Requirements

Tips of the Trade – ELEMENT 10 – Special Concerns	
Tip 1	Special requirements included in your Vested Agreement should not conflict with or counteract Vested principals or restrict the ability of the parties to achieve Desired Outcomes.

PART III

GETTING TO WE

CHAPTER 8

WRAPPING UP YOUR VESTED AGREEMENT

We have already explained that organizations moving to a Vested Outsourcing business model must expand how they think about an agreement—they must have a flexible framework that captures the essence of the relationship between the parties.

Businesspeople, contract professionals, and lawyers typically define the word *contract* too narrowly. For this reason we have intentionally avoided using the word in this manual. Instead, we have focused on the word *agreement* to denote how the company and the service provider work together in a dynamic business environment.

This chapter helps you take the collaborative business agreement you have jointly developed and formalize it into a legally binding contract. This chapter does not take the place of sound legal advice or replace good draftsmanship or common sense. It is meant to help non-lawyers who may not have specialized training in drafting the business requirements needed for a contract. Therefore, we recommend that the company and the service provider consult with their respective legal teams. It is our experience that legal teams welcome well-written agreements outlining all the business aspects of the deal.

WHY YOU NEED A WRITTEN CONTRACT

There are three schools of thoughts on contracts. One says that if you have a good business agreement, you do not need a written contract. The relationship between McDonald's and Coca-Cola is often cited as a classic example of two companies working effectively without a written contract. These companies succeed on the strength of their relationship, the soundness of their business decisions, and their commitment to doing good work together.

In Vested Outsourcing, you incorporate these same three elements into your formal agreements. In fact, one business executive commented, "Vested Outsourcing gets us back to good old-fashioned business sense—the handshake deal where companies worked together in a fair manner."[1]

The second school of thought is to write in stone every trivial aspect of the business agreement. This is definitely the dominant school of thought, with contract size seeming to grow in thickness each year. The bigger the deal, the bigger the desire to go overboard in documentation. We have seen some large information technology and business process outsourcing deals where one or more of the parties spent in excess of $500,000 in legal fees to document and negotiate a contract. Outsourcing advisory firms are notorious for crafting overly complex agreements. One executive told us, "I think my advisory firm gets paid by the page. We ended up with an 800-page contract and the most complex set of metrics I have ever seen. It was no surprise that as we got close to signing the deal the advisory firm recommended they stay on board to help us manage the contract and sell us their software to manage the scorecard." In our view, contracts are not instruments used to bludgeon one another, nor are they ornamental objects that sit on a dusty bookshelf.

Excessively long contracts do not necessarily lead to bad relationships, however. Thomas Atkin, a professor of supply chain management at Sonoma State University, and Lloyd

Rinehart, an associate professor of marketing and logistics at the University of Tennessee, set out to prove that there is a direct and negative correlation between contract formality and relationship satisfaction.[2]

What they discovered proved to be counterintuitive: There was a small, positive correlation between contract formality and relationship satisfaction. Rather than contract formality causing discord, their research suggested that the actual relationship itself may cause dissatisfaction.

The third school of thought is based on Ian Macneil's and Oliver E. Williamson's philosophy, as outlined in chapter 2. A contract should be a flexible framework designed to create "instruments for social cooperation." We strongly advocate for this third approach. This chapter shows you how to take the Ten Elements of your Vested agreement to create a flexible contract framework.

It is important to understand that while we advocate a flexible framework, we also recommend that you distill the agreement into a physical document—a contract. Simply put, a contract is a memorial of the agreement, whether written or verbal. It is true that written contracts are easier to enforce legally, but we advocate writing all of your agreements down and combining them into one contract for business reasons. We want business teams to be able to refer to and modify aspects of the Vested deal over time.

Your contract should act as a roadmap for the business aspects of your agreement and the resulting relationship. Drivers consult a roadmap before starting on their journey (sometimes even if they think they know where they are going) and whenever they reach unexpected roadblocks or traffic jams. On your journey, your Vested contract serves as the roadmap. The written agreement is the one document that all team members consult for the duration of the Vested partnership.

To illustrate, consider this hypothetical example. Two years after finalizing the Vested agreement, the parties recognize an upcoming change in the market that could negatively impact them if they do not act quickly. This market disruption is an unexpected detour. Ideally, the companies have agreed upon a process for addressing such situations and have documented that process in the governance structure. Therefore, *before* the parties meet to discuss the situation formally, each company consults the written contract. The parties also review any number of additional documents, including the Desired Outcomes, the margin matching trigger points, and the contract modification framework. By reviewing the Vested agreement first, however, the company and the service provider know what assumptions drove the initial conversations that led to it, the vision for why they were partnering, and the process for modifying the legal agreement to match changes in circumstances.

Rather than terminating the contract for convenience to solve market disruption issues, we hope that the parties have created a contract that is a flexible, living, breathing document that accommodates market disruptions.

STRUCTURING YOUR CONTRACT

There are two primary and necessary components to include in any outsourcing agreement: a master services agreement (MSA) and the associated attachments that reflect and document Vested Outsourcing's Five Rules and Ten Elements. You should have already documented the business aspects of your deal by completing your homework on each of the Ten Elements of a Vested agreement. The subdocuments you attach to the MSA generally are referred to as schedules, attachments, or exhibits. It really does not matter what you call them. We use the word *schedules* in this chapter to mean the written documents addressing the Ten Elements.

MSAs can be short, as few as 3 or 4 pages, or as long as 150 pages. Long MSAs generally pull the content from each of the Ten Elements into the overall document—more or less creating one very long document. We prefer MSAs to be shorter documents that include just the legal boilerplate rather than incorporating all the moving parts into one document without attachments. Each schedule should represent one of the Ten Elements. Each schedule discusses a specific section of the agreement—for example, the pricing model or the exit management plan.

Thus the MSA is a key component to a Vested Outsourcing agreement. It sets the stage and ties everything, including the schedules and attachments, together. Think of the MSA as a three-ring binder. It literally holds all the individual elements of the agreement together. This concept is graphically depicted in Figure 8.1. The MSA also legally holds all the other documents together.

Some have asked why they cannot just use a group of schedules. Simply put, each schedule could technically become its own "contract" covering that one segment of the deal, thereby excluding the other elements of the deal to the companies' detriment. Without some sort of overarching document—in this case, the MSA—to integrate the schedules, common contractual elements must be inserted into every attachment in order for those provisions to apply to each schedule. That level of redundancy is unnecessary and fraught with dangers. A good agreement consists of a single document that is comprehensive and integrated yet flexible and plain enough so that those executing the deal will understand it easily.

In Figure 8.1, the first hierarchal level represents the Five Rules. The Ten Elements then flow from those Five Rules. To keep the documents logical and orderly, consider organizing the schedules or exhibits in this manner. Some elements, such as the workscope, might have numerous subexhibits (perhaps the various taxonomy and workload allocation for various service offerings under the agreement). By attaching the Ten Elements as schedules to the MSA, it is much easier to modify the agreement one part at a time as needed.

Vested contracts are designed to allow companies to embrace the dynamic nature of business using a flexible

Figure 8.1 MSA Integrates All Supporting Documents

Vested Outsourcing Agreement Structure

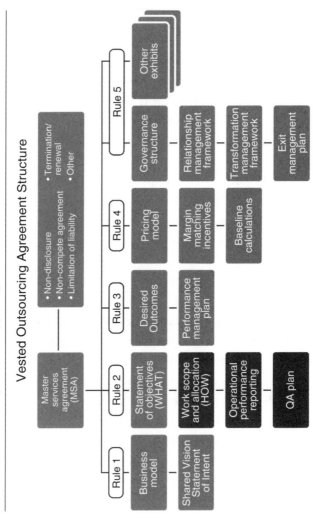

■ Service provider owned

A Vested Outsourcing agreement is structured as follows: A master agreement is combined with subordinated schedules or exhibits that individually outline each of the 5 Rules and 10 elements of Vested Outsourcing.

contract framework that ensures both parties strive to achieve the Shared Vision and operate under the Statement of Intent. As such, Vested agreements should be reviewed, renegotiated, and modified over time as markets change and technology advances.

Your company may wish to document the deal structure differently from what we have outlined. We encourage you to design an agreement that works for you. Our primary point is that you include all Ten Elements that follow Vested Outsourcing's Five Rules as integral parts of the overall outsourcing agreement.

WHAT TO INCLUDE IN YOUR MSA

A good MSA accomplishes three important things:

1. It establishes definitions or specific language that applies uniformly to all of the schedules. For example, a single definition of the term *governance framework* (see glossary) should be applied and understood universally through all Vested agreement documents.

2. It establishes clauses that apply to each schedule. For example, the overall term or duration of the agreement should be included in the MSA because it applies to the entire agreement and all of the schedules.

3. It establishes mutual adherence to all the covenants in one area for signatures rather than having management sign multiple documents.

Next we present possible items to include in a MSA. Each MSA will be different based on the specific type of business being outsourced. The purpose of this list is simply to get you thinking about your MSA.

Definition of Terms

This section lists commonly used terms, or terms with a unique meaning to your specific business, and provides definitions for those terms. This section provides one definition for each term, preventing multiple and conflicting definitions.

Typically, each term is listed in alphabetical order, followed by its definition. Be sure to include any acronyms used in place of the full title of something (i.e., using MSA instead of master service agreement).

Do not underestimate the importance of this section. When working with multiple schedules that may have been negotiated by people different from those tasked with implementing the deal, use of clearly defined terms in all the schedules can eliminate much of the confusion that permeates deal interpretation. (The glossary is a useful resource you can use to create your defined terms.)

General Contract Terms

Many contractual terms are mundane yet critically important. One such term is the *start date* for the agreement. There can be a cascade of consequences associated with something as innocuous as a start date. For example, tax, regulatory, or other legal implications usually are associated with the start of an agreement. The MSA is a great place to outline the start or effective date of the agreement. It is the legal starting point.

Consider placing other important terms and conditions in this section as well. Terms such as *statutory warranties* (those paragraphs that tend to be written in all capital letters), *indemnification provisions,* or *limitations of liabilities* could go in this part of the document. Because each party wants these terms to apply to all provisions of the agreement, including every schedule, we suggest that they be placed in the MSA for both clarity and uniformity. Since many of these terms must be written using very specific language to meet statutory or common law requirements, leave this decision to your company's lawyers. Therefore, your lawyers ultimately will decide on how these terms will be worded and where to place them within the contract. Figure 8.2 presents 12 legal terms that non-lawyers should understand.

Figure 8.2   Legal Terms

Legal Term	Definition
Representation	A statement of fact. For example, a representation might look like this: Company represents that it knows of no legal or regulatory proceeding pending against it as of the execution date of this agreement.
Warranty	A statement concerning quality, quantity or title to something within a company's ownership. For example, service provider warrants that it has full right, title and interest in the software being licensed to company.
Implied Warranties	An implied warranty is a statutory warranty governing the sale of goods only. There are several implied warranties in US law. The implied warranty of merchantability is one example.
Covenant	An affirmative commitment or obligation to perform. Company acknowledges its obligations concerning all tax related consequences resulting from the transfer of buildings to service provider.
Disclaimer	A voluntary repudiation of a legal claim to something, or a denial of any connection with or knowledge of something. For example, there are many disclaimers in an outsourcing agreement, including the parties' right to disclaim warranties and representations.
Indemnification	A commitment by one party to pay for another party's losses arising from wrongful activity associated with the agreement. For example, company may ask service provider to indemnify company against all third party claims that service provider is infringing on third party's intellectual property rights.

Continued

Figure 8.2   Continued

Legal Term	Definition
Mutual Indemnifications	A mutual agreement to protect each other against third party claims and resulting monetary losses.
Limitations of Liabilities	A cap on the amount of money one party will pay to the other party in specific circumstances. For example, a company may want the service provider to pay an unlimited amount of damages if the company's business is halted due to the service provider's actions or inactions. The service provider may want a damages cap equal to some fixed amount should the company's business come to a halt.
Default Termination Rights	The right of one party to terminate if, after notice and a time to cure, the other party does not cure a breach of the contract. For example, the service provider may insert a default termination clause if the customer files for bankruptcy, or becomes subject to receivership.
Force Majeure	An act of God, or other such calamity, that prevents either party from performing. Earthquakes, national workforce strikes, wars are all examples of circumstances triggering a Force Majeure clause.
Alternative Dispute Resolution (ADR)	All forms of dispute resolution outside of the formal court system. ADR can take the form of mediation or arbitration, and may be as informal or formal as the parties wish.

Incorporation of Schedules, Exhibits, and Other Related Documents

The schedules and exhibits section of the MSA literally and legally incorporates all the other documents attached to or related to this agreement in specific and detailed language. List each and every schedule by its proper name (not the shorthand version that you used while actually negotiating its terms), and give each schedule a number or a letter for easy referencing.

Do the same for all other ancillary documents that might apply to the deal, such as related agreements the company may have with the service provider separate from this particular deal.

Contract Termination and Renewal

There are two schools of thought on the contract termination and renewal section. Some place all the termination language into a separate schedule; others incorporate all of this language in the MSA. It is wise to place the end date for the entire agreement and any process for renewal of the agreement in the MSA. Place any specific termination dates or renewal processes for a specific objective in the schedule covering that objective. For example, the Vested Outsourcing agreement might cover four phases, each with its own end date. The MSA would state that the entire agreement, irrespective of the language in the schedules, terminates five years from now. Phase 1 could terminate six months from now, when the company transitions operation "A" to the service provider. Therefore, the schedule outlining phase 1 would have a different termination date specific for that phase, but that date would not impact the other phases of the project or the contract as a whole.

This clause also may include language concerning the process by which the agreement is terminated or renewed. Topics such as how much notice each party must give the other and whether the request to terminate must be in writing also are stated. Although we do not encourage creating a Vested deal that is easy to terminate, circumstances outside of everyone's control could lead to the early termination of the agreement.

Signatures

Every agreement must end with a section designated for signatures all of involved parties. This section is absolutely critical. Without signatures on the written document, the parties have nothing more than a verbal agreement. Courts in different jurisdictions interpret verbal agreements differently than written agreements, simply due to their oral nature. With verbal agreements, you risk falling into the proverbial common law rabbit hole.

Ideally, the MSA is signed in counterparts, which means that each company has its authorized signatory sign the agreement and fax or scan the signature page to the other company. As long as each company has its original signature page and the facsimile signature page from the other party, the agreement is binding. This section would prevent having to bring all the signatories into one room for a ten-minute signing process. It saves time and money while still providing a valid agreement.

Finally, each signature block will be accompanied by that day's date or the effective date of the agreement. In some circumstances, a company may sign the agreement weeks before its official start date (and, realistically, several weeks after the real work has begun). Nevertheless, the effective date is important to the overall interpretation of the contract in many regulatory circumstances and cannot be overlooked.

WORKING WITH LEGAL TEAMS

Now let us shift focus from the nuts and bolts of the contract to working with your company's legal department. Two common problems are unique to working with legal departments. The first problem stems from how lawyers approach discussions about risk. The other problem stems from using contracts from other deals as templates for your Vested deal.

Allocate Risk: Do Not Shift Risk

As mentioned in chapter 2, the April 2010 study by the International Association for Contract and Commercial Management (IACCM) concluded that the classic legal approach of contract law focuses almost exclusively on limiting liability, indemnification, risk mitigation, and liquidated damages.[3] The IACCM findings show that most companies are indeed focusing on shifting risk in their contracts. Figure 8.3 shows the results of the IACCM study of the most frequently negotiated terms (also see Appendix B). Right at the top are terms dealing with limitations of liability, indemnification, and damages—all key terms designed to allocate risks.

By design, contracts seek to legally allocate risk from one company to another.

Unfortunately, companies and their lawyers use contracts to provide (sometimes illusory) protective rights. Old-school contracts try to establish limitations on each party's liability to each other and to third parties, but contracts do not actually prevent negligence or other forms of performance breakdowns. It is a common misperception among non-lawyers that contracts prevent bad things from happening.

Many businesspeople—and especially lawyers—fear non-compliance. Each company's representatives bring this fear to the negotiating table and haggle over terms that try to force cooperation. An example could include charge-backs. Out of

Figure 8.3   2010 Top 10 Negotiated Terms

Terms where internal and external concern increased during 2010
Price / Charge / Price Changes
Payment
Limitation of Liability
Invoices / Late Payment
Indemnification
Service Withdrawal or Termination (cause / convenience)
Service Levels and Warranties
Business Continuity / Disaster Recovery
Confidential Information / Data Protection
Liquidated Damages

Source: IACCM Top Terms Report

fear that a supplier will not try to achieve a performance objective, a company might insert onerous charge-back rights. The theory goes like this: if you make the penalties harsh enough, the service provider will have no choice but to cooperate. As we note several times throughout this manual, "business happens." Performance breakdowns are not necessarily the result of a lack of cooperation.

We believe that one element can prove detrimental to relationship satisfaction: a disproportionate focus on haggling over legal risk and legal liabilities. Lawyers live in the what-if and focus on who is left holding the bag. Lawyers' propensity for finding risk is helpful, to a point.

Most lawyers talk about legal risks and liabilities as if all are accorded the same probability of happening or causing harm. In other words, a malfunctioning switchboard in a call center is much more likely to occur than an aggrieved call center representative maliciously damaging the outsourcing company's internal customer service infrastructure. Yet when lawyers sit down to negotiate which company is liable for what kind of damages, they may place an undue amount of attention on the extreme but far less likely risk event (malicious damage to company infrastructure) than to the more likely but far less damaging risk event (switchboard malfunctions). One likely reason for this focus is that the damage done as a result of the aggrieved call center representative is far ranging and permanent while the malfunctioning switchboard is limited in scope and duration. We know one thing for sure: You cannot avoid the conversation around risk, so it is wise to address it early.

Well-known outsourcing lawyer George Kimball notes five types of risk.[4] These risk types ought to be thoroughly covered during your discussions relating to the Ten Elements.

1. *Operational risks.* These risks relate to workscope and workload allocation. Poor service from the supplier or poor forecasting from the company creates operational risks.

2. *Financial risks.* These risks relate to overconsumption of services (poor assumptions) or inaccurate baselines impacting pricing and margins.

3. *Scope.* These risks result from the actual implementation of the workscope, such as unmanageable workload allocation and unforeseeable project overruns ("business happens").

4. *Compliance and security.* These risks impact highly regulated industries and pose significant legal liability issues for both the company and the service provider. You must address these risks in your discussions throughout your Vested journey. Your company's lawyers will be especially keen to properly document these issues.

5. *Extraordinary risks.* These risks are your worst-case scenarios. Although they have little likelihood of occurring, when they do happen, they can result in financial ruin.

The conventional approach for managing these risks is to provide language that affords protections in the form of detailed representations, overarching warranties, indemnities, termination for convenience rights, and rights to specific monetary damages. We do not entirely agree with this method.

We believe that you should address these five risk types in the Ten Elements at a *business level*. For example, operations people from both companies should meet to discuss the variety and likelihood of problems stemming from performance breakdowns. Likewise, teams from both companies would meet to discuss each and every other type of risk noted. The businesspeople are better suited to understand the level of certainty for a particular risk and discuss the actual monetary impact. Do not leave these important conversations strictly for the lawyers to hash out.

To illustrate our point, let us look at price. Suppose that both parties worked on the pricing model and all of the incentives but left the discussion of various risk factors to the lawyers. The lawyers meet. The company's lawyers advocate for an increased allocation of risk to the service provider. In turn, the lawyers for the service provider agree, *so long as the service provider gets paid more to offset the risk*. Both parties are no longer on a Vested journey. Rather, they are on a traditional transactional journey, a journey in which everything has a price that can be bartered without realizing the impact to the Vested nature of the deal.

We suggest a different approach to addressing risk. First we suggest having processes in place that mitigate risk. As you completed your homework, you would have created these processes. Next we suggest that each party sends a legal representative to meetings at which the business teams address risk throughout the Vested journey. The lawyer learns from the businesspeople the true nature of the threat and the likelihood that monetary damages will actually right the wrong. Equally important, the business team learns about the common-law response to addressing various risks. The risk conversation becomes a two-way street with the businesspeople and the legal teams simultaneously crafting the business and legal terms.

Finally, we suggest allocating risk to the party that is most likely able to mitigate it. Clearly, risk conversations cannot be left to the eleventh hour for the legal teams to hash out. The parties are jointly invested at the business level for understanding and allocating risk.

Think Twice Before Using Templates

Another serious problem threatening your Vested deal comes from cutting and pasting language from other contracts or using an old contract as a template.

Shortcuts can cost you. In this age of electronic advancement, it seems only natural that you, or a member of your company's legal team, would cut and paste language from an existing contract into your Vested contract or find a template using an Internet search engine. Taking this approach is like shooting yourself in the foot at the 25-mile marker of a 26-mile marathon.

What follows is a true story of how two organizations used the wrong template and seriously derailed their deal. A government agency and a nonprofit were tasked with negotiating a complex alliance. The arrangement was designed as far more interdependent than a customer-vendor relationship, but not a legal partnership. The parties would meet to discuss various points to this deal, which had many features that made it multifaceted. The government's representative would then email a document to the executive director at the nonprofit. The document was a concessionaire's agreement, as in granting permission for selling hot dogs at a beach.

Needless to say, the nonprofit was frustrated and would shoot back an email outlining all the hundreds of ways that the document was insufficient, lacked appropriate specificity as negotiated, and was wholly inappropriate. The government's agent would tell the nonprofit that she would see what she could do. *Twelve years later*, the parties were completely stuck. That is when they called the authors.

There were several significant issues, all of which correlated with one or more of the Ten Ailments (see Appendix A). But more important, the government simply refused to create the agreement from scratch and insisted on using a template. No amount of fiddling, massaging, or coaxing could change a concessionaire's agreement into a multifaceted alliance. There was only one person in the organization who had the authority and vision to change the attorney's mind-set about drafting the agreement from scratch—the head of the government agency. It took one meeting between the nonprofit and the head of the government agency to force the government's attorneys to draft an appropriate contract. Further meetings developed a vision statement and various workload allocations. In only nine months, the contract was signed.

This example, while humorous, differs from the business world in only one way. Businesses would have given up on each other long before the 12-year mark; they would never have reached an agreement. Vested deals, if done properly, are very different from all other deals you might have sample language for.

As we noted at length in chapter 1, a Vested deal is more complex and interdependent than transactional deals and yet it is less legally intertwined than equity partnerships and joint ventures. Figure 8.4 illustrates this point.

Vested Outsourcing differs fundamentally from simple outcome-based business models and transaction-based agreements because it uses a hybrid model. Traditional transaction-based contracts are lacking in appropriate language, particularly regarding workload allocation, pricing, and governance. Equity partnerships and joint ventures are legally structured partnerships, which makes their types and responsibilities for risk different from those in Vested deals. The closest type of contract to a Vested arrangement is a simple outcome-based contract. Although Vested Outsourcing is an outcome-based contract, it is a hybrid based on the shared value principle that value found by one party is shared by all. It also follows the WIIFWe

Figure 8.4   Business Mapping Framework

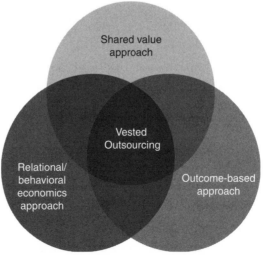

to governance as opposed to a WIIFMe supplier relationship management approach. For this reason, Vested Outsourcing agreements are not easily developed simply by cutting and pasting from other contract templates.

We would deceive ourselves if we believed that you will take out a pencil and a pad of paper and start *writing* the new Vested agreement. Rather, we are asking you to think twice when you cut and paste or use templates. Every lawyer we know uses templates and cuts and pastes language into contracts. Here are some tips to help you draft a Vested deal using sample language.

- *Understand each and every word in any clause that you cut and paste from any existing contract or template.* It took hundreds of hours of negotiations to get to the precise language. Companies and service providers went back and forth over the wording to make sure it fits that specific deal, so do not necessarily assume it will fit your deal.
- *Watch out for conjunctions and qualifiers.* Lawyers write using a complex sentence structure. Phrases like *notwithstanding the foregoing* radically change the meaning of the entire clause.
- *Know where the language came from.* Some in-house legal departments use software that allows the lawyers to track from which contract a clause was copied. This is important in two ways: (1) If the contract is old, it may—legally speaking—be out of date; (2) the language likely is specific to a particular jurisdiction and therefore, could be invalid for your deal.

Be careful as you draft your agreement. You would hate to see many months of hard work go down the drain simply because someone copied the wrong language or used the wrong template as a model.

Remember Who Are You Writing For

We highly recommend that you write each of the Ten Elements of the Vested agreement, all associated documents, and the MSA in plain language. Moreover, we do not advocate writing the contract for some hypothetical judge reviewing the agreement in the event of some hypothetical breach of the contract. Instead, we recommend drafting the agreement for those who will refer to it over the course of many (successful) years as Vested Outsourcing partners. Use simple language. Legal terms of art, specific phrasing, and even the word *shall* have specific legal connotations. The legal department will edit as it sees fit.

Develop the written agreements in the order outlined in this manual. Write your vision statement after both parties have had a meeting of the minds about that vision. Do not come to a verbal agreement, delay writing it down until later, and move on to the next element. The idea is that as you agree and document one element of your Vested Outsourcing deal, the previous work becomes the outline for the next set of homework. Because the parties co-author most of the written agreements, plan to work with several iterations of any one document before both parties feel satisfied with the end product. Throughout the Vested journey, individuals from the companies will encounter many legal issues. For example, when both parties outline the workload allocation, employment regulations and compliance issues may impact certain decisions and resulting allocation choices. Therefore, it is wise for each company to stay in constant contact with its legal department.[5]

Further, we suggest that you consult George Kimball's book *Outsourcing Agreements: A Practical Guide.*[6] Kimball's intended audience is both legal and nonlegal businesspeople. Although *Outsourcing Agreements* runs more than 400 pages in length, it is not a traditional legal text. We particularly appreciate that Kimball never sacrifices accuracy in his quest for simplicity. His explanations are precise and balanced. *Outsourcing Agreements* also includes sample contractual language in the appendixes.

As we have said throughout, organizations need to expand their thinking about contracts to reflect a more flexible framework. This chapter discussed the role of the MSA and how it works together with the various schedules to create that flexible framework. By using this chapter in connection with the others, you have crafted a document that correctly establishes the rights, roles and responsibilities between the parties. By so doing, you will establish a living and breathing document that captures the essence of your Vested agreement.

CHAPTER 9

THE NEXT LEG OF YOUR VESTED JOURNEY

Congratulations! You have finished your homework and crafted your MSA. You have just completed the first leg in your Vested Outsourcing journey. Your company now has a Vested agreement that is sure to pay big rewards in the years to come. We hope you feel very proud of your team and excited about working with your Vested partner.

Closing the deal is just the beginning. The next leg of the journey is living with your Vested Outsourcing agreement in terms of its day-to-day execution and implementation. Imagine that you and your Vested partner just got into the car for a cross-country road trip. Your Vested agreement is the roadmap, but you still have to drive thousands of miles to reach your destination. The trip is wonderful and rewarding, but it will have rough patches too.

For example, how will you respond when your chief financial officer asks for 10 percent off the bottom line and $200 million out of the supply chain? Will you revert to zero-sum thinking and justify demands for cost savings from the service provider? How will you collaborate when the other company's team members change and the new members are not invested in the deal? What happens when adverse market changes loom and the other company's team gets surly?

This is where the rubber of a solid Vested relationship meets the road. To get the promised rewards, the parties must pay attention to the perpetual need to collaborate when these types of questions arise. During the course of your collaborations, you likely will be tempted—even unknowingly—to fall back to self-serving positions when the stakes are high. Here we are in effect telling you to "play nice."

To answer these questions in a Vested environment, your company needs cross-company and cross-functional collaboration. As mentioned in chapter 1, your organization must align across departments and teams (horizontal) and from the top to bottom (vertical). Thus, collaboration must span corporate boundaries to achieve top-level outcomes. Companies cannot expect professional buyers, supply chain management, and account representatives to carry the entire burden of collaboration. Middle management usually will tow the corporate line while senior management, especially when facing contentious issues, will tend to protect their company's interests as the first priority. Everyone must adopt the collaborative spirit of Vested Outsourcing going forward.

There is no doubt that along the way there will be different points of view that will require creative approaches to work through. To get to an agreement, the parties will continue to negotiate—perhaps not on the same scale as it took to get to this agreement, but you will nonetheless negotiate.

To get to your final destination, collaboration and negotiation are more important than ever before. Not only are the stakes higher (you have signed a big deal and increased your mutual dependency), the daily challenges and the frequency of communication may be unlike any relationship you have implemented before. The biggest challenge facing you now is getting to the point where you truly believe that you will collaborate for the duration of the deal and that neither party will creep back to self-interest when faced with all kinds of temptations. Our goal in this chapter is to introduce you to negotiation best practices in the highly collaborative Vested environment. We recognize that readers of this book may represent divergent groups of stakeholders. Nevertheless, you—personally—can adopt collaboration best practices in your own approach to working together, and they will have a positive impact on the next leg of your Vested Outsourcing journey. The techniques discussed in this chapter are not new. They are, however, not always put into practice. What may be new is the idea that you must follow these principles until they become second nature to you as a collaborative negotiator.

COLLABORATION: A PROCESS, NOT AN EVENT

Collaboration is a constant process that includes a lot of give-and-take. By that we mean that you will have countless conversations aimed at reaching a great number of little (maybe a couple of large) agreements over the course of many years. When you fully engage in the back-and-forth conversation, you are negotiating. A negotiation is nothing more than a back-and-forth conversation aimed at reaching an agreement. Unfortunately, many seasoned business professionals consider negotiations to be formal, face-to-face meetings fraught with tension, positioning, and legal technicalities aimed only at closing the most advantageous deal. Once the deal is done, you are done negotiating, right? Wrong! It is your choice whether you see the negotiation process as competitive or collaborative.

We call our negotiation philosophy what's-in-it-for-we (WIIFWe) rather than the traditional what's-in-it-for-me (WIIFMe). Individuals representing varying stakeholders can develop a WIIFWe mentality when working internally with different stakeholders and externally with the other company. In our experience, as one person puts sincere effort into changing his or her negotiation approach to reflect a more collaborative spirit, other people in the conversation make positive changes too.

To embrace the WIIFWe mentality on a daily basis, approach continual collaboration as a process with four repeating steps, as shown in Figure 9.1. This chapter introduces each step. Collaboration is an ongoing process. Using this process as a guide will help companies stay on track for success.

Step 1. Internal Alignment

To work collaboratively with external partners, internal business partners must be on board with the Vested deal. Internal stakeholders must invest in the deal by performing the required daily, monthly, and quarterly activities. Internal disagreements about who does what and why eventually will impact external conversations in insidious ways.

For example, say you negotiated workload allocation, and both companies agreed to a set of metrics requiring monthly data collection. Internally at your company, though, the operations department is not designed to collect that kind of data. For that reason, people in operations just ignore the service provider's requests for the information and make excuses that

Figure 9.1   Vested Collaboration Wheel

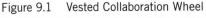
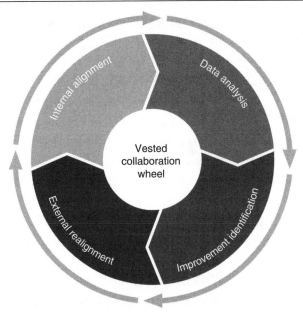

they are too busy. This scenario shows how a small internal misalignment begins to impact external alignment. The company
is not collaborating internally. The messages it sends to the service provider are mixed. In effect, the company is saying, "We
will hold you accountable, but we are unable to hold ourselves
accountable."

The service provider will notice this disconnect. Continuing
with the example, let us fast-forward many months. At meetings
to discuss the metrics, the service provider is upset that the company is not providing the data. The service provider also may
secretly wonder if the company knows something that it will use
against the service provider in some unforeseen way. It is not
a rational thought; thoughts like these are the first signs that
trust is starting to erode. So, the service provider's representatives at the steering committee meeting make a snide comment
about when they can expect the data. The company's representative, noticing the snide tone, might feel like protecting his
or her colleague by responding with another snide comment.
Thus, signs of the first small crack in the relationship appear,
even before the relationship is a year old. The next nine years
of the ten-year agreement will feel like an eternity if something
does not change quickly.

Step 2. Data Analysis

When you created your Vested agreement, you created data collection and sharing processes. Data sharing is not data dump-
ing. In chapter 7, we talk about developing insights, not just
oversight. The next step in the collaborative process is actually
to analyze data to look for patterns, trends, disruptions, maladaptations, and inaccurate baseline assumptions. Both companies have built the agreement on a host of assumptions, but are
those assumptions accurate? The only way to get to operational
insight is to analyze the data in addition to sharing it.

Recall ailment 8, the "driving blind disease" (see Appendix
A). If you have no ability to understand the data you are

collecting, you are driving blind. All the metrics in the world will not help you if you do not know how to interpret them. Besides, the parties signed on to the concept of insight, not merely oversight.

Step 3. Improvement Identification

A Vested deal is premised on the notion that the company gains financial rewards by identifying improvements that the service provider is given incentives to implement. The idea is that the parties always are looking for ways to make or save money.

Most changes you encounter will be minor, but others can significantly change the relationship. As the changes become more complex, your commitment to the Pony—the difference between the value of the current solution and the potential optimized solution—will require an increasing level of data analysis and internal alignment before you meet opportunities for process improvement. When the parties consent to make changes to the agreement, the appropriate governance team needs to meet to formalize those changes.

Step 4. External Realignment

Governance meetings are boring compared to negotiating the deal. Some perennial dealmakers are adrenaline junkies. They love getting to an agreement, but once the ink dries, they are on to the next one. In their opinion, only nerds go to governance meetings to check in on things.

We will not lie to you. Monthly, quarterly, and yearly meetings are *not* as exciting as creating a Vested agreement. Discussing countless agenda points about operational and financial issues can be tedious. Just because it is boring, however, does not mean that you can avoid it. When the parties agreed to the governance structure, they saw the need for a process of constant communication with one another at increasing levels of managerial responsibility.

Of course, it is taken for granted that the various account representatives and supply chain representatives would talk often, but will upper and middle management talk regularly too? How easy is it for the higher-ups to overbook and miss a meeting? Ultimately, people with increasing levels of responsibility and authority will have to make attending governance meetings a high priority for the duration of the agreement. Very important people cannot wait to engage only when a major problem arises. By then it is too late.

———————

Without laying the groundwork in steps 1, 2, and 3, the companies likely are not in the best position to make necessary changes when a problem arises. Any time the parties agree to a realignment, each company will have to realign internally as well, thus beginning the alignment cycle all over again.

Steps 1 and 2 of this process are completely within your company's control. At the end of chapter 1, we asked you to complete a Vested Outsourcing readiness assessment. Review your assessment results now that you have completed the agreement. What areas still require improvement?

Finally, we must mention the need for training aimed at improving individual collaboration skills. All companies expect their employees to know how to work as a team but rarely teach them specific communication skills to foster such collaboration. Is that fair?

Expect to invest time and resources in training members of the various governance committees in collaborative communication skills. It is unrealistic to expect individuals who are rock stars in their area of expertise also to have exceptional communication skills without the appropriate training. After all, most businesspeople have certifications and/or college degrees. They did not reach their position merely by being in the right place at the right time. They *learned* their profession over time.

Just as on any long road trip, a multitude of things can go wrong in any Vested Outsourcing project. As Mark Twain famously said, "I am an old man and have known a great many troubles, but most of them never happened."[1] Most of what you worry about will not happen. We cannot assure you that your business journey will end well, but we can assure you that if you have followed all Ten Elements of a Vested agreement and you play nice, you will greatly improve your odds of success.

FOUR SPECIFIC COLLABORATIVE COMMUNICATION TECHNIQUES

People who collaborate successfully recognize that it is a process and they have good communication skills to help them navigate that process. Not only are they able to express themselves clearly, they also have the skills to defuse tense situations. Often, these people influence others even when they do not have any authority over them. In effect, collaborative people work with others effectively as equals; they do not need to resort to authoritative actions to get results.

Collaboration requires "softer" communication skills than a traditional command-and-control supplier management style. Four specific communication techniques will help individuals collaborate effectively. Using these skills will help you inspire diverse groups of people to work as a team for a common goal.

Shared Vision Continues to Guide

At the beginning of a Vested journey, the parties crafted a Shared Vision statement for the deal. All of the other agreements made during the first leg of the journey align themselves around the vision statement. The Shared Vision statement continues to serve the same purpose now that the deal has closed.

Think of your Shared Vision statement as your North Star on this leg of the Vested journey. For hundreds of years, sailors used a sextant and the North Star to guide them when they lost sight of land, whether they were in charted or uncharted waters. This leg of your journey is similar. Perhaps you are in charted waters because you have worked with this service provider before. Perhaps the organizations are new to each other. It does not matter. The parties will need to check periodically throughout the relationship to make sure they are still on course to their appointed destination. The Shared Vision statement will help you stay on course.

Researchers have studied multiparty negotiations looking for correlations between positive outcomes and the parties' compatibility, such as sharing a common ideology with one another.[2] In a simulated negotiation, parties received the most resources (whether money, people, or machines) when they demonstrated they were better able to use those resources to contribute to the overall mission of the organization. People who use some guiding light, whether it is the mission statement or set of identifiable outcomes, are more successful than those who fly blind. Therefore, continue to focus on the Shared Vision statement as you collaborate with the other company. When used appropriately, the Shared Vision statement is a powerful, collaborative form of leverage.[3]

People want to act consistently with both their individual values and with commonly shared values. In other words, when people disagree, one party can move the other to its way of thinking by asking that everyone act consistently with individual values and common business values. In the Vested agreement, the common values, so to speak, are written down in the Shared Vision statement. Looking back to the Ryanair and Swissport example in chapter 3, safety is a shared value in their guiding vision. All decisions must ensure safety, period. Since the parties equally contributed to the Shared Vision statement, each party acknowledges those values as legitimate and relevant to any situation that might later arise.

Reminding people of shared values and asking them to make decisions and judgments according to those values is both powerful and positive. You are not hitting someone over the head with the Shared Vision statement. Rather, you are using it as a guide. Ask yourself and your colleagues, "Is this decision, no matter how seemingly insignificant, aligned to the shared values?" If not, do not implement the decision. One small misalignment now will lead to a major misalignment in a matter of months. A series of misalignments could lead the parties right back to one of the Ten Ailments.

Using the Shared Vision statement is only part of the collaborative equation. At an individual level, when performing mundane daily activities, you will have to get people—your own colleagues or the other party's team members—to do things for you. Workshop participants often ask us: "How do I get people to do things when I can't force them?" In other words, if you have no obvious power, how do you get things done?

Influence, Not Power Plays

Now that the deal is done, power has changed hands; the parties are on a more equal footing. Since neither company dominates the relationship, each must use subtle forms of influence to get its own people and those from the other company to comply. Businesspeople call this relationship management. We simply call it working together.

It is safe to assume that after you have completed your Vested agreement, each company will have some level of influence over the other company's behavior. That is to say, individuals and teams will exert influence—whether positive or negative—over another individual or team in order to achieve some result. Ideally, that result is mutually beneficial.

Positive influence requires a trust. You must trust them. They must trust you. Trust, while always a factor in any relationship, takes on an increasingly important role in Vested Outsourcing. Unfortunately, people misunderstand how to build trust. Remember the chapter 8 discussion about long contracts including trivial details? Those companies were trying to legislate trust at the contractual level. Trust is not something to demand, measure, or legislate. Trust, which is established through mutual compatibility over time, is one element of influence. Framing your message is another.

Consciously framing your message is the easiest way for anyone to exert influence. Articulating and pitching your message does not depend on any external source of power, nor does it depend on your personality. It depends on your ability to listen carefully to what is and is not being said while at the same time considering how and what you will say to your counterpart. Moreover, frame a difficult message to defuse the situation rather than inflame it.

For example, if you heard the company's supply chain manager repeatedly say in a meeting that your company still had not produced the year-end report even though it was already March, you would directly address her concern in your response. You might say something like "I've heard you say you are concerned about the report not being done. We still need to get certain information from your company before we can complete it. Let's look at what we can do to get that information compiled quickly." Rather than jumping right to the defensive answer that her company did not get your company all the information it needed, you subtly exert influence every time you acknowledge having heard another person's concern. In effect, you are letting her, and all the other people in the meeting, know that you are paying attention and not ignoring, justifying, or shifting the blame for her concern. In the end, you will get people, even frustrated ones, to help you solve the problem.

People often make common mistakes that reduce their level of influence. Here are some mistakes to avoid.

- *Do not frame your conversations from a self-serving perspective.* As soon as you do that, the shame and blame game is on. Do you really want to battle over whose fault it is? Do not revert back to the what's-in-it-for-me (WIIFMe) attitude. Understandably, we all have good reasons for those self-serving statements, but successful collaborators use a more neutral frame of reference. When you spend time spinning things from your company's perspective, you ruin all chances at positively influencing the other party. Look back at the last example. You, the speaker, are influential because you are not making self-serving excuses. Nor are you blaming anyone else, even though the company has not given yours the information it needs for the report. The neutral message is that the report is not done because you need information, and the committee needs to solve that problem. Plain and simple.

- *Watch out for death by PowerPoint slides and unnecessarily long reports.* Slides and reports are only tools; they are not influential in and of themselves. If your message is not framed right, no amount of colorful slides or glossy paper will help you. Your message still will be dead on arrival.

- *Whatever you do, think before you speak.* Do not just say whatever happens to come to mind. Be more deliberate. By doing so, you will be more influential.

Trade-offs Will Get You Some Trade-ups

Collaboration means everyone will have to give something to get something. You can have anything you want; you just cannot have *everything* you want. Making trade-offs and trade-ups is not the same as making concessions. When people talk about negotiating, they often use the word *concession.*

People hate making concessions when they think they did not get anything in return. It is a one-sided gift. Most people giving one-sided gifts start to keep score. It ties back to our human tendency to play WIIFMe games.

In early 2009, Pete, the president of a supplier and one of our clients, got a call from his largest customer's supply chain manager—we will call her Anne—who wanted a 5 percent price cut. Initially, Anne was not willing to give Pete anything of value for that price cut. Asking for a price cut without offering anything of value in return is an example of asking for a concession. Interestingly, Anne thought that she was making a trade-off because Pete's company would keep the business. Sound familiar? A company thinks it is giving something of value by not terminating the agreement, but the service provider feels bullied. This type of behavior will kill your Vested deal in a heartbeat.

The problem is that in an interdependent relationship, the party asking for the concession needs to reciprocate. Rarely do companies agree to make a concession without also (at least secretly) expecting to get something of value in return. Telling a supplier that the company will not terminate the contract is not a form of reciprocity.

A trade-off is a mutual exchange for mutual gain. Trade-offs have a completely different emotional feeling compared to concessions. Trade-offs engender a spirit of trust and respect based on a genuine sense of reciprocity. One company is not giving up value at the demand of another. Instead, both companies work to find a set of meaningful trade-offs. Vested Outsourcing depends on the companies making meaningful these trade-offs.

In Vested Outsourcing, you might even make some trade-ups. A trade-up is more than a mutual exchange of value. It means giving up something of little value in exchange for something of greater value. Let us look at ailment 9, "measurement minutiae" (see Appendix A). That ailment is all about gathering needless and useless information in the hope of managing the service provider through data. If the company releases its demands for copious amounts of useless data (little value), it gets better performance (greater value) in exchange. The service provider no longer collects useless data and in exchange is freed up to perform (greater value). This is a trade-up because it is more than an exchange for mutual value. It is an exchange for *extra* value. Because the value derives from the exchange, each company must be willing to have conversations about what is valuable and not valuable to them.

What if the service provider offers a trade-off that you do not agree with? We recommend that rather than saying no, you make a counteroffer.

Do Not Say No, Make a Counteroffer

Sometimes no is the wrong response. No does not add to the conversation. In fact, it can halt the conversation in its tracks. The person hearing no becomes defensive because he just offered a solution he thinks is the best solution for the situation. Hearing no in response to your good idea can be really frustrating. Because collaboration requires a lot of communication you are better off if you can keep the conversation going. A counteroffer (or counterproposal) says, "Not exactly; what about this instead?"

A counteroffer is a change that you make to an existing proposal. The proposal could relate to anything from changing the date of regular monthly meetings to significant changes in performance metrics. The concept is the same for small and big proposals alike. For example, if you need to change the date for monthly status meetings, you would propose some new days and times. If the other team members responded only with no, you would be left wondering "Well, what days would work?"

A counterproposal says no while simultaneously offering an alternative. There are two ways to suggest an alternative. You could say, "Tuesdays do not work for me. How about Wednesdays instead?" Not bad for minor matters. Remember that messaging is important to collaboration. A better counterproposal might be to say something like "Tuesdays do not work. You have mentioned before that you need us to meet before the quality control committee meeting. Would meeting on Wednesday give you enough time to prepare for the quality control meeting?" The difference is that in the second example, you explicitly state that you are aware of an important issue while also saying no to Tuesdays. This technique might not make a big difference when scheduling dates, but it really matters when big things are at stake.

Returning to the example of the supply manager who asked for a 5 percent price cut, Pete had a trade-off in mind but did not know how to offer it. Rightfully, Pete did not want simply to say no to his company's biggest customer. He wanted to make some sort of counterproposal. He asked for two days to consider the situation and internally analyzed the account. Pete realized that he could shave 3 percent from the overall price if the customer did two things: paid Pete's company by wire transfer, not by check, and shortened the payment period from net 45 days to net 30 days.

Pete's counteroffer explicitly communicated two things:

1. Pete's company was willing to agree to a smaller price cut (meet its customer's need) and what it wanted in return for doing so.
2. On a more subtle level, Pete left Anne with the impression that if this proposal did not work for her, he was open to having a conversation.

The next day Anne agreed to accept the 3 percent price reduction and to pay Pete's company electronically, net 30 days as requested. It is unlikely that these two companies would have reached any agreement at all if Pete had simply said no.

Pete's willingness to request a trade-off in exchange for agreeing to the price reduction paid big dividends to the overall relationship between his company and its largest customer. Months after they negotiated the change, Anne admitted to Pete that she did not agree with her company's request to seek a price cut from Pete's company. She thought the request was unfair and expected Pete to say no. Anne told Pete that she was taken by (pleasant) surprise when he agreed to make a price reduction and said that since he seemed to understand the reason for the request, she was motivated to negotiate internally with her accounting department on his behalf. A less artful counteroffer might not have moved the supply chain manager to go to bat for the supplier.

People make two common mistakes when they make counterproposals.

1. They offer a solution before the other person has explained what is important to them. There is little surprise when the other person says "No, that will not work." Your solution sounds self-serving if it does not explicitly meet your counterpart's needs. How could it if you do not know what those needs are?

2. They fail to consider whether their counteroffer meets the needs of the other person *from that person's perspective.*

Good solutions get shot down because people do not think you actually have solved their problem. Any change to their proposal—even if it makes things better for them—is not always recognized or accepted as a better solution. People are overly invested in their solutions. For this reason alone, people reject perfectly good solutions.

It is your job to offer alternatives in a manner that explicitly signals the fact that your proposal meets the other person's needs and that you are willing to talk about it until the problem is solved. In the example, Pete explicitly met Anne's needs by offering a small discount. Anne got the supplier to reduce its prices without giving much up in return. Pete's company solved a nagging cash flow issue and got something of value in exchange for agreeing to the 3 percent cut. This was a mutual exchange from each company's perspective. Pete also signaled that he was open to have a conversation until the solution met everyone's needs.

Sometimes people get stuck in problem conversations because a situation comes up that does not have an obvious solution. Clients often tell us that they do not want to make any proposals until they know for sure what to do. They are afraid of being held to a suggestion later on even if it turns out that the suggestion cannot solve the problem.

For example, consider this situation in which the company neglects to adequately address services it should have retained in the workload allocation. The service provider wants to make some suggestions but is not certain that its ideas are right. It seems simple enough to tell the company what you think they ought to be doing. But in reality it is not that simple. The company's team may not be receptive to your suggestions unless you lay the appropriate groundwork. More important, your company may make some suggestions that later turn out to be too costly. You cannot take your suggestions back, can you?

If you were to make a counteroffer on behalf of the service provider, you might start the conversation like this: "Since we both agreed that a Desired Outcome was a 75 percent employee utilization rate of the employee cafeteria, we would like to offer the following proposal. We would be willing to...if you would be willing to..." This is a great way to approach the conversation, even when you are thinking "We thought you guys would be doing that job, and now you have us doing that. We did not agree to that. You will need to do that job yourself if you expect to reach your employee utilization rate of 75 percent."

Our suggestion does three important things.

1. It aligns the proposal to the appropriate Desired Outcome. Everyone knows that the statements to come will address that Desired Outcome.
2. The service provider starts with what it is willing to do. It makes a trade-off.
3. The if-then form of the suggestion asks for a trade-off in return while also keeping the conversation flexible and fluid. If the company does not agree with the suggestion, it will be more likely to suggest

an alternative. This formula prevents parties from becoming alienated from one another.

Unsuccessful collaborators miss an important point when they make proposals or counteroffers. It is your job to clearly articulate what your counterpart has to gain from following your proposed course of action. It is not the other person's job to search your proposal for clues. Do not underestimate the difficulty of group collaboration. People tend to avoid difficult conversations, but avoidance is usually destructive. By attempting to avoid difficult conversations, people hope the conflict will go away—but it will not. Organizations must be honest about their ability to behave collaboratively. The tools in this chapter will help any organization work more collaboratively with its Vested Outsourcing partner. Small communication changes can have big impact.

The road ahead will stretch you in ways that you cannot imagine. You have successfully completed the first leg of your journey by creating your Vested agreement. To complete the long journey ahead and reach your destination, *collaborate, do not alienate.* Here is our challenge for you:

Do one thing every day that will make the relationship better. Send an email with praise or accolades. Tell five people about the good work the other company is doing. Return a call with the intention of building rapport with the other person. Do one small thing that will make the relationship stand the test of time. Now go out and play nice.

CHAPTER 10

CONCLUSION: REACHING YOUR DESTINATION

At the start of this manual, we set out to develop a road-map to make it easier for companies and their service providers to tackle one of the hardest parts of Vested Outsourcing: crafting a business-to-business agreement that not only formally binds the companies through a contract but establishes the ten foundational elements for a successful business relationship.

If you are reading this conclusion, we hope you have completed all of the homework and have created your own Vested agreement following the roadmap we have presented.

Along your journey, we hope we have helped you dig deeper into your relationship, enabling you to develop a true win-win agreement where both parties have a vested interest in achieving the mutually defined Desired Outcomes to which you have agreed. Using this manual should have enabled you to create your Vested agreement and to structure it as a flexible operating framework that embraces business changes. You also should have created a governance structure built on insight, not oversight; we hope it will prove valuable as you inevitably encounter the dynamic nature of business. If you have followed the roadmap by addressing each of the Ten Elements in your agreement, you are on your way to an outsourcing relationship that should take you to the real end of your journey: achieving your Desired Outcomes.

Our last bit of advice is to resist the urge to make your Vested agreement a vinyl binder or an ornamental shelf object. Refer to your Vested agreement regularly as a sort of Global Positioning System to help you achieve your Desired Outcomes. Do not be afraid to leverage the change management procedures you have created as needed.

We hope that our collective wisdom as practitioners, academics, and legal professionals coupled with our research, has provided a valuable resource that will take your outsourcing relationships to the next level. Those who have challenged themselves to follow the Vested Outsourcing rules will create innovative solutions that resolve the conflicting goals so often found in conventionally outsourced business models. If you get stuck along the way, we encourage you to visit the Vested Outsourcing website (www.vestedoutsourcing.com) for resources and tools that can help you.

After you begin to play by the rules of Vested Outsourcing, you will fully grasp what we have learned through our research and collective experience: there really *is* a better way to outsource. We hope you will share our enthusiasm for Vested thinking with others who are struggling with their own outsourcing relationships while taking to heart and mind Albert Einstein's maxim:

> *The significant problems we face cannot be solved at the same level of thinking we were at when we created them.*

HAPPY VESTING!

ACKNOWLEDGMENTS

W riting *The Vested Outsourcing Manual* was a truly collaborative effort. We stood on the shoulders of so many talented people that it is hard to know where to begin to express our gratitude. Except, perhaps, at the place where this book began: with the research.

Our deepest gratitude goes to Mike Ledyard and Karl Manrodt—coauthors of the first book on Vested Outsourcing. Without your efforts on the original research and the first book, this book would not have been possible.

A very special thanks to Nobel laureate Oliver E. Williamson for his inspiring research and scholarship.

Thanks to all of the progressive organizations that provided us with case studies, best practices, and a vision for excellence: Many must remain unnamed due to their corporate rules and desire to maintain their competitive advantages. You know who you are, and you have our deepest gratitude.

We would like to thank the University of Tennessee and the International Association for Contract and Commercial Management for their continued support of our zealous research and outreach efforts to spread the word about the transformational powers of a Vested Outsourcing business model. This includes Ted Stank, Bric Wheeler, Chuck Park, Carolyn Cuddy, Karen Hanlon, Alex Miller, and the rest of the UT team and faculty who have supported us along the way. We would like to give Tim Cummins, founder and chief executive of IACCM, a special thanks for tirelessly spreading the message about how contracting and legal professionals need to embrace the thinking behind Vested Outsourcing.

We are deeply indebted to Dr. John Grant Rhode for his thorough review of the manuscript.

Elizabeth Kanna: You offered the vision for what could be and the tools and guidance necessary to make that vision a reality.

Laurie Harting: You were quick to understand the power of Vested Outsourcing and provided valuable strategic direction on this book. With Palgrave Macmillan, we truly have a vested relationship!

Bill DiBenedetto and Debra Manette: Thanks for reining in our jargon, smoothing out our disjointed writing styles, and making us sound like one pleasant voice for change.

Steve Allcock: Thanks for your fabulous design work on the graphics, including the covers of both books.

Steve Symmes and Jeanne Kling: Thank you for your hours of diligent research and documentation of concepts that saved us days and days in our journey.

Thanks also to the following thought leaders who reviewed our work along the way and provided valuable feedback, support, and endorsement that Vested Outsourcing truly is a game-changing business model that will define how companies outsourcing in the future:

Jim Groton—retired lawyer and dispute specialist
George Kimball—HP
Scott Schroeder—Megatech Oregon
Todd Shire—Intel
Richard MacLaren—Unipart
Dr. René Franz Henschel—Professor of Law and Economics, Aarhus School of Business, Denmark

A special thanks to analyst firms and professional organizations that have helped us share the concepts: ARC Advisory Group, Aberdeen Group, the Outsourcing Institute, the International Association of Outsourcing Professionals, the Sourcing Interest Group, and the National Contract Management Association.

Last, we would like to recognize Mike Watts, Rhonda Watts, Laurie Hanley, and Karen Wiley: You keep Kate organized, on time, and everything running in perfect order for her. You are a savior for Kate, and for that we are all indebted.

And last, but certainly not least, a special thanks to our families, for all your support and patience during this fabulous experience:

Greg and Austin Picinich
Jonathan Archer
Tim Lohraff
John, Annie, Kelsey, and Adam Kawamoto. And a special thank you to brother James A. Koslick for being a great sounding board over the years.

APPENDIX A:
THE TEN AILMENTS[1]

AILMENT 1. PENNY WISE AND POUND FOOLISH

This is the easiest ailment to identify: when a company out-sources based purely on costs. We have all heard the warning to not be pennywise and pound foolish. Unfortunately, many procurement professionals still labor in the Dark Ages in this regard. Too many companies profess to have an outsource part-nership, but, behind the scenes, they focus solely on beating up their service providers to get the lowest price.

Organizations with this ailment give outsourcing a bad name—and should not be outsourcing in the first place. Their myopic focus might pay off in the short term, but time and time again it is proved that it does not pay to be pennywise and pound foolish.

When cost and the lowest price are the only incentives to do a deal, there is probably trouble ahead.

AILMENT 2. THE OUTSOURCING PARADOX

The first symptom manifested by sufferers of ailment 2, the "outsourcing paradox," is the development of the "perfect" set of tasks, frequencies, and measures. The "experts" within the company attempt to develop the "perfect" statement of work (SOW). Their goal is to tightly define the expected results. After all, we are taught that we need to clearly define expecta-tions, right? The result is an impressive document containing all the possible details on *how* the work is to be done. At last, the perfect system! However, this "perfect system" is often the first reason why a company will fail in its outsourcing effort. That is because it is the company's perfect system, not one designed by the service provider.

We found a classic example of the "outsourcing paradox" at work in a third-party logistics provider (3PL) that runs a spare parts warehouse. During a site visit, we saw approximately eight people servicing a facility that on average had fewer than 75 orders per day. We asked: Why all the resources? We were told, "That is what the company that is outsourcing requires per our statement of work—so I have staffing at that level to meet the contract requirements."

It is amazing to find that companies have chosen to outsource to the "experts" yet insist on defining the requirements and workscope so tightly that the service provider winds up executing the same old inefficient processes! This disease can be exacerbated when coupled with ailment 4, the junkyard dog factor.

AILMENT 3. ACTIVITY TRAP

Many companies that suffer from the "outsourcing paradox" also suffer from a related malady, the "activity trap." Traditionally, companies that purchase outsourced services use a transaction-based model. Under that model, the service provider is paid for every transaction—whether it is needed or not. Businesses are in the business to make money; service providers are no different. The more transactions performed, the more money they make. There is no incentive for the service provider to reduce the number of non–value-added transactions, because such a reduction would result in lower revenue.

The "activity trap" can manifest itself in a variety of transaction-based outsource arrangements. When the contract structure is cost reimbursement, for example, the outsource provider has no incentive to reduce costs because profit is typically a percentage of direct costs. Even if the outsource provider's profit is a fixed amount, the typical company will be penalized for investing in process efficiencies to drive costs down. In a nut-shell, the more inefficient the entire support process, the more money the service provider can make.

Perverse incentives play a major factor in the activity trap as well. Nineteenth-century paleontologists traveling to China used to pay peasants for each fragment of dinosaur bone (aka dinosaur fossils) that they produced. They later discovered that peasants dug up the bones and then smashed them to maximize their payments.

Inherent in the "activity trap" is a disincentive to try to drive down transactions. (This is another symptom seen in the "zero-sum game," ailment 7.) But does this really happen? Yes, unfortunately it does.

On a site visit, we asked the general manager of a 3PL what the large area full of orange-tagged pallets was for. She replied, "That's some of our customer's old inventory I need to move to an outside storage facility." When we dug further, we found out it was product that was well over five years old—and at the rate it was moving, it would last 123 years. *(This is not a typo!)* When we pressed further, asking why she did not work with the customer to scrap the material, the answer was "Why? I charge $18 a pallet per month to store it. I'd lose revenue if I did that!"

Another victim of the "activity trap," a large technology company, was transferring sales support activities from one outsourced provider to another. It found that the data required to run certain reports was no longer current, and the new data was being stored in a new format in a different location. The current provider had not been made aware of this fact, so the reports that it had produced for the past five months were wrong. In a damage control drill, the team learned good news as well as bad news: The sales manager who had requested this reporting had been transferred, and the new sales manager did not use this (now-inaccurate) report. But it was still a required activity, and the technology company was being charged each month to generate the report. Upon further investigation, the company discovered that over 300 unused reports were being generated each month at $75 a report—a whopping $22,500 per month.

A third example of the "activity trap" comes from outsourced manufacturing. A contract manufacturer performed final kitting and assembly pack-out as a value-added service for an original equipment manufacturer customer that designed consumer electronics. The customer had given the contract manufacturer the bill of materials with detailed instructions to use a specific finished goods "pretty box." This full-color, high-quality box was meant to serve as a kit to hold all of the various components for a particular device, including the manual, cables, charger, and so on. The contractor needed to assemble the box and then insert the parts properly. Building the box required the contractor to have 12 "touches." The contractor charged a flat fee per touch to assemble the box carton, plus a fee of one touch for each item placed in the kit. The contractor knew that the particular box design was not efficient but simply did what it was told rather than suggesting solutions for an improved box design that might eliminate unneeded touches.

AILMENT 4. THE JUNKYARD DOG FACTOR

When the decision to outsource is made, it usually means jobs will be lost as the work and jobs transition to the outsource provider. The result? Often employees will go to great lengths to hunker down and stake territorial claims to certain processes that simply "must" stay in house. We call this ailment the "junkyard dog factor." Even if the majority of the jobs are outsourced, many companies choose to have their "best" employees stay on board to manage the new service provider. These same "best" employees are often the ones who were asked to help write the statement of work. Is it any wonder that SOWs can become such rigid documents of often-less-than optimal ways the company was performing the tasks that are now being outsourced?

Over time, this ailment affects the outsource provider as well. Under a transaction-based model, the service provider is rewarded for work associated with the volume of the transactions. Unless otherwise compensated, the last thing a service provider wants to do is develop process efficiencies that eliminate its own work. So a company that might begin outsourcing to find an efficient and low-cost *total solution* instead achieves the lowest cost for an activity without really achieving its desired outcomes.

AILMENT 5. THE HONEYMOON EFFECT

At the beginning of any relationship, the parties go through the honeymoon stage. The Stamford, Connecticut, research firm Gartner, Inc. studied the honeymoon effect and found that overall attitudes toward an outsourcing contract tend to be positive at the outset, but satisfaction levels drop over time.[2] Outsource providers often jump through hoops as they ramp up and begin to collect revenue for their new client.

AILMENT 6. SANDBAGGING

To prevent the "honeymoon effect," some companies have adopted approaches to encourage outsource providers to perform better over time by establishing bonus payments for them to achieve certain levels of performance. This can work, but unfortunately, and all too often, it creates perverse incentives for the outsource provider, whereby the company achieves just the amount of improvement needed to get the incentive.

Consider Ukrainian Sergey Bubka, who was a world-class pole-vaulter earning $50,000 every time he set a new world record. From 1983 to 1998 he set world records 35 times...but never by more than one centimeter!

AILMENT 7. THE ZERO-SUM GAME

One of the most common ailments afflicting outsourcing arrangements is the "zero-sum game;" companies play this game when they believe, mistakenly, that if something is good for the service provider, then it is automatically bad for them. Of course, service providers also play this game.

Players on each side do not understand that the sum of the parts actually *can* be better when they are combined effectively, which was proven by John Nash's Nobel Prize–winning research in the area of game theory (aka behavioral economics). The basic premise of game theory is that when individuals or organizations play a game together and work together to solve a problem, the results are *always* better than if they had worked separately or played against each other.

AILMENT 8. DRIVING BLIND DISEASE

Another aliment that bedevils a great many outsourcing agreements is "driving blind disease:" the lack of a formal governance process to monitor the performance of the relationship. When we started working with companies more than 20 years ago, most outsourcing arrangements fell into this trap. Companies would develop arrangements but not outline how they would measure the success. Typically the companies would track costs but not measure various aspects of performance. As a result, early outsourcing agreements often failed because of an unclear definition of success.

According to Todd Shire of Intel:

> When we recalculate the ROI [return on investment] of an outsourcing agreement after implementation and stabilization, we sometimes find that anticipated savings were not realized because we needed to change scope or pricing in order to meet service expectations. When this happens, there is often devastating damage done to the customer/service provider relationship

that stops all potential progress toward mutual value creation. If we had agreed with the supplier on specific outcomes like service levels instead of transactions and headcount, the "leakage" could have been avoided.

AILMENT 9. MEASUREMENT MINUTIAE

Most of us probably remember Mom's warning that too much of a good thing can be bad for you, perhaps while you were gobbling up your Halloween candy or Thanksgiving dinner. The same concept applies to measurement of service providers. The hallmark of "measurement minutiae" is trying to measure *everything*. Actually the minutiae that some organizations create are quite remarkable. We have found spreadsheets with 50 to 100 metrics on them. "Measurement minutiae" often is associated with companies that also are suffering from the junkyard dog factor and agreements that are typified by the activity trap.

One company we visited had so many metrics that it needed a binder to keep track of everything on a monthly basis. Managers were embarrassed to tell us the total person-hours across all the organizations required to create these spreadsheets. Now, this is not a wasted effort if the company is getting positive results based on improvements it is making. Unfortunately, our experience has shown that few companies have the diligence to actively manage all of the metrics they have created all of the time.

AILMENT 10. THE POWER OF NOT DOING

The saddest of all ailments is the one we call "the power of not doing." We recently observed a case of this ailment at a Fortune 50 company. A senior manager was demonstrating what a great job her company had done on establishing measures. It had signed up for a seminar to learn how to apply the Balanced Scorecard and had hired a consulting firm to help create a world-class scorecard. The company had invested more than $1 million in an automated scorecard solution to capture and graph performance. Each of the supplier scorecards was posted on an internal Web site. One could quickly click through to look at the current measures and performance.

As this manager pulled up a scorecard, we randomly pointed to a measure and said, "This metric seems to be in the red. [The scorecards were color coded; red indicated poor performance.] When was the last time your team discussed this performance with the outsource provider?" The response? She looked us straight in the eye and answered honestly that she had no idea. She knew they had quarterly business reviews with their "top" suppliers, but the dashboard in question was not for one of these suppliers. We went on to ask "How rigorously do you adhere to quarterly business reviews?" She was embarrassed to say that they were lucky if they met with their suppliers once or twice a year.

This case of the power of not doing is not unusual—many companies have fallen into the trap of establishing measures for the sake of measures but have not thought through how they will be used to manage the business. We have all heard the old adage "You can't manage what you don't measure," but if the metrics compiled are not used to make adjustments and improvements, do not expect results.

APPENDIX B: IACCM
TOP TERMS 2010

**Contract Negotiations Continue
To Undermine Value**

RESULTS OF THE IACCM ANNUAL SURVEY OF THE MOST NEGOTIATED TERMS[1]

Business-to-business contracts are "instruments for social cooperation,"[2] according to Ian Macneil, the recently deceased author and leading legal academic. "Contracts arise because the parties recognize that there is more to be gained by some level of cooperation than by separation."

However, when it comes to the terms on which contact negotiators spend most time, this spirit of cooperation remains notable for its absence. IACCM's 9th Annual Report on the Most Frequently Negotiated Terms indicates that risk allocation and avoidance continue to dominate interactions during the negotiation of formal business-to-business agreements. The effect of the recession was in fact to increase the degree of separation between contracting parties, further threatening the economic value to be achieved from their relationship.

Macneil anticipated a growing number of today's academics and thought-leaders by his appreciation that many contracts can "be governed efficiently only if the parties adopt a consciously cooperative attitude."[3] It would appear obvious that the nature of a contract—and the time invested in its creation and management—must depend on the nature and economic potential of the relationship. The problem appears to be that too many contracting and legal professionals either fail or feel unable to make this distinction and do not alter their negotiation priorities to reflect the potential value or the extent to which its realization depends on cooperation.

As a result, contracts (and the professionals charged with their creation) are frequently seen as obstacles to value creation and are viewed by many as an unfortunate pre-requisite to doing business, rather than as a fundamental asset to successful relationships.

DID WE LEARN FROM THE RECESSION?

In general, the recession was marked by a more adversarial attitude in which contracts often proved themselves of limited value. Many powerful organizations simply ignored inconvenient terms and insisted on their renegotiation. Others made unilateral, non-negotiable changes, in particular in areas such as payment terms (interestingly, the fact that suppliers felt forced to accept such changes led buyers to see "increased collaboration," whereas the suppliers felt that collaboration had taken a hefty negative blow).

The recession did cause some shifts in the areas of emphasis in negotiations—but those areas were certainly not about increased partnership. Over 50% of negotiators felt that openness to risk discussion and balance in risk sharing reduced in 2009. The top terms where IACCM members observed substantial increases in both internal and external focus are shown in Table 1.

Table 1   Terms where internal and external concern increased during 2010
Price / Charge / Price Changes
Payment
Limitation of Liability
Invoices / Late Payment
Indemnification
Service Withdrawal or Termination (cause / convenience)
Service Levels and Warranties
Business Continuity / Disaster Recovery
Confidential Information / Data Protection
Liquidated Damages

While the recession caused some narrowing of the gap in frequency of negotiation for specific terms, there was no movement in the top five. Indeed, our Top Ten continues to be dominated by the risk-related provisions that are primarily about self-protection. Limitation of liability is once again number one—despite Macneil's observation (written some 40 years ago) that "damages and losses are not precisely quantifiable (in business contracts) and it is pointless to try." It would appear that it is this very lack of the ability to be precise that generates so much of the negotiation—and of course causes that aura of "pointlessness" that for so many businesspeople surrounds much of the contracting process.

THE FOCUS OF CONTRACTING PRACTICES TODAY

Much of our negotiation appears driven by classical legal theory that is based more on transactions than it is on relationships. Classical law assumes selfishness and that economic interest is "best served by looking after yourself, at the expense of other parties." This assumption encourages an attitude that approaches negotiation deal by deal, rather than seeking or observing patterns or examining the potential management of risk across relationship portfolios.

Economists have moved beyond this point, with their understanding that people and organizations are in fact able to grasp the benefits of cooperation and team behavior. The law is struggling to catch up and still appears to believe that the best way to manage risk is to allocate it to someone else and the greatest incentive to perform is via threats of dire punishment for failure.

This tendency for the law to be such a dominant feature in defining contractual obligations is not the only factor that undermines the effectiveness of contracting and negotiations. It is further amplified by the methods used in many Procurement organizations. The myopic view that all relationships can be reduced to individual commodity transactions ignores the dependency on relationship quality and governance. Turning again to Macneil, he observes: "Somewhere along the line of increasing duration and complexity, (the contract) escapes the traditional legal model...It is replaced by very different adjustment processes of an on-going administrative kind"(for example, think of governance, performance and change management). "This includes internal and external dispute resolution structures ..."[4]

The contracts community—or at least the top negotiators who have responded to our survey —are well aware of this conundrum. Over 80% acknowledge that today's practices do not result in the best outcome. Their "agenda of the future" closely mirrors the thoughts of Ian Macneil, written in 1969, when he set out "The Five Basic Elements Of Contract:"

1. Cooperation
2. Economic exchange
3. Planning for the future
4. Potential external sanctions
5. Social control and manipulation

As Table 2 illustrates, negotiators would like to focus on the areas of cooperation, economic exchange and planning for the future—for example, what are we trying to achieve together? They recognize the need for clarity in the economic exchange—the costs, the benefits, the responsibilities, and how these will be adjusted when change is needed. They recognize the importance of on-going communication and reporting against clear and specified goals and that then—only then— the need to establish the consequences of failure (the "external sanctions").

Table 2   Terms which would be more productive in supporting successful relationships
Scope and Goals
Change Management
Communications and Reporting
Responsibilities of the Parties
Service Levels and Warranties
Price / Charge / Price Changes
Limitation of Liability
Delivery / Acceptance
Dispute Resolution
Indemnification

A FUNDAMENTALLY WRONG ASSUMPTION

Macneil's work also pinpointed another key reason why traditional legal theory simply does not work in today's business environment. He commented on the point that "Classical law views cooperation as being 'of little interest' and external to the contract. In part, this is because it assumes a common base of presumed rules by the parties." Such an assumption is not only risky in the 21st century global market, but it is downright wrong. We know for instance that the parties frequently have very different presumptions about the "rules" that govern their relationship—legal, ethical, business, and social. Hence once more we can see the critical importance of changing the fundamentals of our debate, both during negotiation and indeed throughout the relationship. "The distinguishing feature of contractual obligations (in business) is that they are not imposed by the law but undertaken by the parties" (Smith, 1993).

The purpose of contracting should be to determine and then maintain the alignment of the parties and their respective capabilities to deliver the expected economic gains. This demands a framework that assumes and encourages cooperation and continuing dialogue. "The word solidarity—or trust—is not inappropriate to describe this web of interdependence and expected future cooperation. The most important aspect of solidarity is the extent to which it produces similarity of selfish interests, whereby what increases or decreases for one does so also for the other" (Macneil).

As Table 3 shows, the focus for today's negotiators clearly fails to achieve this balance of increase and decrease. It is dominated by the "potential external sanctions" that are in fourth place on Macneil's table of priorities. The dominance of risk-averse terms tends to emphasize the things that separate the parties and reflect their selfish interests. Some would argue this is realism; and in a casual encounter where the item of exchange is a one-time commodity, such concerns would be valid. But here we are discussing relationships that are often intended to survive for many years and require a far more sophisticated behavioral framework. Our focus today is failing to deliver this framework and thereby is also failing the business that we seek to protect.

Table 3   The terms that are negotiated with greatest frequency
Limitation of Liability
Indemnification
Price / Charge / Price Changes
Intellectual Property
Confidential Information / Data Protection
Payment
Service Levels and Warranties
Delivery / Acceptance
Liquidated Damages
Warranty

SO WHY NO CHANGE?

Negotiators mostly believe that change is necessary and desirable—almost 75% state this to be the case.[5] They are relatively clear about the areas for increased focus (as shown in Table 2 above). But they are unable to make the change primarily because of "resistance by the other side." Of course, since both sides are represented in our study, one must be rather skeptical about this statement. However, there is certainly truth in the fact that most negotiators are representatives of broad stakeholder groups; in that sense, they are not really decision makers but rather positional advocates. Their room for maneuver is generally quite limited—and this is reflected in their other primary reason for failure to change—internal stakeholder resistance and rules.

In the end, this lack of perceived empowerment is unfortunately accompanied by a lack of will or motivation to push for change. Our investigations suggest that most negotiators do indeed wish to do things better and differently, but they see too many obstacles. For example, what is the business case that could drive executive support? How could you measure the benefit that would flow from greater cooperation and more collaborative management of risk and change? As one General Counsel explained: "The benefits of cooperation would probably be significant nine times out of ten. But unfortunately I don't know how to measure them. The one time out of ten when things went wrong, all hell would break loose. And that is why contracts people and lawyers are reluctant to change."

In part, we cannot measure because we do not in general study contracts as a portfolio. For example, until IACCM introduced this study of the most negotiated terms, no one had thought to measure it. Similarly, very few organizations regularly capture data on the frequency, source and consequence of change; or similar data related to claims and disputes. There is even reluctance in many to monitor cycle times. Yet information of this sort would generate a greater drive for improvement and would help executives understand how the policies and procedures of today frequently stand in the way of good trading relationships.

The Road Ahead

Individual companies can make a difference and those with substantial negotiating power do sometimes break the mould. However, at present these examples are anecdotal rather than fundamental.

IACCM recognizes its responsibility to do more than simply advocate change. As a professional association, we must show leadership. Our research and advocacy of best practices is one example of that. In particular, the work we have done to benchmark the companies "Most Admired" in negotiation and contract management has resulted in a welcome boost in awareness and understanding of good practice and the benefits of developing contracting competency.[6]

At a more practical level, IACCM is undertaking work to develop standard forms of agreement. For example, in the technology sector we are at an advanced stage of producing balanced model terms that could change the face of negotiation and eliminate the traditional "battle of the forms." Our goal is not to prevent negotiation, but rather to ensure that it focuses on the things that really matter and assists parties in reaching trade-offs based on areas and items of value.

We are also involved in initiatives that could change some of the ground rules for contracting. An example is the UNCITRAL initiative (backed by the Organization of American States) to take the courts out of on-line dispute resolution. This proposal would result in the creation of a global arbitration service and has the potential to be just one element of a growing range of global contracting principles and practices for cross-border trade.

Education and awareness is also fundamental to change. The Association's focus on development of a global "body of knowledge" and consistent worldwide training for those involved in contract management is key to improved performance. As with any "community of practice," massive benefits flow from consistent terminology, methods and techniques— not only by facilitating communication and trust, but also by enabling measurement and continuous improvement. Today, there are several thousand professionals undertaking IACCM on-line training; later this year, we will publish the world's first book containing a universal "body of knowledge" for contract management.

In addition to the work on this new book, IACCM has a range of working groups and projects in areas such as complex project contracting, the development of supplier relationship management skills and techniques and improved standards in outsourcing. Overall, there are hundreds of managers and professionals from more than 60 countries who are volunteers in these projects and who are working together to ensure that change and improvement will occur.

A new focus is possible; and it will generate improved results. We are excited by the numbers who are now committed believers in making this journey.

APPENDIX C: TEMPLATES

Note: These templates and other resources are available for download at www.vestedoutsourcing.com/resources/tools.

Figure C.1   Requirements Roadmap Template

| Desired Outcome | Performance | | | Incentive | Inspection | | | |
	Statement of Objective	Standard	Tolerance/ALQ		Who	Data Source	Calculation	How Often Collected

Figure C.2   Risk Mitigation Template

ID Date	Risk Description/ Reason	Probability of Occurence	Impact on Project	Catergory—Red, Yellow, Green	Mitigation Plan	Responsible Party	Target Date to Resolve	Status

Impact on Project	High	Medium	High
Medium	Low	Medium	High
Low	Low	Low	Medium
		Probability of Occurence	

APPENDIX D:
ADDITIONAL RESOURCES

Vested Outsourcing offers a variety of tools and resources for the practitioner.

VESTED OUTSOURCING WHITE PAPER LIBRARY

www.vestedoutsourcing.com/resources/whitepapers

"IACCM and Vested Outsourcing—A Better Way to Structure Outsourcing Contracts"

"Unpacking Oliver—10 Lessons to Improve Collaborative Outsourcing"

"Unpacking Transportation Pricing—A White Paper Challenging Transportation Pricing Models"

JOIN THE DISCUSSION:
VESTED OUTSOURCING BLOG

www.vestedoutsourcing.com/category/from-the-blog

Keep current on Vested Outsourcing topics.

VESTED OUTSOURCING TOOLS

www.vestedoutsourcing.com/resources/tool/

We have complied implementation tools to empower your Vested Outsourcing relationships. Access our website to get the current versions and future updates. Currently available:

Requirements Roadmap Template
Risk Mitigation Template
Stakeholder Analysis and Communication Plan
Vested Outsourcing Evaluation Form
Vested Outsourcing Project Plan

VESTED OUTSOURCING IN A BOX

www.vestedoutsourcing.com

Vested Outsourcing has developed a set of interactive tools and processes that will help companies and service providers in the process of structuring their Vested Outsourcing deals. The toolbox is available through VestedOutsourcing.com.

VESTED OUTSOURCING
EDUCATIONAL RESOURCES

www.vestedoutsourcing.com/resources/educational-resources

The University of Tennessee offers courses as options to learn about and apply Vested Outsourcing concepts.

www.iaop.org

The International Association of Outsourcing Professionals (IAOP) is the global, standard-setting organization and advocate for the outsourcing profession.

VESTED OUTSOURCING RESOURCES

www.vestedoutsourcing.com/resources/program-resources/

Vested Outsourcing offers a variety of program resources to help you with your Vested Outsourcing implementation. University of Tennessee program faculty are ready to help you with research or evaluating your existing outsourcing arrangement.

Vested Deal Certification
Vested Outsourcing Deal Review Program
Integrated Consulting/Coaching Program
Vested Outsourcing Implementation/Consulting
Research Programs
Educational Outreach and Private Events

NOTES

INTRODUCTION: IMPLEMENTING THE BETTER WAY

1. The first book in the series is titled *Vested Outsourcing: Five Rules That Will Transform Outsourcing*. This is the second book. Palgrave Macmillan and the authors plan an additional a book with case studies and a textbook.
2. Grubb & Ellis, "Integrated Corporate Real Estate Solutions," 2010 Brochure.
3. Accenture, Microsoft OneFinance, company profile (2010) 1-2.
4. Grubb & Ellis, ibid.
5. Retrieved March 2011 from the Outsourcing Center: www.outsourcing-center.com/2008-08-growing-the-business-to-drive-value-article-37343.html.
6. Retrieved March 2011 from the International Association of Outsourcing Professionals (IAOP): www.iaop.org/Firmbuilder/Articles/34/187/1820.
7. Retrieved March 2011 from Accenture: www.accenture.com/us-en/company/overview/awards/Pages/outsourcing-excellence-award-2010.aspx.
8. IAOP news release retrieved March 2011 from: www.iaop.org/Content/23/196/3121.
9. Research interview.
10. Nobel Prize Release, retrieved December 2010 from: http://nobelprize.org/nobel_prizes/economics/laureates/2009/press.html.
11. C. John Langley, Jr. "2010 Third-Party Logistics," 15th annual study, *The State of Logistics Outsourcing*. Retrieved December 2010 from: www.3plstudy.com.

1   ARE YOU READY?

1. Kate Vitasek, Mike Ledyard, and Karl Manrodt, *Vested Outsourcing: Five Rules That Will Transform Outsourcing* (New York: Palgrave Macmillan, 2010).

2. Ibid., chapter 6.
3. Most of the deals we reviewed won some type of award. Some were external recognitions from organization such as the Shared Services Outsource Network, Everest Group, and Project Management Institute. A large number won company-specific awards, such as Supplier of the Year or Environmental Supplier of the Year.
4. Malcolm Gladwell, *Outliers: The Story of Success* (New York: Little, Brown, 2008). Gladwell states: "Outlier is a scientific term to describe things or phenomena that lie outside normal experience. In the summer, in Paris, we expect most days to be somewhere between warm and very hot. But imagine if you had a day in the middle of August where the temperature fell below freezing. That day would be an outlier. And while we have a very good understanding of why summer days in Paris are warm or hot, we know a good deal less about why a summer day in Paris might be freezing cold. In this book I'm interested in people who are outliers—in men and women who, for one reason or another, are so accomplished and so extraordinary and so outside of ordinary experience that they are as puzzling to the rest of us as a cold day in August." Quote retrieved December 2010 from: www.gladwell.com/outliers/index.html.
5. Michael E. Porter and Mark R. Kramer, "The Big Idea: Creating Shared Value," *Harvard Business Review Magazine* (January–February 2011). Retrieved January 2011 from: http://hbr.org/2011/01/the-big-idea-creating-shared-value/ar/1.
6. Vitasek, Ledyard, and Manrodt, *Vested Outsourcing*, 114–124.

2 PLAYING BY THE RULES

1. Ian R Macneil, *Contracts: Instruments for Social Cooperation* (Hackensack, NJ: F. B. Rothman, 1968).
2. Ian R. Macneil was the John Henry Wigmore Professor Emeritus of Law at Northwestern University School of Law. Macneil died in February 2010 after devoting his life to advocating that contract law needed to be approached from a collaborative rather than an adversarial approach.
3. Macneil, *Contracts*, p. 91.
4. Oliver E. Williamson, "Outsourcing: Transaction Cost Economics and Supply Chain Management," *Journal of Supply Chain Management* 44, no. 2 (2008): 5–16.

5. Ibid.

6. Oliver E. Williamson, "The Theory of the Firm as Governance Structure: From Choice to Contract," *Journal of Economic Perspectives* 16, no. 3 (2002): 171–195.

7. "Contract Negotiations Continue to Undermine Value," International Association of Contracting and Commercial Management Ninth Annual Top Ten Terms Report, April 2010.

8. Ibid.

9. Ibid.

10. Research interview.

11. Researchers efforts at the University of Tennessee studied progressive companies exploring innovative approaches to outsourcing. Several common themes were identified, no matter what types of services were being outsourced. A key major theme was the shift away from a conventional customer-supplier relationship to a highly collaborative one aimed at developing a broad, true win-win solution. Following the university's lead, we have taken our collective wisdom as academics and practitioners, mixed in our own research, and have distilled all of this into a systematic model to improve outsourcing as a business practice. We call this model Vested Outsourcing.

12. In his 2008 article for the *Journal of Supply Chain Management*, Williamson wonders what benefits might come from the more widespread use of trust among outsourcing buyers and at what cost. He suggests that it is often better to leave money on the table or not insist on winning every negotiating point. This idea goes against the usual low-cost, transaction-based grain in a traditional contract. If each party or even one has a strategic agenda and wants to gain the upper hand—or, as Williamson says, go muscular—asymmetry will result. This "could plainly jeopardize the joint gains from a simpler and more assuredly constructive contractual relationship," he states. "Always leaving money on the table can thus be interpreted as a signal of constructive intent to work cooperatively, thereby to assuage concerns over relentlessly calculative strategic behavior." What can result is a pragmatic and ultimately wise outsourcing agreement with credibility from start to finish. When working toward a strong business relationship, leaving money on the table can signal a constructive intent to work cooperatively that will build an environment that is credible from start to finish.

3   RULE #1: FOCUS ON OUTCOMES, NOT TRANSACTIONS

1. Peter Kraljic first described his Kraljic model or matrix in "Purchasing Must Become Supply Management," *Harvard Business Review* (September-October 1983). The model can be used to analyze the purchasing portfolio of a company with regard to two factors: profit impact and supply risk. The model distinguishes among four product categories: leverage items, strategic items, noncritical items, and bottleneck items.

2. Kate Vitasek, Mike Ledyard, and Karl Manrodt, *Vested Outsourcing: Five Rules That Will Transform Outsourcing* (New York: Palgrave Macmillan, 2010).

3. "Contract Negotiations Continue to Undermine Value," International Association of Contracting and Commercial Management 9th Annual Top Ten Terms Report, April 2010.

4. Retrieved December 2010 from Jaguar's web site: www.jaguar platinum.com/promo/platinum-coverage.

5. In his 2008 white paper, "Outsourcing, Transaction Cost Economics and Supply Chain Management," Journal of Supply Chain Management, Volume 44, Issue 2 (p. 5–16), Oliver E. Williamson quoted James Buchanan's theory that economics as a science of contract is underdeveloped and needs to be rectified. At the very heart of the problem was Buchanan's view that there must be mutuality of advantage from voluntary "exchanges." An *exchange* is defined as: A trade where one party receives something they value in return for something else that they have to give, for example bread for vegetables. The exchange is immediate, simple and transparent. There is a mutual advantage in the transaction.

6. The term catch-22 was coined by Joseph Heller in his famous satirical novel of the same name, published in 1961. A catch-22 is a logical paradox that occurs from a situation in which an individual needs something that can be acquired only by not being in that very situation; therefore, the acquisition is logically impossible.

7. It is generally accepted in the aerospace industry that Rolls-Royce was the first to implement a Power by the Hour program. It is true according to the authors' knowledge as well. Power by the Hour is a registered trademark of Rolls-Royce.

8. Extensive information on the Power by the Hour program at Rolls-Royce is available on the company website: www.rolls-royce.com /site_services/search_results.jsp?search_term=power+by+the+hour &x=5&y=8&AllSections=1.

9. Described in "Cabin Cash In," *The Sun*, December 16, 2010. The article reports on rumors that to increase revenue, gate agents are supposed to identify passengers who violate the "one-bag carry-on rule" and charge those passengers a fee to stow the bag with other checked luggage. Retrieved January 2010 from: www.the-sun.co.uk/sol/homepage/news/money/3278528/Fine-Ryanair-baggage-cheats-or-else-staff-told.html.

10. Ryanair and Swissport initially signed the outsourcing agreement in 2002. In 2006, their agreement was substantially renegotiated. The companies were extremely optimistic and hopeful about the new arrangement. Swissport issued a press release upon completion of the negotiations, retrieved January 2010 from: www.swissport.com/news-media-center/news-releases/news-detail/?tx_ttnews%5Btt_news%5D=151&cHash=28f6984b12ddc1630d4a6ca0189eaf76.

11. "Swissport and Ryanair Conclude a Major Partnership Agreement for Six Years, Commencing February 2006," *Travel Daily News*, February 2, 2006. Retrieved January 2010 from: www.traveldailynews.com/pages/show_page/12235-Swissport-and-Ryanair-conclude-major-partnership-agreement-for-six-years.

12. Dunne quote ibid.

13. The University of Tennessee has a Certified Deal Architect education program.

14. All the authors have performed these functions and can point you to qualified resources to help you find the right deal architect for your project. The University of Tennessee offers a ten-day training course to certify individuals as certified deal architects, and the IACCM offers an e-learning curriculum on service provider relationship management based entirely on collaborative principles and defined collaborative competencies.

15. ARC Advisory Group Brief, "Shared Destiny: Key Lessons from Unipart's Vested Outsourcing Journey with Jaguar and Vodafone," March 2010, p. 6.

16. Ibid.

17. J.D. Power press release, retrieved December 2010 from: www.jdpower.com/autos/articles/2010-Sales-Satisfaction-Index-Study.

4 RULE #2: FOCUS ON THE *WHAT*, NOT THE *HOW*

1. Kate Vitasek, Mike Ledyard, and Karl Manrodt, *Vested Outsourcing: Five Rules That Will Transform Outsourcing* (New York: Palgrave Macmillan, 2010).

2. Yogi Berra's quote is widely cited. Retrieved December 2010 from: www.rinkworks.com/said/yogiberra.shtml.
3. The quote is widely attributed to both men. It is unclear who said it first, but likely Peters did in *In Search of Excellence* (New York: Harper & Row, 1982). Drucker's quote retrieved December 2010 from: www. qualitywriter.com/about-us/famous-quotes-deep-thought-humor-fun-politics-sayings.
4. This discussion is extracted from a 2010 article on outcome-based contracting by David Rosewell, who leads Fujitsu's value governance practice in business consulting in London. Article retrieved December 2010 from: www.fujitsu.com/downloads/EU/uk/pdf /services/business-services/outcome-based-contracts.pdf.
5. Tim Venable, "Procter & Gamble's William Reeves: Driving Leading-Edge Service Delivery," The Leader Vol. 4 Issue 2 (March 2005) 62.
6. "Jones Lang LaSalle Named Supplier of the Year by Procter & Gamble for Second Consecutive Year," Undated news release retrieved February 2011 at www.joneslanglasalle.com/Pages /NewsItem.aspx?ItemID=18183.

5   RULE #3: AGREE ON CLEARLY DEFINED AND MEASURABLE OUTCOMES

1. Governance structures are discussed in chapter 7.
2. Defense Acquisition University, Continuous Learning Center, Online Module CLL011, "Performance Based Logistics," 2005. Available at: www.dau.mil/default.aspx.
3. Retrieved December 2010 from J.D. Power: http://secure.business center.jdpower.com/News.aspx?search=%20customer%20 satisfaction.
4. J. D. Power press release retrieved December 2010 from: www .jdpower.com/autos/articles/2010-Sales-Satisfaction-Index-Study.
5. In chapter 6 you will link incentives to the achievement of the standards.
6. The authors do not generally support the notion of penalties. We find that it is much better to use incentives rather than penalties. We do, however, advocate for fee-at-risk approaches where the service provider "earns" its base margin by achieving SLAs.
7. Kate Vitasek, Mike Ledyard, and Karl Manrodt, *Vested Outsourcing: Five Rules That Will Transform Outsourcing* (New York: Palgrave Macmillan, 2010). Chapter 7 provides more direction and insight

into how to conduct a baseline. It is important to understand that companies can spend as much time or as little time on the baseline as they need to gain a comfort level that helps establish the performance targets.

6   RULE #4: OPTIMIZE PRICING MODEL INCENTIVES FOR COST/SERVICE TRADE-OFFS

1. Excel is a trademarked program of Microsoft Corporation.
2. Gonzalez quote retrieved January 2010 from the Vested Outsourcing website: www.vestedoutsourcing.com/rule-4-optimize-pricing-model-incentives.
3. Michael E. Porter and Mark R. Kramer, "The Big Idea: Creating Shared Value," *Harvard Business Review Magazine* (January-February 2011): 62–77. Retrieved January 2011 from: http://hbr.org/2011/01/the-big-idea-creating-shared-value/ar/1.
4. A good example is with supply chain management services. Say a company developed an agreement with a service provider to provide distribution services to the company's retail stores. Under the original agreement, the workscope included shipping full pallets to the retailer's distribution center. However, the retailer requested the company begin to ship slow-moving items in smaller case quantities. This workload shift meant that the service provider would need to take much more time to pick the product and likely would have to establish new racking to best store cases instead of pallets.
5. From *Supply Chain Quarterly*. Retrieved January 2011 from: www.supplychainquarterly.com/topics/Strategy/scq200702future.
6. Available at the Edmunds website: www.edmunds.com/tco.html.
7. A. Jaconelli and J. Sheffield, "Best Value: Changing Roles and Activities for Human Resource Managers in Scottish Local Government," *International Journal of Public Sector Management* 13, no. 7 (2000): 624.
8. Best Value Second Interim Report, "Linking Best-Value Procurement Assessment to Outcome Performance Indicators," *Cooperative Research Centre for Construction Innovation*, Project No. 2002-035-C (2002).
9. M. Wisniewski and D. Stewart, "Performance Measurement for Stakeholders: The Case of Scottish Local Authorities," *International Journal of Public Sector Management* 17, no. 3 (2004): 222–233.
10. Best Value Second Interim Report.

11. Mark Solomon, "An Inside Look at Valeant Pharmaceuticals' Emergency Shipment Program," *DCVelocity*, September 7, 2010. Retrieved January 2011 from: www.dcvelocity.com /articles/20100907emergency_parcel_shipments.
12. The Global Sourcing Council website is http://gscouncil.org.
13. George Kimball is senior counsel at Hewlett Packard. Kimball is also the author of *Outsourcing Agreements: A Practical Guide* (New York: Oxford University Press, 2010).
14. George Kimball, "Risk Allocation Liability Limits and Disputes in Outsourcing," *Outsourcing 2010: Structuring, Negotiation and Governance* Vol. 1 (Practicing Law Institute, 2010) 257.
15. Oliver E. Williamson, "Outsourcing: Transaction Cost Economics and Supply Chain Management," *Journal of Supply Chain Management* 44, no. 2 (2008): 5–16.
16. " 'Power by the Hour': Can Paying Only for Performance Redefine How Products Are Sold and Serviced?" Wharton School (February 2007).
17. Monte Carlo simulation is a problem-solving technique that uses computers to estimate the probability of certain outcomes by running multiple trial runs, called simulations, using random variables.
18. Defense Acquisition University, Continuous Learning Center, Online Module CLL011, "Performance-Based Logistics," 2005.
19. Kate Vitasek, Karl Manrodt, and Srinivas Krishna, "Vested for Success Case Study: How Microsoft and Accenture Transformed Global Finance Operations," University of Tennessee Center for Executive Education (2010): 47.
20. Kate Vitasek, Mike Ledyard, and Karl Manrodt, *Vested Outsourcing: Five Rules That Will Transform Outsourcing* (New York: Palgrave Macmillan, 2010).

7   RULE #5: A GOVERNANCE STRUCTURE THAT PROVIDES INSIGHT, NOT MERELY OVERSIGHT

1. As reflected in the work of Ian Macneil and Oliver Williamson, and the IACCM's 2010 Top Terms report (see Appendix B).
2. Ian R. Macneil, *Contracts: Instruments for Social Cooperation* (South Hackensack, NJ: F. B. Rothman, 1968).
3. Ibid.
4. Oliver E. Williamson, "Outsourcing: Transaction Cost Economics and Supply Chain Management," *Journal of Supply Chain Management* 44, no. 2 (2008): 5–16.

5. "Wal-Mart takes Control of Inbound Transportation – and Its Vendors Are Wary," *Supply Chain Digest*, May 25, 2010. Retrieved January 2011 from: www.scdigest.com/ASSETS/ON_TARGET/10 -05-25-1.PHP?CID=3485.

6. Florian Moslein and Karl Riesenhuber, "Contract Governance—A Draft Research Agenda," *European Review of Contract Law* 5 (2009).

7. Oliver E. Williamson, "The Theory of the Firm as Governance Structure: From Choice to Contract," *Journal of Economic Perspectives* 16, no. 3 (2002): 171–195.

8. "3PL Management New Tips and Tools," *Operations Leadership Exchange: The Corporate Executive Board*, 2009.

9. As cited by Expense Management Solutions and Sourcing Interests Group in a 2008 presentation at the SIG Global Sourcing Summit.

10. "Telecommunications and Network Services: Ten Steps to Successful Contract Governance," Hudson & Yorke Ltd., White Paper Executive Summary, 2009.

11. Adrian Gonzalez, "Insights from Performance-based Outsourcing Think-Tanks at ARC World Forum." ARC Insights, Insight # 2010-21E. April 29, 2010.

12. "How Are You Effectively Managing Your Partner's Compliance with Alliance Agreements for Maximum Financial Benefit?" PricewaterhouseCoopers' Global Pharmaceuticals and Life Sciences Industry Group (online publication, 2007). www.pwc .com/en_GX/gx/pharma-life…/licensing-management.pdf.

13. Expense Management Solutions, *Complex Outsourced Services: A Strategic Framework*, Institute for Supply Management presentation, May 2007.

14. Research interview.

15. Roger L. Martin, *The Design of Business: Why Design Thinking Is the Next Competitive Advantage* (Boston: Harvard Business Publishing, 2009).

16. Chris Owens and Michele Flynn, "Locking in the Benefits of Outsourcing: Innovation, Cost Reduction, and Continuous Improvement at Microsoft," *Leader* (September 2005): 2–5.

17. Ibid., p. 5.

18. For more on dispute resolution boards and the standing neutral experience, see Groton's website: http://jimgroton.com/index. php?option=com_content&view=article&id=76&Itemid=86.

19. James P. Groton, "The Standing Neutral: A 'Real Time' Resolution Procedure That Also Can Prevent Disputes," *International Institute for Conflict Prevention and Resolution* 27, no. 11 (December 2009).

20. Robert Solow, "Technical Change and the Aggregate Production Function," *Review of Economics and Statistics* 39 (1957): 312–320.

21. Cynthia Barton Rabe, *The Innovation Killer* (New York: Amacon, 2006).

22. A. G Lafley and Ram Charan, *The Game Changer* (New York: Crown Business, 2008).

23. "US: Coca-Cola Co Expands McDonald's deal," retrieved January 2011 from the Just-Drinks website: www.just-drinks.com/news /coca-cola-co-expands-mcdonalds-deal_id97095.aspx.

8   WRAPPING UP YOUR VESTED AGREEMENT

1. Research interview.

2. Thomas Atkin and Lloyd Rinehart, Research Report: The Effect of Negotiation Practices on the Relationship between Suppliers and Customers. *Negotiation Journal* 22, no. 5 (January 2006): 47–65.

3. "Contract Negotiations Continue to Undermine Value," International Association of Contracting and Commercial Management Ninth Annual Top Ten Terms Report, April 2010.

4. George Kimball, "Risk Allocation Liability Limits and Disputes in Outsourcing," *Outsourcing 2010: Structuring, Negotiation and Governance* Vol. 1 (Practicing Law Institute, 2010) 257.

5. We strongly suggest that members of both parties' legal teams attend as many substantive meetings as possible. Since it is not always practical to have your company's lawyers present, be sure to check in with them about issues that could have significant legal implications to the issues you are discussing.

6. George Kimball, *Outsourcing Agreements: A Practical Guide* (New York: Oxford University Press, 2010).

9   THE NEXT LEG OF YOUR VESTED JOURNEY

1. Twain quote retrieved January 2011 from: www.quotedb.com /quotes/1094.

2. J. Polzer, E. Mannix, and M. Neale, "Multiparty Negotiation in Its Social Context," in *Negotiation as a Social Process*, edited by R. Kramer and D. Messick (Thousand Oaks, CA: Sage, 1995).

3. Negotiation scholars refer to this form of leverage as *normative leverage*.

APPENDIX A: THE TEN AILMENTS

1. Kate Vitasek, Mike Ledyard, and Karl Manrodt, *Vested Outsourcing: Five Rules That Will Transform Outsourcing* (New York: Palgrave Macmillan, 2010) 25–36.
2. Kate Evans-Correia, "Gartner: Outsourcing Deals Based on Price Alone Are Likely Doomed," CIO.com, March 15, 2006.

APPENDIX B: IACCM TOP TERMS 2010

1. This is IACCM's 9th annual study of the terms that are most frequently negotiated in business-to-business transactions. It is based on input that represents many thousands of contract specialists and negotiators within procurement, legal and contract management functions. More than 1,000 organizations contributed to this year's study, which was undertaken in the period December 2009–March 2010. All major industries and legal jurisdictions are represented in the results and further breakdown analysis to reflect cultural, jurisdictional or industry variations will be published at a later date.
2. "Contracts: Instruments For Social Cooperation" Ian R Macneil, 1968. Published by F B Rothman.
3. See in particular the work on transaction cost undertaken by a range of academics, and acknowledged by the recent Nobel Prize in Economics awarded to Oliver E Williamson.
4. See page 6 for an example of the continuing evolution of dispute resolution as a key element of trust in trading relationships. Cross-border (and therefore cross-jurisdictional) relationships are increasingly reliant on non-legal mechanisms.
5. When asked "If the aim of contract negotiation is to create a framework for successful business outcomes, do you believe that negotiations today focus on the right topics to achieve that aim?", 26% believe that the focus is right.
6. IACCM undertook a worldwide study of The Companies Most Admired for Post-Award Contract Management (2008) and The Companies Most Admired for Negotiation (2009). This latter study was accompanied by in-depth best practice analysis and reporting undertaken in partnership with Huthwaite International.

GLOSSARY

3PL (third-party logistics). An outsourced provider that performs logistics services on behalf of its clients. A 3PL typically facilitates the movement of parts and materials from suppliers to manufacturers and finished products from manufacturers to distributors and retailers. Among the services 3PLs provide are transportation, warehousing, cross-docking, inventory management, packaging, and freight forwarding.

Behavioral economics. The study of the quantified impact of the behavior of individuals (or organizations). The study of behavioral economics is evolving more broadly into the concept of relational economics, which espouses that economic value can be expanded through positive relationship (win-win) thinking rather than adversarial relationships (win-lose or lose-lose). In short, entities can work together to expand the pie rather than fight over it.

Best value assessment. An assessment that bases pricing decisions *on the value associated with the benefits received, not on the actual prices or cost.* It uses decision criteria that go beyond costs and include decisions on workscope and pricing based on intangibles such as market risks, social responsibility, responsiveness, and flexibility.

Business model-mapping analysis. An exercise that helps a company determine the appropriate business model to use for its sourcing relationship. The exercise also can help service providers consider how to offer added value to customers more closely related to the outcomes their clients desire.

Change management. The process of managing and monitoring all changes to products and processes. A formal change management process typically is instituted to avoid risks associated with ad hoc change and to document any changes to the agreement. A Vested agreement always includes a change management process.

Company. The organization that is outsourcing the process or function.

Continuous improvement. A structured, measurement-driven process with the goal to review performance and make improvements on a frequent basis.

Cost-reimbursement agreement. An agreement in which the company pays its service provider the actual costs to perform a service. By definition, cost reimbursement is a variable price agreement, with fees dependent on the amount of service provided over a given time period. A cost-reimbursement approach is appropriate when it is too difficult to estimate a fixed price with sufficient accuracy and when the service provider will not agree to assume the risks associated with unknowns. Cost-reimbursement agreements often are used to develop a new product or service, because the work cannot be clearly specified.

Desired Outcomes. A description of results a company strongly wants to achieve. Typically, Desired Outcomes include system-wide, high-level results for items such as lowered cost structures, higher service levels, higher market share, faster speed to market, reduced cycle time, more loyal customers, or others.

EBITDA. Earnings before interest, taxes, depreciation, and amortization. EBITDA is a common accounting term to measure profit.

Exit management plan. A plan that facilitates a smooth, effective transition of services delivery, minimum disruption of ongoing delivery, and efficient completion of all agreement obligations. The plan is invoked with the issuance of a formal termination notice under the agreement, specifying:

(1) the portion of services included in the scope of termination; (2) the estimated exit transition period and vendor delivery centers affected; and (3) the period of time following a termination notice that the parties will have to agree on the specific scope of transition services provided by the vendor.

Five Rules of Vested Outsourcing. The name given by the University of Tennessee to the five key rules it has identified to employ when crafting business-to-business agreements that require more than basic market-based exchanges. Although these rules originally were created for outsourcing deals, they are applicable to any business agreement where the parties want to create a shared value relationship to jointly leverage capabilities to innovate, lower costs, and improve service to compete. When applied to an outsourcing relationship, the rules will move the relationship from a conventional relationship to a Vested relationship. The Five Rules are:

1. Focus on outcomes, not transactions.
2. Focus on the *what*, not the *how*.
3. Agree on clearly defined and measureable outcomes.
4. Pricing model and incentives optimized for cost/ service trade-offs.
5. Governance structure that provides insight, not merely oversight.

Fixed-price agreement. An approach in which the service provider's price is agreed in advance and typically is not subject to adjustment. The parties agree on the fixed price, which includes the service provider's costs and profit. A fixed-price agreement eliminates budgeting variation for the company. Because the total fee for the products and services is fixed, the service provider, not the company, absorbs the peaks and valleys.

Gainshare. A monetary incentive where the service provider shares in costs savings. The focus is on driving out costs that are of limited value and sharing the costs savings.

Governance/Vested governance framework. A governance framework that provides consistent management and cohesive policies, processes, and decision rights that enable the parties to work together effectively and collaboratively to manage performance that achieves transformational results throughout the life of the Vested agreement. Vested governance encompasses a joint process and flexible framework that over time defines and structures an enterprise/agreement that in theory and practice works for the mutual benefit of all the parties by ensuring that they act ethically, employ best practices, and adhere to formal laws. (Also see *Vested governance structure.*)

Guardrails. Agreement boundaries or structured parameters that can block the parties from developing a formalized agreement to frame their Vested business relationship. Guardrails provide the team that is drafting the agreement with the authority to develop a deal within the clearly stated boundaries. If the parties establish an agreement within the guardrails, no last minute surprises will occur because, by design, the agreement is within boundaries already established.

Incentive. A type of award for the company or the service provider. Incentives can be monetary or nonmonetary. In a Vested pricing model, incentives should be based on achievement of incremental performance of the desired outcome. In a Vested Outsourcing agreement, incentives motivate service providers to make decisions that ultimately will meet the company's Desired Outcomes.

Incentives framework. The mechanism that the parties use to measure incremental performance and establish incentive payments. Typically this is a mathematical formula. The simpler the formula is, the better.

Investment-based model. An equity partnership in which the parties form a single balance sheet entity, also known as a merged in-source solution. This model can take different legal forms, from buying a service provider, to becoming a subsidiary, to equity-sharing joint ventures. Equity-based partnerships often are born out of a company's need to acquire mission-critical goods and services. Also, these partnerships often require the strategic interweaving of infrastructure and heavy coinvestment. Most equity partnerships are in place on a continuing basis and often conflict with the desires of many organizations to create more variable and flexible cost structures on a company's balance sheet.

Joint Statement of Intent. A document in a Vested agreement that is a working guideline of principles under which the parties commit to operate. (See *Statement of Intent.*)

Key performance indicator (KPI). A critical metric in the outsourcing agreement that reflects performance against the overall Desired Outcomes. In most cases, the company and the service provider must work together to achieve the KPIs.

Lean. A production practice that considers the expenditure of resources for any goal other than the creation of value for the end customer to be wasteful and thus a target for elimination. Working from the perspective of the customer who consumes a product or service, "value" is defined as any action or process that a customer would be willing to pay for.

Logistics. The management of business operations, such as the acquisition, storage, transportation, and delivery of goods along the supply chain.

Margin matching. A technique used to fairly adjust actual prices to be paid. Margin matching includes establishing a trigger point that activates to reset prices when the point is met. For example, the inflation rate might be a trigger point for resetting inventory carrying cost charges. The goal of using a margin matching technique is to establish pricing fairness, which ultimately builds trust and a better working environment.

Master services agreement (MSA). A legally binding contract entered into by two or more parties. The agreement, which is usually service-oriented, goes into great detail regarding all its components. Because the parties intend to enter into future agreements with one another, they document terms that will govern future agreements in one place, the MSA. The same terms need not be negotiated again. Thus, the parties are freed up to negotiate deal-specific terms.

Operational metrics. The lowest level in the metrics hierarchy. These measure results at the task level.

Organizational alignment. Creating relationship and communications mechanisms that enable a company and the service provider in a Vested agreement to work together effectively to achieve the mutually defined Desired Outcomes.

Outcome-based business model. A model in which a service provider is paid for the realization of a defined set of business outcomes, business results, or agreed-on key performance indicators. An outcome-based business model typically shifts risk to the service provider for achieving the outcome. A well-structured agreement compensates a service provider's higher risk with a higher reward.

Outsource/Outsourcing. The transfer of a process or function to an external provider.

Performance management. A process and culture that drives performance and accountability to delivery performance against key performance indicators. A performance management program goes beyond just having performance metrics in place. Metrics are aligned to strategy and linked to the shop-floor or line-level workers. Tools/technology are in place to support easy data collection and use. This often includes the use of a dashboard or scorecard to allow for ease of understanding and reporting against key performance indicators.

Performance-based outsourcing. A simple outcome-based sourcing relationship. It typically pays a service provider for the achievement of agreed-on key performance indicators.

This model typically rewards the service provider for achieving or maintaining performance. It also sometimes includes a gainshare incentive but does not include a value-share incentive. A well-structured performance-based outsourcing deal that follows the Vested Outsourcing's rules is a Vested deal.

Performance-based logistics (PBL). A term used primarily in the aerospace and defense sector to describe the purchase of assets with a complete array of services and support in an integrated, affordable, performance package. This approach is designed to optimize system readiness and meet performance goals for a weapon system through long-term support arrangements with clear lines of authority and responsibility. PBLs use an outcome-based business model but are not Vested deals.

Performance work statement (PWS). Resides between a statement of objectives and a statement of work in terms of specificity. The company defines the expected results in the statement of objectives and solicits solutions from service providers. The service provider then develops a performance work statement. A PWS still expects the service provider to drive innovation to fulfill the company's statement of objectives—but it goes into more detail than a statement of objectives. A PWS allows for input and innovation from the service provider in *how* it meets the Desired Outcomes and associated statement of objectives. It is important to note that using a PWS is *not* a requirement in a Vested agreement. If it is used, it is not part of the formal agreement but an additional resource that helps the companies establish trust as they learn to work together effectively.

Pricing model. The mechanism companies use to establish the price(s) between a company and its supplier. In most cases, the pricing model consists of a spreadsheet. We use the term *model* because in many cases prices change for various business reasons. A good pricing model enables the parties to manipulate the assumptions of the various pricing model components. The pricing model components are:

The compensation method (e.g. fixed price, cost plus, hybrid)
Assumptions
Total costs and best value assessment
Risk allocations
Margin matching
Contract duration

Pony. In Vested Outsourcing, the difference between the value of the current solution and the potential optimized solution. It represents something the outsourcing company wants but was not able to get on its own or with existing service providers.

Process metric. Measures the success of a process.

Relational economics. The study of the quantified impact of the behavior of individuals in a contractual relationship and the direct impact that their collective behavior has on achievement of the Desired Outcomes and realization of mutual gain.

Relationship management. The practice of establishing joint policies and processes that emphasize the importance of building collaborative working relationships, attitudes, and behaviors. The structure by necessity will be flexible and will provide top-to-bottom insights about what is happening with the Desired Outcomes and, just as important, the relationship between the parties. Relationship management is a comprehensive approach to managing an enterprise's interactions with the organizations that supply the goods and services it uses. The goal of relationship management is to streamline and make more effective the processes between an enterprise and its suppliers. This is most definitely not a whose-throat-to-choke exercise; rather, it is the establishment of processes for communication, reporting, and improvement.

Relationship rules of conduct. A firm commitment to constructive working relationships, attitudes, and behaviors. A Vested relationship is, after all, about people working together in new ways to achieve a common goal; it is not about filling seats at the lowest common denominator and bean counting. It must be recognized at the outset that behavior modification is likely necessary for success.

Risk mitigation. The active practice of avoiding predicted events that could cause harm to a business and its operation.

Risk premium. The value (typically in term of a fee) paid to a party that knowingly and willingly bears a risk and is rewarded for doing so in some form or another.

Root cause analysis. A problem-solving method that aims to identify the source of problems or incidents. The focus is to solve problems by attempting to correct or eliminate their basic origins rather than merely addressing their symptoms.

Shared value. A mutual commitment to establish economic benefits for all parties .In essence, shared value thinking involves entities working together to bring innovations that benefit them through a conscious effort to gain (or share) in the rewards. This shared value thinking is what the University of Tennessee researchers have named "what's in it for we" (WIIFWe).

Shared Vision statement. The statement that sets forth the larger, guiding principles for the business relationship and the purposes for going on the Vested journey together.

Service-level agreement (SLA). Specific metrics that a service provider must meet. Often there are incentives for exceeding SLA targets or penalties associated with missing SLA targets.

Service provider. The external company that provides the outsourced process or function.

Standing Neutral. A trusted objective expert selected by the parties at the beginning of their relationship who is readily available throughout the life of the relationship to assist in the prompt resolution of any disputes.

Statement of Intent. A statement that builds the foundation for the agreement by setting out how the parties will work together to achieve it; it establishes how the parties will behave once the agreement is documented in a written contract. Each party must align its intentions with the Shared Vision.

Statement of Objectives (SOO). A statement that establishes the required objectives that the parties will strive to accomplish under the agreement. Under a Vested agreement, the company outsourcing must be willing to allow and enable the service provider to make significant changes to improve overall processes and flow within the scope of work it is assigned.

Statement of Work (SOW). The tool usually used by outsource practitioners to document business requirements. Typically, a company defines and documents the tasks it wants the service provider to accomplish. SOWs are best suited for transaction-based models and not for outcome-based or Vested Outsourcing business models. In Vested Outsourcing, SOWs should be avoided in favor of a Statement of Objectives.

Supplier relationship management (SRM). The practice of creating mechanisms to increase the efficiency and effectiveness of how a company works with its service providers. The goal of SRM is to create effective processes for working together, which in turn yields lower costs of doing business. Some SRM efforts are designed to build deeper relationships that foster improved collaboration efforts and innovation. A benefit of SRM is that it provides a common frame of reference for companies and services providers, thus establishing unified business practices and terminology for how the organizations work together.

Ten Ailments. University of Tennessee research and experience have defined the 10 most common problems seen with outsourcing agreements, which drive perverse behaviors and lead to severe strains in the relationship—or worse, to the failure of vendors or outsourcing companies. The ailments are listed in Appendix A.

Ten Elements. The foundation of Vested agreements. These elements set out how the parties will work together to achieve the agreement and how the parties will behave once the agreement is documented in a written contract. The Ten Elements document the business aspects of an outsourcing contract.

Total cost of ownership (TCO). The foundation for any Best Value decisions that need to be made. A TCO analysis includes determining the direct and indirect cost of an acquisition and operational costs. The purpose of determining the TCO is to help make clear decisions when it comes to pricing.

Transaction-based business model. The business model typically used by companies for all of their commercial agreements when they make buy decisions. Conventional approaches to transaction-based models keep service providers at arm's length. Three types of transaction-based sourcing relationships have evolved over time as businesses wrestle with how to create service provider relationships that are better suited for more complex business requirements: simple transaction providers, approved providers, and preferred providers.

Transaction-based pricing model. An outsourcing model where payments to the service provider are based on the number of transactions executed.

Transaction cost economics (TCE). In its simplest form, the study of the economics of all of the hidden costs associated with the transactions that companies perform, based on research by Oliver Williamson underscoring that businesses should collaborate for mutual interest or face hidden transaction costs. The University of Tennessee's applied research augments their research with evidence of hidden transaction costs in the form of the Ten Ailments of outsourcing.

Transformation management. Management that supports the transition from the old to the new as well as improvement of end-to-end business processes. The focus is on mutual accountability for attaining Desired Outcomes and the creation of an ecosystem that rewards innovation and a culture of continuous improvement.

WIIFMe (what's-in-it-for-me). A relationship approach in which the parties act in their own self-interest with a focus on winning.

WIIFWe (what's-in-it-for-we). A relationship approach in which the parties move toward a partnership that focuses on identifying Desired Outcomes and then aligns the interests of all parties so that all benefit if those outcomes are reached.

Win-win. Negotiation philosophy in which all parties to an agreement or deal stand to realize their fair share (not 100 percent) of the benefits or profit.

Valueshare. The practice of allocating a share of the total value that is derived from an improvement or innovation to the parties. The savings are based on the entire value to all stakeholders, not just the company. Valuesharing encourages service provider innovation for total overall value.

Vested. The use of the common word vested which respects and conveys all the foundational principles of Vested Outsourcing: shared value, behavioral economics, mutual success, and where the size of the pie is not predetermined.

Vested agreement. An agreement between two or more companies whereby the beginning foundation of the agreement determines its future success—shared value. The Vested Outsourcing Five Rules and Ten Elements provide the flexible, customizable framework for the agreement to enable both parties to "contract" for mutual success.

Vested governance. A framework that uses a relationship management structure and joint processes as a controlling mechanism to encourage organizations to make proactive changes for the mutual benefit of all parties.

Vested Outsourcing. An outsourcing relationship where companies and service providers become Vested in each other's success, creating a true win-win solution.

Vested Outsourcing business model. A business model that is a hybrid of outcome-based, shared value, and relational economics approaches. It is best used when a company wants service providers to move beyond just performing a set of directed tasks and instead develop solutions to achieve the company's Desired Outcomes.

Vested pricing model. A pricing model designed to reward both the company outsourcing and the service provider for achieving the Desired Outcomes. When properly structured, the pricing model should generate returns in excess of target margins for both parties when the parties achieve the Desired Outcomes.

Vested principles. Principles describing the Vested approach, in which a balanced partnership based on trust, collaboration, transparency, and value delivery. Companies and service providers establish joint and flexible processes that allow for timely decisions while providing proper controls for ensuring ethical decisions.

INDEX